Making Their Way

Making Their Way

EDUCATION, TRAINING AND THE
LABOUR MARKET IN CANADA AND
BRITAIN

Edited by
David Ashton and Graham Lowe

Open University Press
MILTON KEYNES

Open University Press
22 Ballmoor
Celtic Court
Buckingham MK18 1XW

First Published 1991

British Library Cataloguing in Publication Data

Ashton, D. N. (David Norman), *1942-*
    Making their way: a comparative analysis of
    relationship between education, training and the labour
    market in Canada and Britain.
    1. School leavers. Employment. Equality of opportunity.
    Social aspects
    I. Title.   II. Lowe, Graham
    331.3′4133

ISBN 0–335–09392–2
ISBN 0–335–09391–4 (pbk)

Typeset by Scarborough Typesetting Services
Printed in Great Britain by Biddles Limited,
Guildford and Kings Lynn

Please find enclosed a copy of **Making Their Way**. We asked the publishers to send you a copy of this, but I understand this has not been done. Rather than encountering further details by corresponding with them, I enclose one of the copies which was forwarded to me a couple of weeks ago.

I am pleased with the outcome, as is the Canadian High Commission who provided the funds for Banff.

Yours sincerely

David Ashton

LMS

Labour Market Studies

University of Leicester

103 Princess Road East
Leicester
LE1 7LG

Tel: (0533) 523750
EMAIL: LMS@UK.AC.LEICESTER
FAX: (0533) 523653

7 November 1990

Judith Marquand
Head of Evaluation & Research Branch
Training Agency
Policy & Programmes Div
Moorfoot
SHEFFIELD S1 4PQ

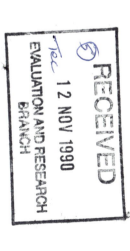

Contents

List of contributors

David Ashton is Professor of Sociology and Director of Research of the Labour Market Studies Group, University of Leicester. He has published widely in the field of labour markets and the school to work transition. His latest book, in collaboration with Malcolm Maguire and Mark Spilsbury of the Labour Market Studies Group, entitled *Restructuring the Labour Market: The Implications for Youth*, was published in 1990 by Macmillan. In 1989–90 he was Visiting Professor, Department of Sociology, University of Alberta, Canada.

Phil Brown is lecturer in Sociology at the University of Kent at Canterbury. His publications include *Schooling for Ordinary Kids* (Tavistock 1987), and is joint editor (with David Ashton) of *Education, Unemployment and Labour Markets* (Falmer 1987), and (with H. Lander) *Education: In Search of a Future* (Falmer 1988).

John Bynner studied Psychology at Bristol and completed his Ph.D. in Social Psychology at Birkbeck College, University of London. From a first appointment in the Central Council for Health Education doing research on the sexual behaviour and attitudes of young people, he moved to OPCS where he worked on studies of smoking behaviour. He was Professor of Education and Dean of the School of Education at the Open University before moving to the Social Statistics Research Unit, City University, to become Director in January 1989. He is also currently National Coordinator of the ESRC 16–19 Initiative.

Jane Gaskell is Professor and Head of Department of Social and Educational Studies at the University of British Columbia. Her publications include many articles on work, education and gender, as well as a book edited with Arlene McLaren, *Women and Education: A Canadian Perspective* (Detselig 1987).

Walter Heinz is Professor of Sociology and Social Psychology at the University of Bremen, FRG. He has published widely in the field of youth and socialization and the transition from school to work. He is currently Chairman of the Special Collaborative Programme 186 of the Deutsche Forschungsgemeinschaft (DFG), a major German research initiative examining status passages and social risks in the life course.

Harvey Krahn is an Associate Professor of Sociology and Director of the Population Research Laboratory at the University of Alberta, Canada. He has published articles in the fields of unemployment, trade unions and labour market segmentation. He is co-author with G. S. Lowe of *Work, Industry and Canadian Society* (Nelson 1988).

Graham Lowe is Professor of Sociology at the University of Alberta, Canada. He has published widely in the area of industrial sociology. His latest book *Work, Industry and Canadian Society*, co-authored with Harvey Krahn, was published in 1988 by Nelson, Canada. He is also editor of the *Canadian Journal of Sociology*, and in 1989–90 was the Social Sciences Visiting Professor at Carleton University, Canada.

Malcolm Maguire is a Research Fellow in the Labour Market Studies Group at the University of Leicester. He has published numerous articles on education, the school to work transition and training, and is a co-author of a number of research monographs on youth and the labour market. His most recent publication (with D. N. Ashton and M. Spilsbury) is *Restructuring the Labour Market: The Implications for Youth* (Macmillan 1990).

Julian Tanner is an Assistant Professor of Sociology at the University of Toronto. He has published articles in the field of youth studies and education. After graduating from what is now the East London Polytechnic and obtaining a post-graduate certificate in education from the University of Leicester, he then completed his Ph.D. at the University of Alberta. Since then he has taught at the University of Toronto. His research interests lie in the fields of work, education and youth.

Foreword

Judith Marquand
Head of Evaluation and Research Policy and Programmes
Division, Training Agency Sheffield*

Canada and Britain have many surface similarities. Both are rich advanced capitalist nations, but neither is among the world's economic and techno-logical leaders today. They have strong cultural links rooted in Canada's historical origins as a British colony. They face common challenges of changing technologies, changing world patterns of trade and growing economic integration with dominant neighbours – the United States in the case of Canada, the European Community for Britain. But despite these shared pasts and current circumstances, the two nations are a study in contrast. In particular, there are major differences in labour markets, educational and training institutions.

International comparative work is difficult to undertake. Single-dimension comparisons are misleading. Instead it is necessary to try to understand the working of the whole system – in this case of the transition from school to work – in each country and then to appraise the adaptation to common problems.

The strength of this book as a comparative study of the transition from school to work is that it sets the transition in the context of the different histories, institutions and individual attitudes to education, training and work in the two countries. On the surface, some current policies to encourage adaptation in the labour market appear similar – the Canadian Jobs Strategy and the British Employment Training, for example. But the

* This Foreword represents the author's personal view and must not be taken to indicate the views of the Training Agency.

weight to be placed on similar policy initiatives differs in each country. Entry to employment has been education-led in Canada and training-led in Britain. Individual aspirations are much higher in Canada, especially among women. In the past, Canada has relied on immigrants to supply its skilled manufacturing workers; it has educated and trained Canadians mainly for the service sector. In Britain the manufacturing tradition remains dominant, despite its small and falling labour-market role.

Making Their Way addresses the implications of these national similarities and differences for the youth labour market. It illustrates the potential of a holistic approach. It represents a significant step forward in the development of comparative analysis of the two societies. It shows the fallacy of attempts simply to translate labour market, training or educational policies directly from one to the other. I hope that *Making Their Way* will lead to further comparisons of Canadian and British society, not just to help each understand the other but to help each understand itself.

Acknowledgements

Our first and foremost debt is to Michael Hellyer and the Academic Relations Section of the Canadian High Commission, London, for funding the project which resulted in this volume. In particular they financed the conference, held in Banff, Alberta, at which the authors of the papers were able to discuss their results and explore the comparative dimension to their findings. In addition, we would also like to thank Betty Jennings (Leicester, UK) for administering the project, and Cliff Kinzel (Edmonton, Canada) for transferring our drafts on to disk. Although the Canadian High Commission funded the project and various research bodies funded the work on which the papers report, the views expressed are the responsibility of the authors concerned.

David N. Ashton
Graham S. Lowe

1

School-to-work Transitions in Britain and Canada: a comparative perspective

David Ashton and Graham Lowe

Introduction

There are clear signs that we are at a major turning point in the relationship between work and society (Pahl 1988). Employment is far more problematic today than in previous decades as the division of labour undergoes fundamental transformation. According to the International Labour Organization (ILO 1988; 6–7), flexibility and mobility between occupations and geographic locations are the major results of rapid technological and structural changes in the global economy. For some young people completing their education and venturing forth into the labour market in search of a meaningful and rewarding 'career', the future may look especially bleak. Demographic factors also complicate the labour-market entry process. The late 1980's youth cohort is in the shadow of the huge 'baby boom' generation. Having faced a tight labour market now, they will be too old to benefit from the labour shortages for entry-level positions predicted for the 1990s. Thus, a pressing issue for many young people is not just whether they will find a job, but whether it will be commensurate with their aspirations. This question is central to understanding change in patterns in the life course at the crucial juncture between youth and adulthood.

The expanding body of literature on young peoples' transition from school into the labour market does not provide a unified analysis of how the transitional process is changing, and the attendant consequences. Some general trends are, however, discernible. For instance, the increasingly insecure nature of employment throughout the industrialized world –

indicated by a rise in the relative numbers of casual or temporary jobs, part-time jobs, marginalized workers, and underemployment – disproportionately affects youth (ILO 1988: 33–4). Moreover, studies in various industrialized countries document considerable difficulties young people face due to diminishing opportunities in the labour market (see OECD 1988; Ashton et al. 1988; Blossfeld 1987; Heinz 1987; Starr 1986; Hartmann 1987). Much existing research focuses on youth unemployment, with less emphasis on those who obtain employment (Reubens 1983; 1: see, e.g., Junankar 1987; Brown and Ashton 1987). This is understandable, given historically high youth-unemployment rates across the industrialized world during the recession of the early 1990s. One consequence of this narrow research focus is a fragmentary image of the types and severity of problems all young people encounter – not just the most disadvantaged – when trying to find a niche in the labour market and, via this, adult society.

Have the harsh realities of the post-recession labour market forced basic changes in the transitional process? Are the institutional arrangements which linked education and training with the job market during the post-war period into the 1970s still appropriate? A number of British researchers (e.g. Willis 1986), including some contributors to this volume, argue that transitional mechanisms have broken down. This assumes, of course, that at one time the transition was indeed a smooth and sequential progression out of school and into a job. There is a lengthy debate about this question in the literature (e.g. Williams 1974; Ashton and Field 1976). In a recent contribution to that debate, an American study of the high-school graduating class of 1972 suggests that deviation from the 'normal' pattern of educational and work activities was prevalent in the 1970s (Rindfuss et al. 1987). These researchers disagree with the assumption that life-course transitions were at one time orderly and linear. Instead, they advocate that 'disorder' be incorporated into analytic models of life transitions. Transition models must also take into account demographic aspects of the youth transition: will the youth unemployment problem of the late 1970s and early 1980s be overtaken by a labour-shortage crisis with the relative shrinkage of the youth cohort in the 1990s (see, e.g., Howe 1988; Foot and Li 1986)?

One of the main contributions of the papers in this volume is to highlight the fact that the above studies can be interpreted only within the confines of specific national settings. Given the hazards of generalizing from national studies, we need to develop a comparative perspective on young people's transitions to work. The existing comparative literature on the topic is scant and only partially clarifies the questions we have raised about the school–work transition. Compare, for example, the optimistic prospects for youth employment suggested in two cross-national surveys (Braungart and Braungart 1986) with the pessimistic picture of joblessness and ineffective state-sponsored training and employment schemes (Rist 1986; Fiddy 1985; OECD 1984). The introduction of a comparative perspective means that we can begin to resolve these contradictions. For the value of a comparative perspective lies in its ability to identify how specific institutional and cultural contexts condition an individual's passage through the life course. This sort of contextualized analysis of national similarities and differences is largely missing from existing comparative studies. As Gill Jones (1988: 716–17) has argued, current research fails to locate youth within the structures and values of society – a criticism especially true of comparative studies. In much grander fashion, Charles Tilly (1984: 14) has implored sociologists to develop 'concrete and historical analyses of the big structures and large processes that shape our era'. Tilly's challenge, we believe, needs to be taken up by youth researchers.

The single contribution of this volume then is to advance our understanding of the school–work transition through a comparative analysis of how macro-level structures shape the educational and work opportunities of individual youth in two countries, Canada and Britain. Three themes integrate the chapters which follow, offering insights into national variations in how education, training and labour markets are interrelated. The first theme emphasizes the importance of opportunity structures defined by the organization of education and the structure of labour markets.

The second highlights how cultural values, which young people more or less assimilate, both reflect and reinforce these opportunity structures. The third identifies how transitional patterns are rooted in particular national combinations of work and education-related institutions and values. Contributors to this book share the assumption that the transitional process has profound implications for the 'life chances' of the next generation. The following chapters address the basic sociological question of how social inequalities are being reproduced within the next generation, viewing the school–work transition as a key mechanism in this process.

Our general perspective is consistent with a growing body of cross-national research which suggests that labour-market structures result from the complex interactions of economic, political and social forces. Researchers are now grappling with how specific factors produce national differences, emphasizing common influences, such as the economic crises of the 1970s and 1980s, and the connections between work structures and class inequalities (Kalleberg 1988: 205). Representative of this approach is the comparison of work structures in France and West Germany by Marc Maurice and his colleagues (Maurice et al. 1986). Their thesis is that the relationship between work and society is determined by the interactions among the organization of firms, educational institutions and the industrial relations system within a society. In sum, basic socio-cultural factors influence how a nation's workforce is stratified.

This volume points towards what ideally should be included in a rigorous comparison of cross-national patterns of school–work transition. In other words, readers will not find an explicitly comparative study using systematically comparable data. Such a project on the topic at hand has yet to be conducted. But as Melvin Kohn (1987) notes, implicit comparisons are none the less a useful means of sketching out a more general picture of social phenomenon. If one accepts that comparative sociology by definition uses the society as the key explanatory unit (Ragin 1982), then the thrust of what follows is indeed comparative.

This book emphasizes the marked differences in how British and Canadian youth make their way from school into the labour force. Our collective interest in these remarkable differences between two of the advanced industrial nations motivated the conference out of which the book grew. But we approach this comparison with some trepidation, well aware that cross-national differences are more difficult to interpret than similarities (Kohn 1987: 716). What is really required – and what this volume hopefully may stimulate – is further study of the factors we identify within a unified comparative research design.

Focusing on Britain and Canada

If we turn now to our two national cases, in Britain the transition occurs early, at age 16 for most, and is characterized by an abrupt departure from school and considerable difficulty for some in finding suitable employment. The Canadian pattern from school to work is more prolonged and two-way, due to much higher levels of educational attainment and opportunities to combine school and work or move back and forth between the labour market and educational institutions. The labour-market problems Canadian high-school and university graduates encounter are more likely to take the form of short-term unemployment and possibly protracted underemployment rather than, as in Britain, long-term unemployment, marking time in a government job-training scheme, or entry to a dead-end job with no training.

Underlying these two national models of transition are differences in class structure, political institutions, state policies, the pattern and timing of industrialization, present industrial structure, and the cultural milieux (see Ashton 1988). These differences shape the opportunities available for young people to obtain an education or training and find a job suited to their aspirations and abilities. The focus of much of the analysis to follow is on these two major institutional spheres – education and training, and the labour market – and how their organization and interrelations underlie the transitional process.

As a backdrop to a comparative discussion of the papers, it is useful to outline briefly the positions of Canada and Britain within the volatile international economy. Canada and Britain are members of the 'Group of Seven' leading industrial nations and share the basic features of advanced capitalism, such as a large service sector, a high standard of living, an educated labour force with high participation rates, and a fairly extensive social-welfare system. Both are adapting to new global economic trends: Britain through the European Economic Community's move towards an integrated market in 1992; Canada by having entered into a free-trade agreement with the United States in January 1989.

Equally important, Canada and Britain have been affected, albeit in different ways, by other powerful forces of industrial restructuring. The flight of capital to low-wage developing nations, the explosion of service industries and the decline of manufacturing, the rationalization of production systems through the application of new employer strategies and microelectronics, rising female-labour-force participation rates, the increasing prevalence of part-time and casual jobs, unemployment rates that remain historically high – such are the winds of economic change sweeping across the capitalist world (see ILO 1988). Precisely how these macro trends affect specific nations, regions, industries or organizations is a matter for careful empirical investigation. History offers the necessary corrective to any tendency to deduce theoretically any general laws in this regard. Britain was the first industrial nation and a great imperial power that entered a prolonged economic decline early in the twentieth century (Barnett 1988). Canada emerged as a resource hinterland under French and British colonial rule. Never fully escaping the role of a junior partner supplying raw materials to more dominant economies, Canada industrialized relatively late and failed to establish an independent, manufacturing-based economy (Laxer 1989). These divergent trajectories of economic development shape the differences we have found in how British and Canadian youth make their way from school to work.

Labour markets

Malcolm Maguire outlines how the 1980s' recession accentuated the basic restructuring of British industry under way since the 1960s. The shift from manufacturing to services created much worker dislocation, with the loss of 3.5 million manufacturing jobs since 1960. The decline of blue-collar employment was partly offset by the expanding white-collar sector, increasingly inhabited by women. Inequalities in the labour market grew wider as the recession combined with advancing workplace automation, management's quest for the 'flexible firm', and state deregulation of employment conditions. The social polarization induced by growing labour-market segmentation created winners and losers, with young people tending to end up among the latter.

Harvey Krahn's chapter presents a profile of the Canadian labour market, highlighting its differences with Britain. Canada has always had a considerably smaller manufacturing sector than Britain and, conversely, a somewhat larger service sector – outdistancing even the US in terms of the services' share of total employment. The female-labour-force participation rate is higher than in Britain. Canadian women have more opportunities in managerial and professional occupations, although inequalities persist despite employment equity initiatives. Prominent in any discussion of Canadian society are regional disparities, particularly in terms of employment opportunities. Comparatively speaking, the north–south polarization in Britain is a more recent phenomenon. Finally, one of the most notable differences between Britain and Canada (and the US as well) is the tradition of part-time work among students in North America. Most Canadian high-school students obtain considerable work experience through part-time and summer jobs. The implications of this for transitional patterns are explored in chapters 6 and 7. Unemployment rates also vary between the two countries. Canada headed into the recession with a higher overall unemployment rate than Britain, recovered more rapidly.

Unlike the British state, Canadian federal and provincial governments responded to youth unemployment passively, leaving educational institutions to fill the breach. The Canadian Jobs Strategy that grew out of the recession is aimed at specific disadvantaged groups (Native Canadians, single mothers, the disabled, high-school dropouts, etc.), not the mainstream of youth as in Britain's YTS scheme. But despite their generally higher educational attainment, Canadian youth face the contradictions of a labour market that, on one hand, places a premium on post-secondary credentials, while, on the other hand, increasingly provides them with low wage, dead-end, insecure service-sector jobs.

Educational institutions

The next three chapters focus on different aspects of education as it influences the transition to work. What stands out is how the different labour-market experiences of Canadian and British adolescents and young adults result largely from the organization of education in each society. But as a recent OECD report concluded, comparative analysis must extend further: 'short-term demand for education and skills may be significantly influenced by traditions and institutions which are more or less independent of current economic trends' (OECD 1988: 74). This volume's three chapters on education emphasize that Canada and Britain have contrasting class structures, educational values, and patterns of state educational policy. These different combinations of institutions and supporting values help to explain Canada's more extensive system of post-secondary institutions and programmes and the ideology of equality of opportunity through education and, by contrast, the more stratified British system in which schools play a direct role in reproducing class inequalities across generations. In short, as Julian Tanner's chapter reminds us, the two societies are exemplary of Turner's well-known distinction between sponsored (Britain) and contest (Canada) mobility.

When viewed within the broader context of the eighteen Organization for Economic Co-operation and Development (OECD) nations, Canada and Britain represent polar extremes in basic aspects of their educational systems (OECD 1987: chapter 1). The majority of adolescents in OECD nations receive general or vocational education until at least age 18. When the OECD nations are ranked by total enrolment at age 17 in 1984 (including secondary schools, apprenticeships and state training schemes, and post-secondary institutions) Germany and then Japan are at the top (97 and 90 per cent), Canada is half way down the ranking with 76 per cent, and the United Kingdom is ranked fifteenth with 65 per cent. However, when only secondary-school enrolments are examined, the gap between Canada and the UK widens to 67 per cent and 30 per cent respectively.

At the post-secondary level national trends are even more accentuated. Enrolment (1984 figures) in post-secondary institutions is highest in the US, Canada and Japan, where just under one-quarter of the comparable age group obtains a bachelor's degree. The figure for the UK is 15 per cent. The entire school system in Britain is geared for minority participation in higher education. Specifically, only 37 per cent of secondary-school students obtain credentials needed to enter higher education, compared with three-quarters of Canadian (and American) students.

The basic patterns then are clear; the early routeing of students in Britain into different streams and the tradition of leaving at age 16; the Canadian (indeed North American) goal of attempting to provide large numbers of students with a general high-school education and the possibility of studying at the post-secondary level. Beyond this, two additional features need to be considered. First, Britain's system of élite private schools traditionally has conferred advantages on children of the upper and upper-middle classes. Roughly 18 per cent of British 16-to-19-year-olds are in private institutions, whereas in Canada these schools account for 5 per cent of all elementary and secondary enrolment. Second, the more universal concept of education found in North America is now extending throughout adult life. Adult enrolment in Canadian post-secondary institutions is high and steadily rising. In 1983, for example, 16.5 per cent of university students were 25–29 years old and 25.2 per cent were 30 or older. Comparable figures for the UK (1981 data) were 8.6 per cent and 11 per cent respectively. In making these comparisons, we must be careful not to overemphasize the 'equality of opportunity' and 'universality' of the Canadian system. These features of the educational ideology reflect reality only to a degree; a sign that the system is far from egalitarian is that an estimated one-third of high-school students drop out before graduating.

What impact do such divergent educational systems have on young people's transition into the labour market? Moreover, how do the school experiences of British and Canadian adolescents shape their overall orientation towards education and, more generally, society? Finally, how are these national differences in schooling reflected in state policy responses to ongoing policy debates about education?

Phillip Brown argues that current political debates in Britain over the future of education threaten the post-war rise of comprehensive schools founded on liberal democratic goals of equality of educational opportunity. While Thatcher's Conservatives have pushed for a more industry-relevant vocational education, the implications of their policies for social inequalities have overshadowed vocational goals.

Against this background of educational reform, Brown examines how students' responses to school contribute to the reproduction of social inequalities. This has been a dominant theme in British educational research since Paul Willis's (1977) seminal study of how working-class boys' rejection of school at a cultural level contributed to their ending up in working-class jobs. But as Brown is quick to note, the economy has changed dramatically since Willis conducted his study in the mid-1970s. No longer can a student assume that there is a job waiting for him or her. Indeed, a recurring theme in this volume is that Britain's youth labour market is in a state of crisis, given that entry-level positions have all but disappeared in areas outside London and the affluent south-east.

Brown's study of pupils' attitudes towards school in an industrial area of South Wales goes beyond Willis in several important respects. For one thing, Brown's analysis incorporates both gender and class. Perhaps even more significantly, his fieldwork identified the close interaction between students' orientations to school and the labour market.

Jane Gaskell's analysis of how the Canadian education system is tied into the labour market offers an insightful counterpoint to Brown's article. Unlike the central control exercised by the British government, educational policy in Canada is a provincial responsibility. The resulting differences in provincial education systems are exacerbated by pronounced regional economic disparities, which are defining features of Canadian society. While neo-conservativism is less pronounced than in Britain, the ascendancy of right-wing ideology in Canada during the 1980s (especially since the Conservative party's 1984 and 1988 federal election victories) has influenced educational policy debates. The nature of this influence is more muted than in Britain, being constrained by the greater value Canadians place on equality of opportunity and universal access. Unlike the highly polarized debate in Britain surrounding Thatcher's single-minded policy thrust, Gaskell argues that in Canada two contradictory issues underpin discussions of educational policy. On one hand, growing public concern about the problem of high-school dropouts (the subject of Julian Tanner's chapter) has sparked demands for more job-relevant education. On the other hand, fears about declining educational standards and quality have prompted calls for a return to academic 'basics', standardized exams, and streaming based on ability.

Gaskell's research among working-class girls enrolled in high-school business education also underscores parallels between British and Canadian schools. In both societies a major role of the educational system is preparation for the labour market. Similarly, both systems stream students according to their class background or sex. As Gaskell suggests, the mechanisms of vocationalism and streaming differ, as do the particular groups affected and the consequences for them. Thus in Canada, the logic of vocationalism is clearly manifested in high-school business education which affects mainly working-class girls.

Both Brown and Gaskell highlight the lack of an oppositional youth culture among the students they studied. This theme of young peoples' responses to the educational system and a rapidly changing job market is explored further by Julian Tanner. Tanner begins with the observation that the North American ideology of mass participation in school treats the dropout problem as a failure of the schools. According to this view, dropouts' alienation from the dominant view that education is the route to personal success exposes the inequalities inherent in a system espousing equality of opportunity. In challenging these assumptions, Tanner dismisses Willis's deterministic position, noted above, in favour of a more balanced approach revolving around the question: has school rejected the dropouts or have they rejected it?

Evidence from Tanner's case study of dropouts in Edmonton, a western provincial capital city with a highly cyclical energy-based economy, offers an important corrective to Willis. Tanner found mixed motives for leaving school, mostly related to the operations of the school and negative experiences with teachers. There was no overall rejection of school, however. Interestingly, Tanner's respondents articulated a lingering commitment to education, especially in light of their subsequent labour-market difficulties.

This chapter thus draws our attention to major differences in young people's school experiences in Britain and Canada. Tanner's dropouts present a marked contrast to the situation described in much British research. No doubt the deeply rooted achievement ethic in Canadian society, coupled with opportunities to return to formal education as an adult, are major contributing factors. Yet as Brown's study of South Wales shows, even in Britain the view that working-class pupils uniformly reject school needs to be modified in light of a more pluralistic reaction in the post-recession 1980s. If anything, Willis's thesis is culturally and historically bound, applying narrowly to British working-class boys in the mid-1970s.

Transitional patterns

The focus thus far on national differences in labour markets and schools begs the question: how do these factors influence transitional pathways? The next two chapters report results from two major longitudinal studies, one British, the other Canadian, on the school–work transition. John Bynner presents findings from the first phase of a study of two cohorts of youth, with average ages of about 16 and 19 respectively, in four contrasting British labour markets. Juxtaposed to this are Harvey Krahn and Graham Lowe's results from a two-year panel study of 1985 high-school and university graduates (with average ages of 18 and 23 respectively in 1985) in three Canadian cities. The age and educational-attainment differences between these two studies reflect key variations in when and how the transition occurs in each society. The studies share a common concern with education and work values, links between school and work, and labour market outcomes. Thus, while not directly comparable, the two studies are sufficiently similar in design to permit some basic comparative conclusions to be drawn. Given the above discussion of the distinctive character of labour markets and educational institutions in Canada and Britain, it would not be surprising to find fundamentally different transitional patterns. Indeed, one of the main contributions of this volume is a documentation of these contrasting transitional patterns.

Turning first to Britain, Bynner in his findings leaves little doubt that school and labour market have become decoupled. The crisis of youth joblessness obviously has been compounded over the last decade by an educational system that pushes the majority out its doors at age 16. Rather than extending the school-leaving age, state policy has emphasized job training through the Youth Training Scheme. YTS may be better than the dole, but local economic conditions determine the probability of finding a job. Indeed, the impact of local labour markets on the 'career trajectories' of young people – especially occupational destinations – is overwhelming. Of the four research locales, only booming Swindon still supports the traditional trajectory of moving out of school into full-time employment. For a growing number of young people in economically depressed regions, the dominant trajectory mixes YTS with unemployment.

Given such adverse job prospects, why do British youth not clamour to stay on in school? Part of the answer is a strong commitment, especially among the working class, to paid employment. For this large group, school holds out little prospect of improving their earnings. Ironically, Bynner reports that those least likely to obtain employment clung the most tenaciously to the values of work and money. Other factors buttressing this anti-education ideology include little encouragement or opportunity to return to school after one has left, and a financial incentive to leave at age 16 in the form of a YTS weekly stipend. These values, Bynner points out, are a hallmark of the early (attempted) transition into the labour market among British youth.

A strikingly different picture emerges from Krahn and Lowe's chapter. Their Canadian evidence suggests that the school–work transition is undergoing fundamental change, becoming more prolonged, circuitous and fraught with personal disappointments than previously. Despite these changes, however, transitional mechanisms and institutions have not collapsed (at least not yet) in the way British commentators claim has occurred in their country.

High-school graduates in the Canadian study placed greater value on education, planning to obtain more schooling before seeking out a career. These educational plans reflected occupational goals as well as a view of the labour market in which human capital matters. Among those high-school or university graduates who did enter the labour market after graduating in 1985, sizeable numbers returned in the fall of 1986 to pursue their education. In short, the break with the educational system is not as decisive as it is in

Britain. Good evidence of this is the fact that one-third of the high-school sample and over one-quarter of the university sample combined education and work during the two years following their 1985 graduation. One of the big issues this ongoing research is now examining is whether the relative pay-offs to higher education reaped by preceding youth cohorts will diminish, giving way to widespread underemployment.

This merging of the roles of student and worker and a commitment to further education reflect two essential differences between Canadian and British institutions. First, North American students generally have high participation rates in the labour market in 'student' jobs, thereby lessening the pressure to leave school and earn money, as is the case in Britain. Second, both the organization and underlying values of the Canadian (and American) educational system encourage the attainment of credentials at the post-secondary level and provide more opportunities to do so throughout one's adult life. Thus we find in both societies strong contrasts in transitional patterns.

This is not to deny similarities in transitional patterns. There is little doubt, for example, that gender is a major source of variation in educational and labour-market experiences. In both countries females are clustered in stereotypically 'female' educational programmes and jobs. It is also the case that local economic conditions strongly influence the labour-market experiences of youth, although the effects of locale seem to be more pervasive in Britain than in Canada. Similarly, educational attainment has a major impact on labour-market outcomes. Early school-leavers are perhaps the most disadvantaged segment of the youth population in either country (compounded, of course, by class and race or ethnicity). So too, post-secondary credentials confer advantages. The basic difference, however, is that the Canadian system offers more chances to upgrade one's education and, with that, an increased probability of finding a better job. Clearly these institutional features contribute to the greater salience of the 'contest mobility' model in Canadian society.

Conclusion

In bringing together this collection of papers our intention is not to provide a full-blown account of the relationship between education and the labour market in the two societies. Our aims are to use the studies reported here to highlight the similarities and differences in transitional structures and patterns; to explore how these contextual factors may influence young people's experiences of the transition; and to examine how the ensuing pathways from school to work are being affected by the changing international division of labour, not least by the recession of the early 1980s and its aftermath.

As we have already noted, the common factors and processes of the school–work transition across societies are, at one level, more easy to explain than the differences. Yet the existence of different institutional linkages between education and the labour market means that we cannot, as has so often been done, generalize from research findings in one society to others. For example, if we contrast the movement back and forth between education and the labour market in Canada with the sharp break in the transition found in Britain, then we can see how these institutional differences exert a major influence on the life course and hence the experience of the transition. Thus, if we are to provide an adequate account of the reproduction of the respective class structures, we must explain the origin and persistence of these differences.

When we turn to this task, we are building on a number of traditions. The first is historical sociology, with its focus on the development of institutional structures through time (Elias 1982). Here we refer to the different institutional forms of the state in the two societies, for example, the decentralized Canadian state and the highly centralized British state, and their impact on education and labour-market policy. Also of significance from this tradition is the concern with industrialization trajectories (Moore 1967; Laxer 1989), and their influence not only on the structure of the economy but also on subsequent political developments. To these we add Lipset's concept of organizing principles which he used to characterize the defining events which created a given constellation of values, in his case those of Canadian as opposed to US society (Lipset 1986).

In this paper we extend the concept to refer not just to constellations of values but also to the creation of the distinctive interrelationships between the educational and labour-market institutions which characterize Canadian and British society. The concept helps highlight the way in which institutions and values once formed shape subsequent changes. With regard to values, it helps to explain how the greater consensus on the Canadian values of equality of opportunity and universality have led to the more extensive provision of state education. In Britain, the dominant, but contested values have been those of selectivity and the use of education to prepare each status group for its place in the labour market. Hence the more limited provision for the working class in Britain and the more extensive use of private education by the upper class.

Finally, in the traditions of historical sociology, we point to the significance of internal class relations as an explanatory factor. For example, the presence of a hereditary aristocracy and upper class in Britain helps explain the dominance of the values of selectivity and the use of education as means of preparing different groups for their place in the social order. The absence of such a class in Canada and the unfettered dominance of the manufacturing and financial capitalist class helps explain the greater consensus on the values of universality and equality of opportunity.

The second tradition on which we build is that of comparative sociology, especially recent developments which focus on the interconnectedness of educational systems and labour markets (Maurice *et al.* 1986). Indeed, it is difficult to understand either the structure or functioning of the educational system without considering how it is integrated with the labour market, especially the system of training and recruitment adopted by employers. Nor can we understand employers' recruitment and training practices without reference to past and present links between industry and the educational system. For example, the institutions through which educational provision is delivered have been influenced, both in their formative years and in their subsequent development, by labour-market institutions, especially the system of training and the recruitment practices of employers. In Britain the apprenticeship system has traditionally been regarded as the main agency of occupational socialization, leaving the schools to concentrate on the provision of basic literacy and 'academic' education. In Canada the absence of such a widespread system of occupational socialization left a greater space for the incorporation of vocational education into the curriculum and the organization of the educational system.

In sum, this volume is a modest attempt to grapple with some big questions from a comparative perspective. Admittedly we can sketch out only a provisional explanation for the similarities and differences between Britain and Canada in the school–work transition. We now invite the reader to examine basic features of the transition in greater detail through the chapters which follow, formulating his or her own comparative insights. The Conclusion picks up the comparative themes raised above, pointing in the direction of a full-fledged comparative explanation which may spark imaginative approaches by others.

References

Ashton, D. N. (1988). 'Sources of variation in labour market segmentation: a comparison of youth labour markets in Canada and Britain'. *Work, Employment and Society*, 2(1): 1–24.

Ashton, D. N. and Field, D. (1976). *Young Workers: The Transition from School to Work*. London, Hutchinson.

Ashton, D. N., Maguire, M. J. and Spilsbury, M. (1988). 'The youth labour market in the United Kingdom and the 1979–82 recession: the effects of cyclical and structural change'. *Labour and Society*, 13: 415–41.

Barnett, C. (1988). *The Pride and Fall: The Dream and Illusion of Britain as a Great Nation*. New York: Free Press.

Bendix, R. (1963). *Work and Authority in Industry*. New York: Harper & Row.

Blossfeld, H. P. (1987). 'Entry into the labour market and occupational career in the Federal Republic: a comparison with American studies'. *International Journal of Sociology*, 17: 86–115.

Braungart, R. G. and Braungart, M. M. (1986). 'Youth problems and policies in the 1980s: some multinational comparisons'. *International Sociology*, 1: 359–80.

Brown, P. and Ashton, D. N. (eds.) (1987). *Education, Unemployment and Labour Markets*. Lewes, Falmer Press.

Elias, N. (1982). *State Formation and Civilization*. Oxford, Blackwell.

Fiddy, R. (ed.) (1985). *Youth, Unemployment and Training: A Collection of National Perspectives*. Lewes, Falmer Press.

Foot, D. K. and Li, J. C. (1986). 'Youth employment in Canada: a misplaced priority?'. *Canadian Public Policy*, 12: 499–506.

Hartmann, J. (1987). *Transition from School to Work: the Swedish Case 1976 to 1985*. Research report, Department of Sociology, University of Uppsala.

Heinz, W. R. (1987). 'The transition from school to work in crisis: coping with threatening unemployment'. *Journal of Adolescent Research*, 2: 127–41.

Howe, W. J. (1988). 'Education and demographics: how do they affect unemployment rates?' *Monthly Labor Review*, III (1): 3–9.

ILO (1988). *World Employment Review*. International Labour Organization, Geneva.

Jones, G. (1988). 'Integrating process and structure in the concept of youth: a case for secondary analysis'. *Sociological Review*, 36: 706–32.

Junankar, P. N. (ed.) (1987). *From School to Unemployment? The Labour Market for Young People*. London, Macmillan.

Kalleberg, A. L. (1988). 'Comparative perspectives on work structures and inequality'. *Annual Review of Sociology*, 14: 203–25.

Kohn, M. L. (1987). 'Cross-national research as an analytic strategy'. *American Sociological Review*, 52: 713–31.

Laxer, G. (1989). *Open for Business: The Roots of Foreign Ownership in Canada*. Toronto, Oxford University Press.

Lipset, S. M. (1986). 'Historical traditions and national characteristics: a comparative analysis of Canada and the United States'. *Canadian Journal of Sociology*, 11: 113–55.

Maurice, M., Sellier, F. and Silvestre, J. J. (1986). *The Social Foundations of Industrial Power: A Comparison of France and Germany*. Cambridge, MA, MIT Press.

Moore, B. (1967). *Social Origins of Dictatorship and Democracy: Lord and Peasant in the Making of the Modern World*. Boston, Beacon Press.

Nardone, T. (1987). 'Decline in youth population does not lead to lower youth jobless rate'. *Monthly Labor Review*, 110 (6): 37–41.

Organization for Economic Co-operation and Development (1984). *The Nature of Youth Unemployment*. Paris, Organization for Economic Co-operation and Development.

Organization for Economic Co-operation and Development (1987). *Structural Adjustment and Economic Performance*. Paris, Organization for Economic Co-operation and Development.

Organization for Economic Co-operation and Development (1988). *OECD Economic Surveys. Canada*. Paris, Organization for Economic Co-operation and Development.

Pahl, R. E. (1988). 'Introduction', in R. E. Pahl (ed.) (1988). *On Work: Historical, Comparative and Theoretical Approaches*. Oxford, Basil Blackwell.

Ragin, C. (1982). 'Comparative sociology and the comparative method'. *International Journal of Comparative Sociology*, 22: 102–20.

Reubens, B. G. (1983). 'Perspectives and problems' in B. G. Reubens (ed.) *Youth at Work: An International Survey*. Totowa, NJ, Rowman & Allanheld.

Rindfuss, R. R., Swicegood, C. G. and Rosenfeld, R. R. (1987). 'Disorder in the life course: how common and does it matter'. *American Sociological Review*, 52: 785–801.

Rist, R. C. (ed.) (1986). *Finding Work: Cross National Perspectives on Employment and Training*. Lewes, Falmer Press.

Starr, J. M. (1986). 'American youth in the 1980s'. *Youth and Society*, 17: 323–45.

Tilly, C. (1984). *Big Structures, Large Processes, Huge Comparisons*. New York, Russell Sage Foundation.

Williams, W. M. (ed.) (1974). *Occupational Choice*. London, Allen & Unwin.

Willis, P. (1977). *Learning to Labour*. Farnborough, Saxon House.

Willis, P. (1986). 'Unemployment: the final inequality'. *British Journal of Sociology of Education*, 7: 155–69.

2

The changing Canadian labour market

Harvey Krahn

Industrial patterns

In broad terms, Canada's economic history is similar to that of other western countries, with primary industries giving way to manufacturing and then to service industries. But there are also some important differences. First, the process of industrialization began later in Canada (Laxer 1985). In 1891 primary industries still accounted for almost half the Canadian labour force (49 per cent), with the secondary sector employing 20 per cent, and the service sector 31 per cent (Matthews 1985: 36). Second, compared to other industrialized countries, the service sectors were more developed by the time manufacturing became a prominent part of the economy. Substantial commercial, financial, and transportation sectors were part of Canada's colonial legacy (Lowe 1987: 29). But despite the late start, industrialization, consolidation of business ownership, and the emergence of large work organizations were trends well under way by the time the twentieth century began (Heron and Storey 1986).

By mid-century, the primary industries had declined significantly, accounting for only 22 per cent of the labour force. Manufacturing and construction now employed 31 per cent, with the remainder (47 per cent) in the service sectors (Picot 1987: 11). The service industries continued to expand in the post-war years, with annual employment growth averaging 4 per cent (1951 to 1981), compared to only 1 per cent in the goods-producing sectors. During the 1950s and 1960s, the most substantial growth was in the public services (education, health and public administration). Since then, commercial services (particularly consumer and business services) have been the growth industries (Picot *et al.*, 1987a: 7–8).

Service-industry growth continued throughout the recession of the early 1980s. While goods-producing industries declined by 2.9 per cent between 1981 and 1986, the 1986 Census revealed that service industries, as a group, had grown by 10.8 per cent. Most noticeably, community, business and personal services showed a 16.7 per cent increase over this five-year period, alone employing almost one in three Canadians in 1986 (Statistics Canada, *The Daily*, 1 March 1988). The other service industries (transportation and communication, trade, finance, insurance, real estate, public administration and defence) had also expanded, but much less so. Thus, by 1987, seven out of ten Canadians worked in the service sectors (Gower 1988b: 18). The 1986 Census found only 16.4 per cent of the labour force employed in manufacturing and a very small minority (3.8 per cent) in agriculture. These two sectors had declined from 24.7 per cent and 15.6 per cent of the labour force in 1951, respectively (Picot 1987: 11).

Canada also differs from other western industrialized countries in the degree to which the production and export of raw materials contribute to the economy. As a colony, Canada provided a succession of unprocessed staple products for world markets – furs, fish, and timber being among the first. Wheat, coal, oil and natural gas, and a variety of other minerals have continued to be mainstay exports. While some economists extol the comparative advantage in resource extraction which Canada enjoys, others have expressed concerns about the economic and social consequences of over-reliance on export of raw materials (Watkins 1982). In particular, vulnerability in world markets due to limited export diversification, relatively few forward and backward linkages to other industries, and the lower proportion of skilled, well-paying jobs in manufacturing are seen as serious drawbacks.

Certain regions of the country are much more reliant on primary industries while, elsewhere, secondary industries are stronger. The geographic distribution of natural resources and transportation routes, historical patterns of colonization and settlement, the earlier experience of industrialization in eastern and central Canada, along with political influences, have all played a part in the evolution of Canada's economic landscape (Krahn and Lowe 1988: 14–21, 48–53). Thus, today, agriculture remains important in the prairie provinces, particularly in Manitoba and Saskatchewan (table 2.1). Other primary industries provide a significant amount of employment in the Maritimes (forestry and fishing), in Alberta (oil and natural gas), and British Columbia (forestry). While the different service industries vary only little across regions, in terms of relative shares of the labour force, it is obvious that Ontario and Quebec are the dominant manufacturing provinces.

Manufacturing has been concentrated in central Canada for a century, despite some industrial diversification efforts by the federal and provincial governments, and regional economic disparities reflect this concentration

Table 2.1 Labour force by industry and region, Canada 1988

Industry	Maritimes	Quebec	Ontario	Man./Sask.	Alberta	B.C.	Total
	%	%	%	%	%	%	%
Agriculture	2.1	2.3	2.3	11.6	7.3	2.6	3.6
Other primary	6.0	1.5	1.2	2.2	5.8	4.2	2.5
Manufacturing	13.0	20.4	21.1	9.4	8.1	12.0	17.1
Construction	7.1	6.1	6.1	5.6	6.6	6.8	6.3
Transportation/ communication	7.8	7.3	6.6	8.3	7.6	7.6	7.3
Trade	18.1	16.9	17.4	17.6	18.0	18.4	17.5
Finance/insurance/real estate	3.8	5.2	6.5	4.8	4.9	6.3	5.7
Service	32.3	32.9	32.2	32.2	34.0	35.3	32.9
Public Administration	8.7	6.5	6.0	7.3	7.3	6.0	6.6
Unclassified[1]	–[2]	0.9	0.3	–[2]	0.4	0.8	0.5
Total	98.9	100.0	99.7	99.0	100.0	100.0	100.0
N (1000s)	(1019)	(3311)	(5118)	(1023)	(1291)	(1514)	(13276)

Source: Statistics Canada, 1989. *Labour Force Annual Averages 1981–1988* (cat. no. 71–529) table 11. p. 157. Small sample sizes in some of the smaller provinces lead to less reliable estimates for less prominent industries. Since Statistics Canada does not publish estimates of less than 4,000, the four Maritime provinces have been combined as have Manitoba and Saskatchewan.

[1] Unemployed persons who, while considered part of the labour force, have never worked for pay and those who last worked more than five years ago.

[2] Provincial estimates of less than 4,000. These omissions, as well as rounding errors, lead to total percentages of less than 100 per cent.

(Phillips 1982). Adult- and youth-unemployment rates have generally been much higher in provinces more reliant on primary industries and have influenced interprovincial migration flows. With the exception of a decade of heavy migration to Alberta during its oil boom in the 1970s, Ontario has been the primary recipient of job-seeking migrants from other provinces. Between 1981 and 1986, it had a net gain of close to 100,000 people from other provinces (Statistics Canada, *The Daily*, 1 March 1988).

The school–work transition in Canada is conditioned by the regional industrial structure. Limited economic diversification in some regions means a higher probability of unemployment and a more limited range of employment opportunities. In particular, young labour-force entrants in Canada's many single-industry communities often encounter difficulty finding work (Krahn and Lowe 1988: 51–3). In the past, the local mine or mill might have provided an opportunity for a reasonably well-paid, secure job. But technological change has led to workforce reductions and fewer entry-level jobs. For example, in 1986 the Canadian mining industry employed almost 22,000 fewer people than in 1981 – a 10.4 per cent decline (Statistics Canada, *The Daily*, 1 March 1988). Alternatively, young people living in Ontario and Quebec are more likely to find entry-level jobs in manufacturing establishments and in a broader range of service industries.

Labour-force participation

The Canadian labour-force participation rate (LFP)[1] remained relatively constant (near 55 per cent) for several decades in the middle of this century, but then began to rise, reaching 58.1 per cent in 1971, and 64.8 per cent by 1981. Since then, it has gone marginally higher (66.7 per cent in 1988). This increase is primarily a result of the rapid movement of women into the paid labour force. The male LFP dropped from 80.8 per cent in 1961 to 76.6 per cent in 1988, but the female LFP almost doubled (from 29.1 to 57.4 per cent) during this time (Statistics Canada 1989: 87; Krahn and Lowe 1988: 40).[2]

A rise in female LFP has also been observed in other industrialized countries. For example, between 1960 and 1980 female LFP in Britain rose from 39.5 per cent to 46.6 per cent. But the increase in these two decades was much more dramatic in Canada, from around 30 per cent to over 50 per cent (Boulet and Lavallee 1984: 6). Consequently, by 1981 the typical Canadian family of the 1950s had been replaced by the two-earner family. Thirty per cent of all families (including single-parent and childless families) had two parents in the labour force, while one-earner two-adult families (with children) made up only 24 per cent of the total (Supply and Services Canada 1987: 4).

As one would expect, LFP is highest among those aged 25 to 44 (84.9 per cent in 1988), and lower in the older age categories. But youth (ages 15 to 24) LFP is also high in Canada (72.2 per cent for males and 66.9 per cent for females in 1988). This is not because young people leave school early to enter the labour force. Some do, but finishing high school remains the norm, and concerns about the labour-market future of high school dropouts arise frequently (Radwanski 1987). Furthermore, large numbers of Canadian youth continue on in colleges, technical schools, and universities. Youth LFP is high, then, because many hold jobs (frequently part-time) while attending school. This trend towards greater employment of young students has been a second (but less important) factor contributing to the general LFP increase observed in Canada over the past decades.

While youth LFP is generally high, there are distinct differences within the youth category. The LFP for males aged 20 to 24 was 85.0 per cent in 1988, while 76.5 per cent of females in this more narrow age category were in the labour force. The comparable rates for youth aged 15 to 19 were 58.5 and 56.1 per cent, respectively (Statistics Canada 1989: 13). Older youth would be more likely to have left school completely and might also have married, both of which would increase the probability of labour-market entry. But considering only full-time students, LFP was higher for 15-to-19-year-olds (44.0 per cent), compared to 38.2 per cent for 20-to-24-year-olds (Statistics Canada 1989: 101).

Finally, multiple-job holding has increased to 4 per cent of all labour-force participants in 1988 (Akyeampong 1988: 102). In addition, there has been a small increase in self-employment in the 1980s. Recent surveys show around 13 per cent of the labour force as self-employed, with about one-half of this group being individuals who employ others and one-half having no paid help (Statistics Canada 1985: 9; Cohen 1988). It is tempting to interpret these trends as direct responses to the high unemployment and declining real incomes of the 1980s, particularly among young labour-force partici-pants. Unfortunately, detailed information on reasons for holding more than one job or for self-employment, and on the age-distribution of multiple-job holders, is not available.[3] As for self-employment, in 1986 only 5.6 per cent of 15-to-24-year-old labour-force participants were self-employed (Cohen 1988), suggesting that this is not a common solution to youth unemployment.

Occupational structure

The shift from primary to secondary and service industries has been accompanied by a transformation of the Canadian occupational structure. In 1901, the national Census found 45 per cent of the labour force in agricultural occupations. In 1986, the figure was 3.9 per cent. Blue-collar occupations in manufacturing and construction accounted for between 25 and 30 per cent of the labour force in the first half of the century. The second half has been one of slow decline in these occupations, to 22.3 per cent in 1986. And when the century began, about 15 per cent of labour-force participants were working in white-collar jobs. In 1986, over half were employed in managerial, professional, clerical and sales jobs (Krahn and Lowe 1988:44; Statistics Canada, *The Daily*, 1 March 1988).

White-collar employment has continued to grow in the 1980s. Between 1981 and 1986, the social science and managerial/administrative categories increased the most (29 and 26.6 per cent, respectively). Strictly 'service' occupations (e.g. food or personal services) had also grown by 13.1 per cent (Statistics Canada, *The Daily*, 1 March 1988). Since 1986, these trends have continued, although there is now some evidence of greater growth in clerical and sales occupations than in the higher-status managerial and professional categories (Akyeampong 1988: 96).

Pronounced differences in female and male occupational distributions are highlighted in table 2.2. Larger proportions of men are in managerial/ administrative and in manufacturing and construction occupations. Women are much more likely to be found in clerical, sales, and service occupations (57.2 per cent in total), and in teaching and medicine. While comparisons to the 1981 Census reveal a slow movement away from gender-specific occupations (Statistics Canada, *The Daily*, 1 March 1988), the male–female differences observed here would be larger if detailed occupational categories were examined. Women are still much more likely to be found in lower-level managerial positions, for example, and, in the medicine and health category, in the traditionally female occupation of nursing.

Concentration of women in clerical, sales, and service occupations translates into lower incomes since these types of work tend to be low pay, low status and, frequently, part-time. But even when considering only full-time, full-year employees, women in Canada earn, on average, about two-thirds of what men earn. Very little of this gender difference can be attributed to direct pay discrimination. Instead, occupational segregation of women in low-pay types of work is largely responsible (Gunderson 1985: 231). The female–male wage ratio has increased only marginally over the past decade, despite the entry of more women into non-traditional areas of work. The rapid increase in female labour-force participation has also meant that many more women moved into clerical, sales, and service occupations (Krahn and Lowe 1988: 135).

Table 2.2 also demonstrates the degree to which age influences occupational location in Canada. Very few of the youngest labour-force participants of either sex are in managerial or professional occupations. But 11 per cent of males aged 25 to 34 have moved into these higher status occupations, showing the effect of educational credentials and experience which this group would have had the chance to obtain. Women in the same age category are actually slightly more likely than those 35 and older to be in managerial and administrative occupations. This may reflect a cohort effect, that is, a decline in gender imbalances over time as larger proportions of young women move into non-traditional occupations. On the other hand, it may simply mean that gender imbalances take time to emerge, with males in a variety of other occupations having more opportunities for career advancement into managerial positions. As for the other white-collar

Table 2.2 Labour force by occupation, age and sex, Canada 1986

	Age						Total		
	15–24		25–34		35+				
Occupation	Female	Male	Female	Male	Female	Male	Female	Male	Total
	%	%	%	%	%	%	%	%	%
Managerial/ administrative	3.1	3.0	9.1	11.1	8.8	16.7	7.5	12.4	10.3
Natural science	1.4	3.3	2.3	6.7	0.9	4.6	1.4	5.0	3.4
Social science	2.0	0.8	3.1	1.6	2.5	1.5	2.6	1.4	1.9
Teaching	2.2	0.7	5.9	2.3	8.0	3.9	6.0	2.8	4.2
Medicine/health	5.1	0.9	10.2	2.0	9.3	1.9	8.6	1.7	4.7
Religion/artistic/ recreational	1.8	1.8	2.0	2.2	1.5	1.9	1.7	2.0	1.8
Clerical	34.0	9.9	34.7	6.8	30.3	5.3	32.5	6.6	17.8
Sales	12.2	10.4	7.0	8.1	8.9	8.2	9.1	8.6	8.8
Services	23.0	16.8	12.1	8.3	14.1	8.3	15.6	10.0	12.4
Primary occupations[1]	2.2	9.3	1.8	6.5	3.0	7.8	2.4	7.7	5.4
Processing/ manufacturing	5.0	17.0	6.1	20.0	7.3	16.9	6.4	17.8	12.9
Construction/ transportation	0.8	13.1	1.0	16.7	1.0	16.2	1.0	15.7	9.4
Other occupations/ Occupation NA[2]	7.2	13.0	4.7	7.7	4.4	6.8	5.2	8.3	7.0
Total	100.0	100.0	100.0	100.0	100.0	100.0	100.0	100.0	100.0
N (1000s)	(1332)	(1487)	(1674)	(2118)	(2602)	(3836)	(5609)	(7441)	(13050)

Source: Statistics Canada. *Census of Canada 1986. The Nation: Occupation* (cat. no. 93–112), table 1.

[1] Includes occupations in agriculture, fishing, forestry and mining.

[2] Includes material handling and related occupations not elsewhere classified, other crafts and equipment-operating occupations, occupations not elsewhere classified, and unemployed individuals who have never held a job or who only held a job prior to 1 January 1985.

occupational groups, the gender differences within the 25-to-34 category are quite similar to those among older workers (table 2.2).

Age has little effect on the probability of women's being employed in primary-sector construction, or transportation occupations (table 2.2). The opportunities for women in manufacturing appear to increase slightly with age but, like the primary and other blue-collar occupations, these tend to be male preserves. For young men, particularly those aged 15 to 24, primary-sector occupations are quite common. Unskilled work in these areas provides one form of entry-level employment for young males. But so do manufacturing and construction occupations which were reported by a sizeable proportion of the youngest male workers. However, it is in the 25-to-34 age group that manufacturing (20.0 per cent) and construction jobs (16.7 per cent) were most common among males.

It is clear from table 2.2 that gender-based occupational segregation is pronounced among Canadian youth. Largely excluded from professional/ managerial and blue-collar positions, the youngest female workers are most heavily concentrated in clerical, sales and service occupations (69 per cent in total), but particularly so in the clerical and service categories. For women aged 25 to 34, sales and service jobs are somewhat less common, but over one-third (34.7 per cent) of these young women are still in clerical occupations. Despite some shifts over time in the gender distribution of occupations, the chances of young Canadian women's finding employment in clerical occupations are still about one in three.

As already noted, the cross-sectional data in table 2.2 cannot adequately distinguish career from cohort effects. Other things being equal, we would expect significant numbers of young workers to move into a broader range of higher-status occupations as they accumulate more education and labour market experience. The decline, with age, of females in service and sales occupations (table 2.2) could be read as evidence of such a career effect. However, other things are changing. Community, business and personal service industries have been expanding much more rapidly than have other industrial sectors. Part-time work has become much more common, and unemployment rates have risen. These trends suggest that young workers today may be experiencing more difficulty moving out of the youth labour market into better-paying and higher-status occupations.

In Britain and other countries where entry into the adult labour market has been more institutionalized (via apprenticeships, for example), the breakdown of the traditional system may be more obvious (see chapter 2). But in Canada, individual efforts (part-time work while in school, 'getting an education', and 'looking for work' after leaving school) have always played a larger part in the transition into the adult work world. Thus, a more problematic process of transition, as a consequence of industrial restructuring and changes in work patterns, may not be as immediately apparent, particularly since part-time work by students and post-secondary enrolments remain high.

Part-time employment

In 1953, only 3.8 per cent of employed Canadians were in part-time (less than 30 hours per week) jobs (Weeks 1980: 69). But in the last two decades, full-time job creation has lagged far behind that of growth in part-time positions (Kaliski 1985: 86). Between 1977 and 1986, this trend was most pronounced, with part-time employment increasing by 60 per cent, compared to only 15 per cent for full-time jobs. Thus, in 1977, part-time work accounted for 11.7 per cent of total employment. By 1986, this had increased to 15.6 per cent. A small reversal in this trend was observed in 1987 when full-time jobs increased somewhat faster than part-time positions, (Gower 1988a: 92). However, data from the first half of 1988 show a return to the trend of greater part-time employment growth (Akyeampong 1988: 100), with the 1988 annual average being 15.4 per cent (Statistics Canada 1989: 213).

Almost all (90 per cent) of the part-time jobs created in the last two decades have been in the service industries (Kaliski 1985: 86). Retail sales and restaurant, entertainment and recreation industries have moved furthest in this direction. Employment of part-time workers reduces direct and indirect (part-time workers receive few fringe benefits) labour costs, and allows much greater flexibility in labour utilization, both of which are highly desirable, from an employer's viewpoint, in the competitive service sectors.

While one-quarter (25.2 per cent) of employed women were in part-time jobs in 1988, only 7.7 per cent of employed men reported part-time work (Statistics Canada 1989: 213). In total, 1.36 million women were working part-time, representing 72 per cent of the 1.88 million part-time workers. About one in three young (ages 15 to 24) workers were in part-time jobs in 1988, compared to about one in ten workers in the 25-to-44-year-old category. Among the young workers, women had a higher probability of being employed part-time (37.3 per cent) than did men (29.1 per cent).

In 1988, 64 per cent of part-time employed young women (ages 15 to 24) and 75 per cent of their male counterparts identified educational reasons for their shorter hours of work (Statistics Canada 1989: 221). Part-time work appears to complement continued education for a large majority of young labour-force participants. However, most of the rest of these young workers had not chosen to work part-time; 22 per cent of the women and 18 per cent of the men reported that they could not find a full-time job. 'Involuntary part-time employment' was higher among women aged 25 to 44 (26.7 per cent), although the majority of these women identified personal or family reasons, or simply stated that they did not want a full-time job. While few men in this age category were in part-time jobs (78,000 in total), most (56.4 per cent) were not there by choice.

Thus, while the flexibility of part-time work may be attractive to students, young parents and older workers, many part-time labour-force participants would prefer full-time employment (Akyeampong 1986). In 1975, only 11 per cent of those in part-time positions were classified as 'involuntary part-time workers' (Boulet and Lavallee 1984: 12). By 1986, this group had grown to include 28.4 per cent of the part-time employed. Since then, it has declined somewhat (Statistics Canada 1987a: 119; Akyeampong 1988: 100), but it is probably too early to take this reversal as evidence of a significant trend.

Unemployment

In the three decades between 1946 and 1976, the Canadian unemployment rate fluctuated between 2.2 per cent (1947) and 7.1 per cent (1961, 1976), but averaged 4.7 per cent. The experiences of the late 1970s and early 1980s put a new meaning on the term 'recession' as unemployment rates rose to 8.3 per cent in 1978, dropped down to around 7.5 per cent for a few years, and then jumped to 11.0 per cent in 1982. They peaked (11.9 per cent) in 1983 when almost one and a half million Canadians were without work. Between 1981 and 1984, almost one-half million long-term workers lost their job (Picot and Wannell 1988).

The economy has recovered since then, and unemployment rates dropped to 8.9 per cent in 1987, and further to 7.8 per cent in 1988. But long-term unemployment has been more persistent (Parliament 1987). Many of those who became unemployed during the recession had difficulty finding new jobs. By 1986, 17 per cent had left the labour force, and 20 per cent were still unemployed. Over half (56 per cent) of those who had found new jobs were earning less than in their old position (Picot and Wannell 1988). Only recently have we begun to see a drop in the percentage unemployed for more than a year (Akyeampong 1988: 105). Some of this may be due to economic recovery, while higher rates of labour-force exit by older displaced workers are probably also part of the explanation (Lindsay 1987; Picot and Wannell 1988).

Canada's high level of unemployment over the last decade needs to be viewed comparatively. In 1979, Canada's unemployment rate of 7.4 per cent was higher than that of the United States (5.8 per cent), France (6.0 per cent), and the United Kingdom (5.4 per cent). All of these countries were affected by the global recession of the early 1980s, but some more than others. Unemployment peaked at 9.7 per cent in the US in 1982, a year earlier than the highest point (11.9 per cent) in Canada. Since then, the US rate has dropped to 6.4 per cent in 1987. But the French and British economies have not recovered as quickly, maintaining 1987 unemployment rates in excess of 11 and 10 per cent respectively (Gower 1988a: 101). To put the Canadian and British experience into context, we should note that over this same period (1979 to 1986), the West German rate of unemployment never went above 7.5 per cent, the Swedish rate peaked at 3.5 per cent, and the Japanese rate failed to reach 3 per cent at any time (Moy 1988: 41; rates adjusted to correspond to US definitions).

Regional industrial patterns significantly affect unemployment rates. The Maritime provinces have a long history of high unemployment while the manufacturing provinces of Ontario and Quebec have generally had lower rates. The western provinces of Alberta and British Columbia, heavily dependent on resource-extraction industries, have been most volatile in this respect. Alberta, for example, had very low levels of unemployment (around 3 or 4 per cent) during its oil-boom of the 1970s. But unemployment rose quickly to above national averages when oil prices dropped in the 1980s and have only begun receding in the past few years.

These regional patterns, with a few variations, have been reinforced as Canada recovered from its recession of the early 1980s. While the country as a whole has experienced five years of economic growth (Gower 1988b: 17), most of the job-creation benefits have been in Ontario, which reported a 5.0 per cent unemployment rate in 1988. In contrast, the unemployment rate in Newfoundland was 16.9 per cent. Prince Edward Island (13.1 per cent) and New Brunswick (12.1 per cent) also reported very high rates, followed by Nova Scotia and British Columbia (both 10.4 per cent), Quebec (9.4 per cent), and Alberta (8.0 per cent). During this last recession, unemployment never went as high in Manitoba and Saskatchewan as in the other western provinces. But 1988 saw marginal increases in joblessness in both provinces (from 7.4 and 7.3 per cent a year earlier to 7.9 and 7.5 per cent respectively).

Unemployment rates also vary considerably across occupational categories. Compared to lower-status occupations, managers and professionals have many more labour-market shelters shielding them from unemployment (Ashton 1986: 53). Hence it is not surprising that, in 1988, unemployment was very low (4.1 per cent) within this group (Statistics Canada 1989: 189). On the other hand, unemployment was much more common in 1988 among Canadians with service (9.8 per cent), construction (13.0 per cent), and primary occupations (10.3 per cent). While service occupations are less often unionized, and so more at risk of job loss, unions are more prominent in construction, mining and forestry. But the seasonal nature of construction, forestry, and other primary-sector work leads to frequent unemployment and clearly contributes to the higher levels of unemployment in regions heavily dependent on resource extraction. Furthermore, global market trends have led to high unemployment in the Canadian forestry and petroleum industries, while industrial restructuring has had a negative impact on employment levels in other parts of the mining industry.

As one would expect, the more educated labour-force participants are much less likely to experience unemployment. University graduates had the lowest chance of unemployment (4.0 per cent) in 1988, compared to 9.1 per cent for those with only a high-school education and 10.7 per cent for those with eight or fewer years of education (Statistics Canada 1989: 92). However, age interacts considerably with this pattern. For example, recent (1982)

Table 2.3   Unemployment rates by age and sex, Canada, 1979, 1983, 1988

Age	1979			1983			1988		
	Female	Male	Both	Female	Male	Both	Female	Male	Both
	%	%	%	%	%	%	%	%	%
15–19	15.8	16.3	16.0	20.1	24.2	22.2	12.0	14.2	13.2
20–24	10.4	11.0	10.7	15.2	21.4	18.5	10.4	12.1	11.2
25–34	8.5	5.5	6.7	11.5	12.1	11.8	8.6	7.4	8.0
35–44	6.8	3.9	5.0	9.2	8.1	8.5	7.2	5.4	6.2
45–54	6.0	4.0	4.7	8.0	7.4	7.6	6.9	4.8	5.7
55–64	4.9	4.5	4.6	7.8	8.2	8.1	6.0	6.3	6.2
Total	8.8	6.6	7.4	11.6	12.1	11.9	8.3	7.4	7.8

Source: Statistics Canada (1984) *The Labour Force, Annual Averages 1975–1983* (cat. no. 71–529), table 1, pp. 13, 17. Statistics Canada, 1989. *The Labour Force, Annual Averages 1981–1988* (cat. no. 71–529), table 1, p. 13.

university graduates reported an unemployment rate of 8.6 per cent when surveyed in 1984, two years after graduating (Picot *et al.* 1987b: 38). In 1988, university graduates under age 25 were still reporting an unemployment rate of 7.5 per cent. Less educated young people are much more disadvantaged. The small minority of Canadian youth (ages 15 to 24) with eight or fewer years of education had an extremely high rate of unemployment (20.8 per cent) in 1988 (Statistics Canada 1989: 92).

When unemployment was at its highest in 1983, male rates were slightly higher than female rates (table 2.3). Since then, the pattern has again reversed, but today the gender difference is not as large as it was in 1979. The relative decline of manufacturing and primary industries which have traditionally been male preserves and continuing growth in the service sector where more women are employed appear to have left their mark on gender-based patterns of unemployment. Nevertheless women (all ages combined) continue to have a somewhat higher probability of unemployment (8.3 per cent in 1988) than do men (7.4 per cent). However, table 2.3 also demonstrates that, within the youth categories, the opposite pattern is observed – young males are more likely to be without work.

In fact, unemployment differences by age are much more pronounced than gender differences. Youth unemployment rates peaked around 20 per cent in 1983. The youngest age category (ages 15 to 19) experienced the highest level of joblessness (22.2 per cent), followed closely by those aged 20 to 24 (18.5 per cent). Youth unemployment suddenly became a national concern. Since then, relatively fewer young labour-force participants have been unemployed, but youth rates still remain considerably higher than adult rates of unemployment. The youngest members of the labour force (ages 15 to 19) are most likely to be without work (13.2 per cent), as they have been in the past, while those aged 20 to 24 reported a 11.2 per cent rate of unemployment in 1988 (table 2.3).

Part of the decline in youth unemployment can be attributed to the general economic recovery, but there is an additional explanation. With declining birth rates, the relative number of new labour-force entrants has been reduced, compared to the 'baby-boom' cohort of a decade earlier (Foot and Li 1986). In 1987, there were one-half million fewer 15-to-24-year-olds in the population than there were in 1980 when this age group was at its largest size (Gower 1988a: 93). Consequently the demand for entry-level positions in the labour force has been significantly reduced.

One of the implications of this demographic shift is that there now may be greater competition for jobs within a slightly older cohort. Comparing 1979 and 1988 rates of unemployment for the two youth categories (table 2.3), we note that unemployment among 15-to-19-year-olds has dropped from 16.0 to 13.2 per cent, even though the overall level of unemployment is still higher in 1988 than it was in 1979. Conversely, unemployment among 20-to-24-year-olds is higher in 1988 (11.2 per cent) than it was eight years earlier (10.7 per cent), although it has dropped from its high of 18.5 per cent in 1983. Thus, as Foot and Li (1986: 499) note, we may be seeing the problem of youth unemployment replaced by one of young adult unemployment.[4]

Organized labour

In the first few post-war decades, union membership in Canada (the percentage of non-agricultural paid workers belonging to a union) remained around 30 per cent. But membership began to rise in the 1960s when civil servants won the right to bargain collectively. With the rapid growth of public-sector unions, membership increased to 37 per cent by 1976 and peaked at 40 per cent in 1983. Thus, while organized labour has been declining for some time in the USA, union membership remains relatively high in Canada (Lipset 1987; Neill 1988: 13). However, high levels of unemployment in the 1980s reduced the ranks of some industrial unions, employment cutbacks in government have slowed the growth of public-sector unions and, to an extent, some of the anti-union tactics of American employers have been imported into Canada. Consequently organized labour in Canada has encountered setbacks in the past few years, reflected in a decline in membership in the last half decade to 36.6 per cent in January 1988.

Union membership has long been high in the manufacturing and transportation industries where large industrial unions have had their base, and at about the national average in construction and the primary industries. But today the unionization rate is highest in the public-administration industry where two out of three workers are union members. In 1986 the three largest unions in the country were public-sector unions (Krahn and Lowe 1988: 196–8). On the other hand, unionization rates are very low in the trade and finance industries. Some of the less unionized industries rely more heavily on part-time workers. Thus, while

40.9 per cent of full-time workers were unionized in 1985, only 18.8 per cent of part-time workers belonged to a union (Rose and Chaison 1987: 578).

These industry differences obviously influence the level of female unionization in Canada since women are much more likely to be working part-time and are underrepresented in manufacturing, construction, transportation and the primary industries. However, women are also much more likely to be employed in government, education and health-related industries where unionization has been increasing. Hence the large gender differences in union membership observed in the past have been shrinking. In 1985 the female unionization rate in Canada was 31.9 per cent, compared to 41.5 per cent for men (Rose and Chaison 1987: 578).

Union membership among young workers (ages 15 to 24) is much lower (18.6 per cent in 1985) than the national average (Rose and Chaison 1987: 578). Again this age difference has less to do with the union receptivity of youth than with their labour-market location. Young workers are more likely to be employed in part-time jobs in service industries where unions are not present. In the past, such entry-level jobs might have been discarded as young workers moved into better-paying, permanent jobs in other industries or government. But the recession of the 1980s meant that many large firms and government departments reduced their labour force. Hence positions for recent graduates were less common. To the extent that these were unionized workplaces, the chances of becoming a union member were reduced.

Post-secondary education

Elementary education in Canada is fairly general, although some 'streaming' of students by academic ability may occur. The growth of 'french immersion' programmes (all instruction is provided in French) in English Canada over the last decade has increased the amount of streaming (Parliament 1986). Somewhat more defined academic and vocational programmes are in place in most secondary schools (high schools). But even here the streaming process is less obvious than it was in the past, given the degree to which high-school students can choose among alternative course offerings (see chapter 4). Nevertheless, the technical or commercial emphasis in vocational programmes is aimed more directly at employment in specific occupations. It may also provide the background for subsequent post-secondary training in community colleges or technical schools. Academic programmes, on the other hand, are aimed directly at university entrance requirements (Statistics Canada 1988c: 22).

Completing secondary school (twelfth grade in most provinces) is the norm in Canada, although substantial numbers do 'drop out' before graduating. Reliable statistics are difficult to obtain, but estimates that roughly two-thirds of those who begin ninth grade eventually complete high school are common (see chapter 4). However, high-school completion rates have been going up. In 1986–7, 90 per cent of 14-to-17-year-old Canadians were enrolled in elementary or secondary schools, compared to 85 per cent a decade earlier (Statistics Canada 1988c: 45). Thus, while youth labour-force participation rates are high, much of this employment is part-time and in conjunction with school attendance. Job creation and training programmes have consequently tended to focus on somewhat older youth than is the case in Britain where school-leaving typically occurs earlier.

Despite predictions that university and college enrolments would begin to decline as the large 'baby-boom' cohort moved into full-time employment, post-secondary enrolments have continued to rise in the 1980s. A total of 796,400 students were enrolled full-time in post-secondary institutions in 1986–7, with 475,400 attending universities and 321,000 enrolled in community colleges (Statistics Canada 1988c).[5] Preliminary enrolment statistics for the 1988 fall term showed 500,000 full-time university students, making this the tenth straight year in which registration increased (Statistics Canada, *The Daily*, 5 January 1989). Full-time enrolment in community colleges increased by 46 per cent between 1976 and 1986 (Statistics Canada 1987b), but declined slightly in 1986–7. Part-time attendance, particularly in universities, has also been rising over the past decade. A total of 287,500 people were attending university part-time in 1986–7, and another 161,600 were part-time college students (Statistics Canada 1988c).

In 1986–7, 53 per cent of full-time male university undergraduates and 60 per cent of full-time female undergraduates were under 22 years of age. Most of the rest were less than 30 years old (Statistics Canada 1988c: 61). Thus, while there is a trend towards more widespread university attendance among older adults, a large majority of Canadian post-secondary students are young adults. In fact, one in four (25.5 per cent) of 18-to-24-year-olds were engaged in some form of post-secondary education during the 1986–7 school term (Statistics Canada 1988c: 123–35). It has been argued that Canadian youth have been continuing on in school in record numbers because of their awareness of a tight labour market. While there is little direct evidence to date to support this contention, it would be fair to conclude that most young Canadians believe higher education improves their chances of obtaining a better job.

Between 1975–6 and 1985–6, female university enrolment increased by 35 per cent compared to a 10.8 per cent increase for males. Hence, while women made up 47 per cent of undergraduate enrolment a decade earlier, in 1985–6 a total of 51.8 per cent of undergraduates were women (61.7 per cent of part-time students and 48.8 per cent of full-time students). Consequently, the percentage of bachelor's and first professional degrees awarded to women has grown from 38 per cent in 1970 to 44 per cent in 1975, 50 per cent in 1980 and 53 per cent in 1986. But men still received the majority of master's degrees (57 per cent) and doctoral degrees (73 per cent) awarded in 1986, although these differences have also declined significantly in the previous decade (Statistics Canada 1986–7: 67–74).

The 1986 Census (Statistics Canada, *The Daily*, 1 March 1988) revealed that commerce, management and business administration were the fields of study for 20 per cent of the university-educated males, followed by engineering/applied science (17 per cent) and social science and related fields (17 per cent). For women with a degree, education, recreation and counselling services were the most common area of study (28 per cent), followed by social science (17 per cent) and humanities (16 per cent). Thus, if we consider the total adult population, university-educated women and men appear to have distinctly different types of academic credentials which, no doubt, contribute to the gender segregation of the occupational structure.

Recent enrolment patterns have seen relatively more young women registering in traditional male faculties such as engineering and business but, at the same time, women remain heavily concentrated in education and nursing faculties. Consequently educational choices continue to play a part in the perpetuation of gender segregation within the labour force. For example, among 1982 university graduates, 12 per cent of the women compared to 4 per cent of the men reported clerical occupations in 1984. Almost one-third (32 per cent) of the women and only 14 per cent of the men were in teaching and related occupations. A total of 23 per cent of the male graduates were employed in natural science, engineering and mathematics occupations, but only 6 per cent of the female graduates reported these types of work (Statistics Canada 1984b).

Overall, the last few decades have seen a rapid increase in educational credentials in Canada. The 1986 Census found 9.6 per cent of all Canadians aged 15 and older reporting a university degree, doubling the figure recorded in 1971. A total of 15.1 per cent of those aged 24 to 44 reported a degree (Statistics Canada, *The Daily*, 1 March 1988). Taking both university degrees and college certificates and diplomas into consideration, 22.4 per cent of the adult Canadian population possessed some post-secondary educational credentials in 1986 (Statistics Canada 1988c). The important question is whether the demand for such post-secondary credentials has expanded as fast as the supply. If not, the most recent highly educated labour-force entrants may be forced into a position of relative underemployment.

Labour-market legislation and programmes

Labour-market legislation and programmes can be separated into 'active' and 'passive' categories (Smucker and van den Berg 1988). Active policies involve direct interventions in the labour market. These might consist of little more than attempts to match workers with jobs through information provision and placement programmes but would also include supply-oriented (training schemes, relocation subsidies) and demand-oriented programmes (wage subsidies, direct job creation). Passive programmes, on the other hand, are responses to, but not attempts to influence, labour-market trends. An unemployment-insurance system would be an example.

If we look back over the decades, it is apparent that the Canadian government has tended to rely more heavily on passive labour-market programmes.[6] Immigration, rather than training, has been the preferred vehicle for increasing skilled labour stocks. Apprenticeship programmes have been maintained but have not become central parts of the overall education system as they have in some other countries. Relatively few direct job-creation programmes have been implemented. Instead, fostering a business climate that might encourage private-sector investments and hence job creation has been a common concern of legislators.

On the other hand, unemployment-insurance schemes have been in place since the Depression. Government-funded employment centres have been operating for just about as long but, up until the mid-1960s, they provided little more than information. When they became part of the new Manpower and Immigration Department, some training and relocation programmes were introduced. However, these programmes tended to focus more on reducing unemployment in specific regions and communities than on increasing the overall stock of skilled workers.

By the late 1970s the renamed Canada Employment and Immigration (CEIC) department began to develop some additional job-creation programmes. Since then, the government has continued to move further in this direction with a number of programmes (frequently short-term in nature) aimed at specific groups such as youth, women, native Canadians or the disabled. In 1985 the federal government introduced the Canadian Jobs Strategy (CJS), a six-programme package designed to replace all existing federally sponsored labour-market programmes. In some ways, the CJS was more interventionist than the programmes it replaced. But it also shifted more of the responsibility for training and job creation away from government-funded employment centres to the private sector.

Two of the six programmes are directly relevant to young people encountering labour-market entry problems. The Job Entry programme has three components. The first, Entry, provides funds for job-training ventures aimed at unemployed early school-leavers, as well as financial assistance for secondary and post-secondary co-operative education programmes. The Re-entry programme is targeted at a very specific group, women who are re-entering the labour force. The Challenge programme subsidizes employers who will provide summer career-related jobs to students. The Job Development programme was set up to subsidize employers willing to hire the long-term unemployed, some of whom might be young labour-force participants.[7]

Systematic evaluations of these programmes are unavailable, so it is difficult to assess their impact on the Canadian labour market and on young labour-force participants. Concerns about chronic shortages of skilled workers continue to be expressed by employers. Complaints about restrictive eligibility rules for programme participation, the provision of public funds to individuals and firms making a business out of training, the quality of training provided, and the inflexibility of the programmes have also been voiced (Senate Sub-Committee on Training and Employment 1987: 12–17). In addition, critics have suggested that the Job Development programme has been little more than a way of subsidizing service-sector employers who pay low wages for work in relatively dead-end jobs. In short, reliance on private-sector initiatives does not, to this point, appear to be more effective than previous government-run labour-market programmes.

Whatever the final assessment of its effectiveness, the selective approach to identifying programme participants (unemployed high-school dropouts, the long-term unemployed, or women re-entering the labour force, for example) in the CJS distinguishes it from some of the more universal labour-market programmes targeting youth in countries such as Sweden or Britain. Finally, compared to previous Canadian government labour-market programmes, the CJS represents a somewhat more 'active' orientation. But compared to countries like Sweden, Canadian labour-market programmes have involved, and continue to involve, relatively less direct intervention in the economy (Smucker and van den Berg 1988: 44).

The Canadian labour market–future trends

Canada's labour market has been transformed since the middle of the century. Jobs in the primary sectors have declined to just a fraction of the labour force, although the export of raw materials continues to play a prominent part in the economy. A decline in the manufacturing sector has also occurred. Hence, today, over 70 per cent of Canadian labour-force participants are employed in the service industries. Growing female labour-force participation and high levels of youth participation have accompanied this industrial change, as has a significant rise in part-time work. Consequently, women and youth are considerably more likely to be working part-time in the various service industries, and involuntary part-time work has increased.

The very high rates of unemployment recorded in the first half of the decade have begun to decline, although this economic recovery has been much more dramatic in central Canada than elsewhere. Whether or not the economy expands further in the next few years, and forecasts are mixed, we will not see a return to the labour market of the 1970s. Service-sector growth will continue with sales, food service, clerical and janitorial positions topping the list of occupations expected to contribute most to employment growth up to 1995 (Krahn and Lowe 1988: 62–3). While part-time employment growth appears to have slowed, there is little evidence that the proportion of part-time jobs in the Canadian labour market will decline in the near future.

This last recession clearly left its mark on employment patterns in Canada. Most obvious were layoffs in or shutdowns of large manufacturing establishments (Grayson 1985) and massive layoffs in mining communities affected by unstable world markets. While a majority of the displaced workers found new positions as the economy slowly recovered, many were earning less than before. Large numbers remained unemployed for long periods of time, and many left the labour force completely (Picot and Wannell 1988). The secondary industries have seen better times in the last few years of the decade, but full-time employment growth has been limited due to corporate reorganizations and mergers, and the introduction of new technologies. The effects of the new Free Trade Agreement with the United States remain to be seen.

Cutbacks in public-sector employment paralleled these workforce reductions in industry. Declining tax revenues and calls for fiscal restraint in government led to the elimination of civil-service jobs at various levels of government or, at best, restrictions in filling vacant positions. Precise numbers are not available, but it is becoming apparent that the use of limited-term contract positions in government hiring has increased. Such practices give employers considerable flexibility without providing any long-term job security (or fringe benefits) to employees. A decade ago, few young job-seekers would have asked, in a job interview in a government department, 'Is this a permanent position?' Today, this is often a first question.

The incomes of labour-force participants have clearly been affected by the changing economy. After some years of expanding real incomes, the period of 1975 to 1987 saw almost no increase in purchasing power for Canadian workers. Over this twelve-year span, average annual labour income rose by 140 per cent. After taking inflation into account, the increase was only 1.5 per cent (Statistics Canada, *The Daily*, 20 October 1988). Even though unemployment rates were dropping and the economy was expanding, average earnings (adjusted for inflation) still declined in 1987 (Gower 1988a: 104). The increase in two-earner families has probably tempered this downward push on household incomes in Canada (Akyeampong 1988: 102), as it has in the United States (Levy: 1987).

Debate continues about whether growth of the service sector (and part-time jobs), the relative decline in well-paying blue-collar and public-sector positions, and reductions in real income are leading to a 'declining middle class' in the United States (Kuttner 1983; Blackburn and Bloom 1985) and in Canada (Finn 1983; Steed 1986). Myles (1988) has linked this debate to the Braverman (1974) thesis of growing 'deskilling' throughout the North American occupational structure. His analysis of Canadian occupational distributions in 1961, 1971 and 1981 demonstrates that skill levels, in general, actually increased during the 1960s and 1970s as more management, professional, and technical white-collar jobs were created (1988: 340–3). But Myles also notes the distinct segmentation of the service sector into high-skill positions (e.g. health, social and educational services) and low-skill jobs (e.g. food and accommodation services), and questions whether service-sector employment growth in the 1980s will have led to a net increase or decrease in skilled jobs (1988: 353).

More importantly, Myles (1988: 341) shows that young Canadian workers (ages 15 to 29) benefited from the skill expansions in the 1960s, but not during the 1970s, even though they continued to invest heavily in higher education. In a more recent study, he demonstrates that a large majority of new jobs created between 1981 and 1986 were in the lowest pay ranges (Myles *et al.* 1988). Most of these jobs had been filled by young workers. More detailed analyses reveal that growth in part-time jobs and industrial shifts in employment had little to do with this pattern of young workers obtaining the new low-paying jobs. Among the alternative explanations suggested by the researchers are declines in 'real' minimum wages, greater privatization and contracting-out of jobs, and a decline in union membership among recent cohorts of labour-force entrants.

It is becoming apparent that substantial labour-market changes and demographic shifts have affected the school to work transition of Canadian youth, and will continue to do so. The extremely high youth unemployment rates of the early 1980s were the product of a recession and a distinct bulge at the bottom of the labour force age distribution. We may now be starting to see more labour market entry problems for slightly older and more educated youth as a large cohort competes for a declining number of well-paid and secure jobs.

In turn, this could have an impact on high-school graduates as university and college-educated youth take lower-level jobs in the absence of better positions. There is some evidence that this has been occurring in the US over the last two decades (Howe 1988). In the past, such entry-level positions might have been accepted and then quickly discarded, as well-educated youth left school permanently and found their appropriate niche in the occupational structure. In the future, larger proportions of young workers may be forced to continue to work in the less rewarding and less secure youth labour market.

Trends toward earlier retirement, more rapid expansion of high-technology industries and high-skill service occupations, further declines in fertility leading to even smaller cohorts of labour-force entrants in the future, continued growth in university and college enrolments – all of these could ease the school–work transition of this and the next generation of young Canadians. These are the optimistic possibilities. We might also see more rapid expansion of low-skill service-sector jobs (current projections point in this direction), or another recession. In short, the transition from school to work in the Canadian labour market has become more problematic and complicated than it was several decades ago. It remains unclear whether current economic and demographic trends will significantly ease this transition for future cohorts of school leavers.

Notes

1 The labour-force participation rate is the percentage of those aged 15 and older who are working for pay, self-employed or employing others, or unemployed.

2 Cross-sectional survey results (and annual averages) underestimate the proportion of the adult population which participates, to some extent, in the labour force. The 1986 Labour Market Activity Survey revealed that 70 per cent of Canadian women aged 16 to 69 and 90 per cent of men in this age range had been in the labour force at some point during the year (Statistics Canada, 1988a: 7; 1988b: 7).

3 Other sources suggest that the self-employed tend to come from the ranks of wage earners, particularly technical, managerial and professional workers (OECD 1986). And while some multiple job holders may be individuals struggling to maintain their household income, others may simply be taking advantage of opportunities in an expanding labour market (Akyeampong 1988: 102).

4 Part of the explanation may also involve the continued expansion of part-time service-sector jobs which, while attractive to teen-agers still in school, are not that satisfactory for older youth seeking full-time, long-term employment.

5 The 'community colleges' category also includes CEGEPs (colleges d'enseignement général et professionnel) in Quebec, agricultural, art, and technical schools, and other non-university post-secondary institutions.

6 This brief overview of labour-market policies relies heavily on Smucker and van den Berg (1988), and addresses only federal-government initiatives. Most provincial governments have also developed some additional labour-market programmes. With respect to young workers, a number have introduced student summer-employment programmes which provide some short-term jobs for secondary and post-secondary students, but only a small minority of young people participate in these programmes.

7 The other four CJS programmes are: Skill Shortages, intended to promote training of workers in occupations where skill shortages are identified; Skill Investment which provides financial assistance for relocation, retraining, or job-sharing to individuals in danger of layoff; Innovations which is meant to fund pilot projects aimed at new solutions to labour-market problems; and Community Futures which focuses on communities faced with persistently high unemployment.

References

Akyeampong, E. (1986). ' "Involuntary" part-time employment in Canada, 1975–1985'. *The Labour Force*, Statistics Canada (December), 143–79.

(1988). 'A mid-year look at labour market developments: 1988.' *The Labour Force*, Statistics Canada (July): 87–117, (cat. no. 71–001).

Ashton, D. N. (1986). *Unemployment Under Capitalism: The Sociology of British and American Labour Markets*. Brighton, Wheatsheaf Books.

Blackburn, M. L. and Bloom, D. E. (1985). 'What is happening to the middle class.' *American Demographics*, 7: 18–25.

Boulet, J.-A. and Lavalee, L. (1984). *The Changing Economic Status of Women*. Ottawa, Supply and Services Canada (Economic Council of Canada).

Braverman, H. (1974). *Labor and Monopoly Capital: The Degradation of Work in the Twentieth Century*. New York, Monthly Review.

Cohen, G. L. (1988). *Enterprising Canadians: The Self-Employed in Canada*. Ottawa, Supply and Services Canada (cat. no. 71–536).

Finn, E. (1983). 'Decline of the middle class'. *The Facts*, CUPE (November): 4–7.

Foot, D. K. and Li, J. C. (1986). 'Youth employment in Canada: a misplaced priority?'. *Canadian Public Policy*, 12: 499–506.

Gower, D. (1988a). 'The 1987 labour market revisited'. *The Labour Force*. Statistics Canada (January): 84–111.

Gower, D. (1988b). 'Annual update on labour force trends'. *Canadian Social Trends*. (Summer): 17–20.

Grayson, J. P. (1985). *Corporate Strategies and Plant Closures: The SKF Experience*. Toronto, Our Times.

Gunderson, M. (1985). 'Discrimination, equal pay, and equal opportunities in the labour market'. In W. Craig Riddell (ed.), *Work and Pay: The Canadian Labour Market*. Toronto, University of Toronto Press.

Heron, C. and Storey, R. (1986). 'On the job in Canada', pp. 3–46 in Craig Heron and Robert Storey (eds). *On the Job: Confronting the Labour Process in Canada*. Kingston, McGill-Queen's University Press.

Howe, W. J. (1988). 'Education and demographics: how do they affect unemployment rates?'. *Monthly Labor Review*, 111(1): 3–9.

Kaliski, S. F. (1985). 'Trends, changes and imbalances: a survey of the Canadian Labour Market.' in W. Craig Riddell (ed.), *Work and Pay: The Canadian Labour Market*. Toronto, University of Toronto Press.

Krahn, H. J. and Lowe, G. S. (1988). *Work, Industry and Canadian Society*. Toronto, Nelson Canada.

Kuttner, B. (1983). 'The declining middle.' *Atlantic Monthly* (July): 60–72.

Laxer, G. (1985). 'Foreign ownership and myths about Canadian development.' *Canadian Review of Sociology and Anthropology*, 22: 311–45.

Levy, F. (1987). 'Changes in the distribution of American family incomes, 1947 to 1984.' *Science* 236 (May 22): 923–7.

Lindsay, C. (1987). 'The decline in employment among men aged 55–64, 1975–1985.' *Canadian Social Trends*, (Spring): 12–15.

Lipset, S. M. (1987). 'Comparing Canadian and American unions.' *Society*, 24(2): 60–70.

Lowe, G. S. (1987). *Women in the Administrative Revolution*. Toronto, University of Toronto Press.

Matthews, R. A. (1985). *Structural Change and Industrial Policy: The Redeployment of Canadian Manufacturing, 1960–80*. Ottawa, Supply and Services Canada.

Moy, J. (1988). 'An analysis of unemployment and other labor market indicators in 10 countries.' *Monthly Labor Review* (April): 39–50.

Myles, J. (1988). 'The expanding middle: some Canadian evidence on the deskilling debate.' *Canadian Review of Sociology and Anthropology* 25(3): 335–64.

Myles, J., Picot, G. and Wannell, T. (1988). 'The changing wage distribution of jobs, 1981–1986.' *The Labour Force*, Statistics Canada (October): 85–138.

Neill, S. (1988). 'Unionization in Canada.' *Canadian Social Trends*, (Spring): 12–15.

OECD (1986). *OECD Employment Outlook*. Paris: Organization for Economic Co-operation and Development.

Ornstein, M. (1983). 'The development of class in Canada.' In J. Paul Grayson (ed.) *Introduction to Sociology: An Alternative Approach*. Toronto, Gage.

Parliament, J. (1986). 'French immersion.' *Canadian Social Trends*, (Autumn): 22.
(1987). 'Increase in long-term unemployment.' *Canadian Social Trends* (Spring): 16–19.

Phillips, P. (1982). *Regional Disparities* (2nd ed.). Toronto, James Lorimer.

Picot, W. G. (1987). 'The changing industrial mix of employment, 1951–1985'. *Canadian Social Trends* (Spring): 8–11.

Picot, W. G. and Wannell, T. (1988). 'Job displacement.' *Canadian Social Trends*, (Spring): 6–11.

Picot, W. G., Wannell, T. and Lynd, D. (1987a). *The Changing Labour Market for Postsecondary Graduates*. Ottawa, Statistics Canada (cat. no. 89–518).

Picot, W. G., Wannell, T. and Lynd, D. (1987b). '1976 and 1982 postsecondary graduates: selected highlights of their labour force experience.' *Canadian Social Trends*, (Autumn): 38–42.

Radwanski, G. (1987). *Ontario Study of the Relevance of Education, and the Issue of Dropouts*. Toronto, Ministry of Education.

Rose, J. B. and Chaison, G. N. (1987). 'The state of the unions revisited: the United States and Canada.' In H. C. Jain (ed.) *Emerging Trends in Canadian Industrial Relations*. Proceedings of the 24th Annual Meeting of the Canadian Industrial Relations Association, McMaster University, June 1987.

Senate Sub-Committee on Training and Employment (1987). *Only Work Works* (Report of the Sub-Committee on Training and Employment of the Standing Senate Committee on Social Affairs, Science and Technology). Ottawa, The Senate.

Smucker, J. and van den Berg, A. (1988). 'Capitalism vs. socialism? Canadian and Swedish labour market policies compared.' Montreal, Working Papers in Social Behaviour 88–8, Department of Sociology, McGill University.

Statistics Canada, *The Daily* (various issues).

Statistics Canada (1984a). *Labour Force Annual Averages 1975–1983* (cat. no. 71–529).

Statistics Canada (1984b). *National Graduates Survey* (cat. no. S2–168. 1986).

Statistics Canada (1985). *Self-Employment in Canada*. Ottawa, Labour and Household Surveys Division (cat. no. 71–582).

Statistics Canada (1986–7). *Women in the Labour Force* (1986–87 edn.) (cat. no. LO16–1578/87B).

Statistics Canada (1987a). *The Labour Force, Annual Averages* (cat. no. 71–001). December 1987.

Statistics Canada (1987b). *Education in Canada: A Statistical Review for 1985–6*. Ottawa, Supply and Services Canada (cat. no. 81–229).

Statistics Canada (1988a) *Canada's Women: A Profile of Their 1986 Labour Market Experience*. Ottawa, Labour and Household Surveys Division (cat. no. 71–205).

Statistics Canada (1988b) *Canada's Men: A Profile of Their 1986 Labour Market Experience*. Ottawa, Labour and Household Surveys Division (cat. no. 71–206).

Statistics Canada (1988c). *Education in Canada: A Statistical Review for 1986–87*. Ottawa, Supply and Services Canada (cat. no. 81–229).

Statistics Canada (1989). *Labour Force Annual Averages 1981–1988* (cat. no. 71–529).

Steed, J. (1986) 'The middle class is under pressure and losing ground as the rich get richer and the poor get more numerous.' *Globe and Mail* 4 October: D5.

Supply and Services Canada (1987). *Posing the Questions: Review of Demography and its Implications for Economic and Social Policy*. Ottawa, Health and Welfare Canada.

Watkins, M. (1982). 'The Innis tradition in Canadian political economy.' *Canadian Journal of Political and Social Theory*, 6(Winter–Spring): 12–34.

Weeks, W. (1980). 'Part-time work: the business view on second-class jobs for housewives and mothers.' *Atlantis* 5: 69–86.

3

British labour-market trends[1]

Malcolm Maguire

In common with other industrialized nations, the United Kingdom has witnessed a radical transformation in its pattern of employment in recent years. Long-term trends affecting the composition of the labour force and the industrial and occupational structures have gathered pace as a result of the recession of the early 1980s, the policies pursued by the Thatcher government, and the continuing impact of the introduction of new technology. There have also been notable developments in companies' employment strategies.

The trajectory taken by the process of industrialization in Britain has had a number of consequences for the contemporary structure of the labour market. As it was the first nation to industrialize, British manufacturers were able to establish themselves across a wide range of industries. However, the family firms which developed were slow to modernize when faced with increasing competition from the USA, Germany and other societies in the second wave of industrialization. Unlike the Canadian experience, a new system of corporate ownership only emerged slowly in the first half of the twentieth century (Chandler 1976). Britain's large manufacturing base was able to sustain production by virtue of the political domination of the British Empire (Hobsbawm 1968). As a consequence, Britain, in contrast to Canada, is still characterized by a large manufacturing base. However, it was precisely this characteristic which rendered British industry vulnerable to the impact of recent changes in the international division of labour, the emergence of global markets, the relocation of labour-intensive industries and the intensified competition from Japan and

Table 3.1 Breakdown of United Kingdom working population: 1960–1988

Year	Employees in employment:			Self-employed (with or without employees)	HM Forces	Employed labour force	Unemployed	Working population
	M	F	All					
			1000s		1000s	1000s	1000s	1000s
1960 (May)	–	–	23,559	–	521	24,080	314	24,394
1965	–	–	23,127	1,673	423	25,223	309	25,532
1970	–	–	22,397	1,743	524	24,663	414	25,077
1975	13,547	9,163	22,710	1,886	336	24,932	912	25,844
1980	13,103	9,384	22,487	1,866	323	24,696	1,659	26,355
1985	11,797	9,479	21,276	2,588	326	24,190	3,237	27,427
1988 (Dec)	12,275	10,466	22,741	3,048	313	26,513	2,037	28,556

Source: Various *Employment Gazettes*, Department of Employment

Table 3.2   Estimates of civilian labour-force activity rates 1971–83, females: Great Britain

Age	1971	1973	1975	1977	1979	1981	1983	1986
	%	%	%	%	%	%	%	%
16–19	65.0	62.9	61.6	67.8	70.7	70.7	70.2	71.1
20–24	60.2	61.3	63.8	66.3	67.5	67.9	68.6	69.2
25–34	45.5	48.9	51.8	56.3	56.2	56.2	57.4	62.8
35–44	59.6	63.0	66.1	68.6	68.5	68.0	68.0	71.8
45–54	62.0	64.8	66.3	66.7	67.0	68.1	68.3	70.2
55–59	50.9	51.4	52.4	56.1	53.8	53.4	50.8	51.7

Source: *Employment Gazette*, Department of Employment, August 1984: 362 *Labour Market Quarterly*, June 1987

the new industrial countries. The vulnerability of its old industrial base in the face of a world recession was enhanced by the early exchange-rate policy of the Thatcher administration which left the pound overvalued.

From a societal perspective, the income from North Sea oil provided some form of economic cushion during the 1980s but the reduction of manufacturing capacity by over one-fifth, with the losses being concentrated in the engineering and steel industries in the Midlands and North, left the country with a high level of unemployment and a growing division between the relatively affluent South-east and a depressed Midlands and North. While the period of economic recovery in the mid to late eighties has increased the living standards of many of those in work, the redistribution of income which has been a feature of the Thatcher administration has left a legacy of a widening gap between rich and poor.

The labour force

The size of the total working population rose by almost 4 million from 1960 to 1988 (table 3.1), with significant increases occurring from the latter half of the 1970s.

The most striking change in the composition of the labour force in that time has been the increased participation of women. While the total number of male employees fell steadily between 1970 and 1980, and then dipped more rapidly before recovering slightly, the total number of female employees has continued to rise (see table 3.1). Consequently females, who accounted for 36 per cent of total employment in 1961 and 30 per cent in 1971, now comprise 46 per cent of employees. The 1983 Labour Force Survey reveals that between 1971 and 1981 the female labour force grew by 1.25 million, whereas the male labour force rose by only 100,000 (*Employment Gazette*, August 1984: 363). Table 3.2 shows that activity rates for females, particularly in the 25–34 and 35–44 age groups, rose considerably between 1971 and 1977 but stabilized thereafter, before increasing rapidly again in

Table 3.3   Total employees in manufacturing industries: Great Britain

	1000s
June 1960	8,662.9
June 1965	8,846.7
June 1970	8,650.0
June 1975	7,378.6
June 1980	6,660.1
June 1985	5,371.1
March 1989	5,147.0

Source: Various issues *Employment Gazette*, Department of Employment

Table 3.4   Total employment in services: Great Britain

	1000s
June 1970	11,335
June 1975	12,433
June 1980	12,981
June 1985	13,857
Dec 1988	15,318

Source: Various *Employment Gazettes*, Department of Employment

recent years, particularly among the 25–34 age group. This period of increasing female participation in the labour force coincides with the upsurge of employment opportunities in the service sector. Recently a concern over labour shortages has led to exhortations to employers to consider recruiting females for a wider range of jobs.

These figures in themselves may understate the true increase of females' willingness to seek employment, for the official statistics of the working population are composed of the addition of the employed labour force to the registered unemployed. The United Kingdom alone among Western European countries has an official female unemployment rate considerably below that of males, due to the criteria required for inclusion on the unemployed register. If other, possibly more appropriate methods of measurement were used, the female unemployment rate, and thereby the female activity rate, would be considerably higher.

Industrial and occupational change

In common with other industrialized nations there has been a pronounced shift in the proportions of employees in manufacturing as opposed to

Table 3.5 Changes in total employment 1971–81

	1971	% of total	1981	% of total
	1000s		1000s	
Non-manual occupations	8,749	37.1	9,759	43.1
Manual occupations	14,805	62.9	12,859	56.9

Source: University of Warwick, Institute for Employment Research

service-sector employment. The decline in the number of jobs in manufacturing was established well before the onset of the recession,which accentuated the trend. From table 3.3 it can be seen that the total number of jobs in manufacturing in Britain has been reduced by over 3.5 million since 1960. While the numbers employed were relatively stable during the 1960s, the decline began in the early 1970s. However, the most dramatic loss occurred during the 1980–3 recession when one-third of the manual jobs in the engineering industry were lost and manufacturing capacity was reduced by 20 per cent. Although the engineering industry suffered some of the most extreme job losses, all manufacturing industries have been affected to a greater or lesser extent.

The loss of these manufacturing jobs has been compensated for partly by the increase of almost 4 million jobs in the service sector between 1970 and 1988 (table 3.4). It is misleading, however, to suggest that the jobs generated by the growing service sector have been adequate replacements for those lost in manufacturing. The jobs lost in manufacturing were predominantly full-time jobs previously filled by males, whereas the jobs gained in the service sector have been predominantly part-time and filled by females. It has also been suggested that half the increase in service-sector employment between 1979 and 1985 was created as a result of increased sub-contracting by the manufacturing sector (Rajan and Pearson 1986).

Leaving aside the impact of technological advancement, these shifts have inevitably produced profound changes in the type and distribution of occupations. From 1971 to 1981 there was an overall reduction of almost 2 million workers in manual occupations, with an increase of just over a million in non-manual occupations (table 3.5). Although in number terms the decline of manual jobs was predominantly in unskilled or semi-skilled occupations, there were also significant reductions of skilled operatives and craft workers. It would appear that there were signs, during this period, of the adverse effect of new technology on clerical occupations, although this must be qualified, as there was an increase of over 100,000 females in those occupations and a reduction of 173,000 males. The main areas of growth were among managers, administrators, professional workers, engineers and scientists.

Analysis of the Labour Force Survey data shows that during the period of the recession, this trend continued. In a period when there was a major contraction in the overall size of the labour force, the three orders of professional, administrative and scientific workers increased by some 16.6 per cent. In addition, the number of managerial and selling workers increased by 11.6 per cent, although some of this may have been due to reclassification and the shift to self-employment (Spilsbury, Maguire and Ashton 1986). Other studies have documented this trend (Goldthorpe and Payne 1986), while independent occupational forecasts based on different methodologies (the Institute for Employment Research at Warwick, 1987, and the Occupational Study Group Institute of Manpower Studies, 1986) have predicted its continuation into the 1990s. While this prospect has not triggered off a debate over the 'declining middle thesis', it is clear that the shape of the occupational structure, the configuration of labour market segments (Ashton, Maguire and Spilsbury 1990) and the British class structure are undergoing substantial change.

At the other end of the occupational hierarchy, unskilled manual jobs, especially those of operatives in manufacturing, have been in long-term decline. Again this is a trend common to all industrial societies. Whereas in 1971 operatives and labourers accounted for 29 per cent of total employment, by 1986 this figure had fallen to 20 per cent and is projected to decline further to 16 per cent in 1995. The loss of less skilled jobs in manufacturing was particularly pronounced in Britain during the recession when the three main manual occupations, the two processing and the miscellaneous orders, were each reduced in number by over 25 per cent. Rajan and Pearson (1986) identified a decrease in the less skilled occupations in production industries, as one of the major trends currently affecting the labour force in the 1980s. They saw this trend as a net effect of a combination of larger employers' technological innovations which demand a more highly skilled labour force and smaller employers' growing demand for less skilled employees.

Gender segregation in the labour market

One of the features of the labour markets in all advanced industrial societies is that of gender segregation. Males and females are disproportionately concentrated in different parts of the labour market. In general terms males are concentrated in the manufacturing sector and females in the service sector. Thus in Britain in 1970, the manufacturing sector employed 42 per cent of males and 29 per cent of females. By 1983 this had fallen to 34 per cent of males and 17 per cent of females. In a part of the service sector where employment grew most rapidly, business and miscellaneous services, the proportion of the male labour force employed increased from 13 per cent of males in 1970 to 19 per cent in 1983, while that of females increased from 35 per cent in 1970 to 45 per cent in 1983. However, this concentration of female employment within the service sector is not uniform throughout the various occupational categories. Within occupational categories women are further concentrated in the low-paid relatively unskilled jobs in cleaning, catering and sales, whereas males are more highly concentrated in the more well-paid full-time jobs in management, administration and professional and scientific services.

While there has been some change in gender segregation in that employers are now, in the face of a potential shortage of highly trained labour, creating greater access to some managerial and professional jobs to women, these actions have not produced a major shift in gender segregation and what evidence there is (OECD 1985) suggests that the British labour market remains more highly segregated than the Canadian labour market.

Unemployment

Table 3.6 outlines how the gradual rise in the numbers of unemployed during the 1960s became more pronounced during the 1970s, and then rose steeply from 1979 before reaching levels in excess of 3 million during 1984. Since then, however, there has been a fall of over one million. There is a good case for believing, however, that these figures seriously understate the true level. In the United Kingdom the official rate of unemployment has always been a byproduct of the provision of state welfare benefit. Until 1982 people had to register as available for work in order to qualify for unemployment benefit. Even those who were unemployed but not eligible for benefit could register and be included in the count. These regulations were amended in October 1982 for ease of computerization, so that now those included in the count are composed only of recipients of unemployment benefit. It was estimated that this immediately caused a reduction in the official total of some 190,000 (*Observer*, 15 September 1985). Many other alterations to the regulations have been implemented since then. For instance, the deregistration of men over 59 reduced the numbers by a further 200,000.

A long-standing argument about the figures surrounds the registration of females. When comparing the United Kingdom rates of unemployment with those of other industrialized countries, it is noticeable that the latter have rates of female unemployment at least as high as those for males. This is because other countries have different ways of measuring official levels of unemployment. The USA, for example, uses a household survey method which takes account of all those who have sought work in the previous month. It is likely that, if the United Kingdom adopted a similar technique, the rate of female unemployment would be nearer to that of males. The 1983 Labour Force Survey estimated that 1.09 million women could be identified

Table 3.6   Unemployment levels: Great Britain (annual averages, except where marked *, including school leavers and seasonally unadjusted)

Year	Male No. (thousands)	%	Female No. (thousands)	%	All No. (thousands)	%
1960	248.3	1.7	97.6	1.2	345.8	1.5
1965	240.6	1.6	76.4	0.9	317.0	1.4
1970	495.3	3.5	86.9	1.0	582.2	2.5
1975	681.6	4.9	149.7	1.7	831.3	3.6
1980*	1,180.6	8.3	484.3	4.8	1,664.9	6.8
1985* (June)	2,196.8	15.7	981.7	9.6	3,178.6	13.1
1986	2,125.5	13.2	978.0	8.7	3,103.5	11.4
1987	1,931.5	12.0	848.3	9.4	2,779.8	10.1
1988	1,547.7	9.6	677.5	5.9	2,225.1	8.1
1989 (April)	1,350.8	8.1	532.8	4.5	1,776.0	6.4

Source: Various *Employment Gazettes*, Department of Employment

as unemployed, at a time when the official count was 0.82 million (*Employment Gazette*, August 1984: 367).

A significant trend in recent years has been the growing proportion of the unemployed who could be classed as long-term unemployed. Whereas in the 1960s most unemployment could be regarded as frictional, in that very few people stayed on the register for more than a few weeks at a time, the 1980s saw the numbers unemployed for over six months rise to almost two million in July 1985. As a result of the economic recovery which occurred in the late 1980s, there has been a reduction in the numbers of long-term unemployed. The number has since fallen to just over one million (April 1989) of whom 744,000 had been unemployed for over 12 months. This phenomenon of the reduction in the numbers of long-term unemployed occurring well after the worst of the recession is over is a well-established consequence of economic recovery (Ashton 1986). The long-term unemployed are vulnerable as they are regarded as more of a risk by employers when hiring than candidates with current or more recent employment experience. In Britain, however, it is more difficult than elsewhere to establish just how far the fall has been due to the effects of a growth in jobs and how much has been due to the effects of administrative changes in rules governing employment registration and social-security benefits. Indeed, the geographical distribution of long-term unemployment suggests that they are concentrated in parts of the towns and cities with high unemployment rates and that these communities are not benefiting from the upturn in the economy.

Continuing high levels of unemployment have also heightened workers' awareness of the dangers involved in voluntarily quitting a job. Table 3.7 shows the trends in labour turnover from 1973 to 1989. This data is only

Table 3.7   Labour turnover in manufacturing industries: Great Britain

Year	Month	Engagement rate			Leaving rate		
		M	F	All	M	F	All
		%	%	%	%	%	%
1973	February*	2.2	3.8	2.7	2.2	3.5	2.6
1974	February	1.8	3.1	2.7	2.2	3.5	2.6
1975	March	1.8	2.6	2.0	2.4	3.9	2.8
1976	March	1.4	2.4	1.7	1.7	2.8	2.0
1977	March	1.8	2.8	2.1	1.9	2.6	2.1
1978	March	1.7	2.5	1.9	1.8	2.6	2.1
1979	March	1.5	2.5	1.8	1.7	2.5	1.9
1980	March	1.2	1.9	1.4	1.8	2.9	2.1
1981	December	0.7	1.4	0.9	1.5	2.5	1.8
1982	March	0.8	1.6	1.0	1.4	2.2	1.6
1983	March	1.0	1.6	1.2	1.5	2.1	1.7
1984	March	1.3	2.0	1.5	1.5	2.1	1.7
1985	March	1.2	2.0	1.5	1.3	2.1	1.6
1986	March	1.1	2.0	1.3	1.4	2.2	1.7
1987	March	1.3	1.9	1.5	1.4	2.1	1.6
1988	March	˙1.4	2.3	1.7	1.5	2.3	1.8
1989	March	1.4	2.1	1.6	1.6	2.5	1.8

* Excluding shipbuilding and ship-repairing
NB The engagement rate and the leaving rate show the number of engagements and discharges (and other losses) respectively in the four-week period ending June, as percentages of the numbers employed at the beginning of the period. The figures do not include persons engaged during the periods who also left before the end of the period and, to that extent, the engagement and leaving figures underestimate the intake and wastage during the period.
Source: Various Employment Gazettes, Department of Employment

available for the manufacturing sector. It can be seen that both engagement rates and leaving rates tend to reflect the level of economic activity, although, while engagement rates dropped noticeably between 1979 and 1981, there was a later and less pronounced response from leaving rates. The scarcity of vacancies greatly reduced the incidence of voluntary labour turnover. This was particularly true among young people. Whereas in the late 1960s the main problem associated with the employment of young people was perceived to be that of chronic job-changing, or 'job-hopping', in the mid 1980s it became one of finding a job (Raffe 1987).

Although young people were traditionally more susceptible to unemployment through changes in the economy during previous peaks and troughs (Makeham 1980), their experience in the 1980s was one of greater difficulty in finding employment. Again, the official statistics do not necessarily reflect the true extent of youth unemployment, because of the numbers on government schemes, notably the Youth Training Scheme (YTS), which was introduced in 1983 as a one-year scheme and extended in 1986 to two years. This was a major policy innovation with the declared aim of providing a bridge to work for every 16-year-old school-leaver. The scheme provides work experience and a minimum period of off-the-job training. Trainees receive a grant of a fixed amount which may be 'topped up' by the employer if desired. In its first year it catered for 24 per cent of 16-year-olds and a similar proportion (27 per cent) in 1987.

Not only are particular groups more prone to unemployment (Ashton 1986), but the degree to which individuals may expect to become un-employed is to a great extent determined by where they live. For many years now South-east England has had lower levels of unemployment than other regions. Generally the effects of the recession have been to increase the rates by a greater proportion in the more economically buoyant regions, while widening the overall disparity. For example, in 1976 unemployment in the South-east stood at 4.2 per cent compared to 7.5 per cent in the Northern region. By June 1985 the comparable figures had risen to 9.6 per cent and 18.5 per cent, before dropping to 5.3 per cent and 12.1 per cent in July 1988. Exceptionally the West Midlands, where the engineering industry was particularly badly hit by recession, was transformed from an area with a level of unemployment below the national average, to one above. More recently, however, there has been an upturn in the economy.

Youth unemployment is also characterized by significant regional vari-ations, although for 16-to-18-year-olds, its immediate impact is masked by the provision of places on the Youth Training Scheme. In August 1988 the imminent launch of the government's all-age Employment Training Scheme was advertised in full-page spreads in national newspapers. The message being projected was that employers were already suffering from a lack of skilled labour, and that this position would be exacerbated by reduced numbers of 16-year-olds entering the labour market, due to demographic trends. While this situation is undoubtedly true of some of the economically buoyant areas of the South-east of England, it would certainly not hold for areas such as Liverpool and North-east England which suffer from a shortage of jobs rather than a shortage of labour. The chasm which exists between locations in terms of the availability of employment opportunities, is one element of a disparity which has been popularized as a North/South divide. Government policy, however, appears to be founded on a southern perspective, whereby the provision of training to alleviate skill shortages is the solution, rather than the creation of jobs.

Unlike in Canada, where the control of training has been placed almost exclusively in the hands of the employers, Britain inherited a system of apprenticeship training with its origins in the medieval guilds. This had two important consequences. First, trade unions were able to use the guild tradition to influence training practices and, second, the new industrial employers of the later eighteenth and early nineteenth century had to adapt to a pre-existing system. Moreover, this was a system which, having been established in an era of slow social and economic change, placed the emphasis on providing the new recruit with a body of knowledge at the beginning of the work career. As a consequence, training for manual work took place in the teenage years. The 'system', albeit in a modified form, provided the basic framework for training into the twentieth century. However, it came under increasing pressure during the latter part of the twentieth century and especially during the collapse of parts of manufacturing industry in the early 1980s, when employers virtually stopped the training of apprentices.

Training

It has long been argued that British employers have neglected training. This neglect has produced periodic skill shortages with a high proportion of manufacturing firms reporting skill shortages during periods of economic boom, e.g. during the mid 1960s and 1970s, and is again increasing in the late 1980s. This pattern is a product of firms' investing in training during boom periods but cutting back on that investment during the economic downturn. Typically firms increased the proportion of apprentices and technicians they recruited as the order books expanded but reduced that training at the first sight of a recession. It was partly in an attempt to counteract this cyclical effect and so increase the numbers of bricklayers, carpenters, engineers and electricians that the Industrial Training Boards were established. However, many of these have since been disbanded.

This cyclical pattern is, however, only one aspect of the problem. We have already seen how recent structural change in the economy is increasing the demand for managerial, professional and scientific expertise rather than the skills associated with the traditional apprenticeship. For example, the employment of information-technology professionals grew by 5–10 per cent per annum between 1986 and 1988. As mentioned earlier, many of the occuaptions which are expected to grow in the next few years are to be found in this category. All these occupations require skills in processing information rather than manual skills. This contrasts with the fact that the number of apprentices has fallen from 120,000 in their heyday to 40,000 (Bynner 1987). Such evidence suggests that the underlying changes in the structure of the economy are going to produce an increasing demand in the future for intellectual skills. It is within this context that we need to examine the supply of educated youth entering the labour market.

Just over half the young people in Britain leave school at the minimum school-leaving age of 16. Of the total school-leavers in 1986 only 54 per cent had achieved passes in O-levels or their equivalent. In that year, 45 per cent stayed on in education; of the remainder, 27 per cent entered YTS, 13 per cent were unemployed and 15 per cent were in employment. The contrast is particularly striking with Canada, USA, Sweden and Japan, where more than 85 per cent of all 16-year-olds were in full-time education. Alone among the major industrial nations, Britain is distinguished by the low level of qualifications of its labour force. Even at the level of higher education, Britain remains behind its major competitors. Thus, of the 18-year-olds in the USA, 55 per cent were in higher education, compared to 17 per cent in Britain (Bynner 1987). The British system is characterized by the production of a small highly educated élite and a large mass of relatively poorly qualified leavers. Neither is the situation improved much when we include part-time education, for whereas 89 per cent of young Germans were either in full-time or part-time education the corresponding figure for Britain was 60 per cent.

In the last two decades, countries such as Canada have chosen to expand their system of higher education to produce a highly educated labour force, with the majority staying on in school until the age of 18 and many of those continuing on into higher education. By contrast, the British system has remained élitist, with only a small higher-education sector and the majority leaving school at the earliest opportunity.

It was against this background, of a reluctance on the part of employers to train and a poorly qualified labour force, that the Manpower Services Commission sought to improve the situation by introducing the New Training Initiative. One of the major components of this has been the Youth Training Scheme. However, the scheme was also seen by the government as a means of reducing the extremely high levels of youth unemployment that were present in the early 1980s. As a result the scheme had to serve a dual purpose, namely to raise the skill level of the labour force while at the same time providing a solution to the problem of mass youth unemployment.

Coupled with YTS was an initiative directed at the school population and those young people staying on in full-time education, the Technical and Vocational Education Initiative (TVEI). This was to be concerned with practical work, problem-solving skills and new technology, and was aimed at the whole ability range, although in practice it has turned out to be more important for those who left school at 16.

The achievement of the YTS has been to raise the level of training of those 16-year-old school-leavers who would previously have received very little. Some apprenticeships have been incorporated into it, although the level of apprenticeship training is still far below that achieved in the 1970s. YTS remains largely a scheme for those who have difficulty in securing employment and is not being so extensively used in the more affluent areas of the South where employers face a labour shortage. In an attempt to enhance its credibility, the Training Agency (formerly the Manpower Services Commission) has undertaken a drive to encourage employers to offer YTS trainees employed-status places, so that, while on the scheme, they are employees of the employer, with the guarantee of continuation of employment at the end of their training period. The impact of TVEI has been to make school life more enjoyable for young people, but it has not encouraged them to remain at school for longer periods (Bell and Howieson 1988).

The most recent government initiative in the field of adult training, the Employment Training Scheme, faces many of the same problems encountered by YTS. It is aimed at the long-term unemployed and has the task of upgrading their skills and reducing the skills shortage mentioned above, while at the same time reducing the level of long-term unemployment. Like the YTS, the training it will deliver will be of a relatively low level and will be able to be accomplished in a short period of time. Neither of these schemes is likely to solve the problem identified above, of a mismatch between the underlying direction of change in the economy, calling for a more highly educated labour force and the structure of the educational/training system which produces a high proportion of poorly qualified new entrants to the labour market.

The contrast between the strategy adopted by the British government and that of the Canadian government is marked. While the Canadian government was faced with a problem of 'training' unemployed groups, the British government, in order to contend with what amounted to a virtual collapse of the youth labour market, had to intervene directly to support the best part of a whole cohort of school-leavers (Raffe 1987a, Finn 1987). Moreover, the experience obtained there was later used to devise a similar scheme for the adult unemployed. Yet despite these differences in the magnitude of state intervention in the labour market there are similarities in the direction of state intervention. Like the Canadian government the British government has tried to push responsibility for training on to employers, firstly by delivering YTS and the Employment Training programme through employers, and more recently by introducing the idea of the local Training and Enterprise Councils, which will be controlled by employers and be responsible for administering the state's programmes. However, given the traditional reluctance of British employers to train, the omens for the new TECs are not good.

Trade unions

The existence of a large number of relatively small employers across a range of industries in the nineteenth century provided a fertile ground for the development of trade unionism in Britain. Following the unionization of semi-skilled and unskilled workers in the late nineteenth and early twentieth centuries, the British union movement became a relatively powerful political force. However, the collapse of large parts of manufacturing industry, the loss of manual jobs and the reduction of trade-union power through mass unemployment and legislative changes have led to a rapid decline in the numbers of trade unionists in the last decade. This decline is illustrated in table 3.8. The strength of trade unions, as measured by the size of their membership, has always shown fluctuations over the years but there are a number of reasons to suggest that the recent changes have represented a significant shift in the appeal of unions. The 1970s witnessed considerable successes in both union-bargaining strategies and in the incorporation of British unions into the government's decision-making process. This was reflected in the continued growth of union membership

Table 3.8   Trade unions: numbers[1] and membership[1] (United Kingdom)

Year	Number of unions	Total membership		Percentage change in membership since previous year
		Millions	As a percentage of working population	
1974	507	11.8	46.6	+2.7
1975	501	12.2	47.9	+3.6
1975[2]	470	12.0	47.2	–
1976	473	12.4	48.5	+3.0
1977	481	12.8	50.1	+3.7
1978	462	13.1	50.7	+2.1
1979	454	13.3	51.1	+1.3
1980	438	12.9	49.5	−2.6
1981	414	12.1	46.6	−6.5
1982	408	11.6	44.8	−4.2
1983	394	11.2	41.6	−3.1
1984	375	11.0	39.9	−2.2
1985	373	10.7	38.4	−2.5

[1] As at December each year.
[2] Thirty-one organizations previously regarded as trade unions are excluded from 1975 onwards because they failed to satisfy the statutory definition of a trade union in Section 28 of the Trade Union and Labour Relations Act, 1974.
Source: Employment Gazette, Department of Employment

which peaked at the end of the decade, when approximately 51 per cent of the labour force was unionized. Since then there has been a dramatic fall, such that by 1985 the percentage of the labour force in unions stood at 38.4.

Union membership has never been uniformly distributed throughout the labour force. The main strength has always been among manual workers. It reached its peak in the manufacturing sector, especially in the nationalized industries where in the early 1980s 97 per cent of manual workers were unionized, whereas in private manufacturing firms the figure was 68 per cent. Among white-collar workers trade unions have traditionally been weaker, with only 31 per cent of those in private firms being union members, as opposed to 61 per cent in the public sector.

The rapid decline in union membership from its peak of 12.9 million members in 1979 to 10.7 million members in 1985 is the result of a number of factors. The rise of mass unemployment made union recruitment difficult. While firms either collapsed or laid off large numbers of workers, those in work were struggling to hang on to whatever job they had. In these circumstances their concerns shifted from collective advancement to individual survival. In addition, the recession had its main impact on the manufacturing industries such as engineering, and metal goods where the unions were strongest (table 3.9). The unions found it difficult to recruit in the service industries, which continued to grow after the worst of the

Table 3.9   Trade union membership by industry: United Kingdom

	1982	1983	1984	1985
	1000s	1000s	1000s	1000s
Metal goods, engineering and vehicle	1,819	1,779	447	404
Energy and water supply	413	359	301	213
Extraction of minerals and ores other than fuels, manufacture of metal, mineral products and chemicals	144	140	122	96
Other manufacturing	686	710	691	675
Construction	267	265	255	254
Distribution, hotels, catering and repairs	460	445	434	424
Transport and communication	742	701	687	712
Banking, finance, insurance business services and leasing	337	343	344	349
National government	552	541	529	481
Local government	1,521	1,563	1,538	1,513
Education	745	733	761	794
Medical/health	658	670	686	686
Other	151	150	150	153
Membership of unions covering several industries	3,097	2,937	4,048	3,962
Total[1]	11,593	11,337	10,994	10,717

[1] Includes agriculture, forestry and fishing where there were 0.5 thousand members in 1982, 1983 and 1984 and 0.7 thousand in 1985.
Source: Department of Employment

recession was over. The main areas of job growth, other than the professional occupations, were the relatively unskilled jobs in hotels, catering and leisure, many of which were part-time. These are areas where the unions have traditionally encountered difficulty in recruiting. The unions succeeded in retaining their membership in parts of the public sector, such as local government, education and health.

At a time when unions were facing these adverse changes in the economy, they were also confronted with a government intent on, as they saw it, redressing the balance of power between management and workers. The Thatcher government brought in two Employment Acts and a Trade Union Act which curtailed the scope of industrial action, opened union funds to legal action and enforced ballots on the election of executives, strikes and the maintenance of political funds. At the same time it reduced the unions' influence in the management of the economy and industrial relations.

Unlike many of the other changes discussed here, the decline of union membership, although evident in other industrial societies such as the USA and France, is not a universal feature. In countries such as West Germany and Canada, which have undergone similar structural changes in their economies, the level of union membership has been maintained or increased.

The effect of these changes on young people's perceptions and attitudes towards trade-union membership remains largely unexplored. Work by Spilsbury *et al*. (1987) has shown that young people's membership of trade unions is determined primarily by whether or not unions have succeeded in organizing the industry in question rather than by the attitude of the individual. Thus, the relatively low level of unionization among young people is a result of their concentration in small firms and the service sector where unions have traditionally been weakly organized.

New technology

Given the much larger size of Britain's manufacturing industry relative to that of Canada, the impact of new technology could be expected to be that much greater. Indeed, much of the blame for the loss of jobs has been attributed to the introduction of new technology (Gill 1985).It is certainly true that the increasing use of computer numerically controlled machines, flexible machining systems and robotics have transformed some manufacturing firms from being relatively labour intensive to something approaching a process-technology situation. However, their impact to date on numbers employed may not have been as far reaching as is sometimes suspected. A Policy Studies Institute report in 1984 estimated the net loss of jobs attributable to the introduction of microelectronics in manufacturing industry to have been 34,000 between 1981 and 1983 (*Employment Gazette*, May 1984: 211). This would account for only 5 per cent of the total job losses in manufacturing in that period. Indeed, in their survey, Northcott and Rogers (1984) found that 69 per cent of all firms using microelectronics claimed that this technology had not affected the number of jobs available. Nevertheless, new technology is likely to have a much more significant impact in reducing the numbers employed in the future, as it assists in generating considerable increases in productivity and output without the need for additional staff. A substantial part of recent productivity increases in British industry may be attributed to this. The Policy Studies Institute report suggested that, while in 1981 30 per cent of British manufacturers were using, or about to use, microelectronics, this proportion had risen to almost 50 per cent by 1984. The penetration of this technology will continue at an increasing pace. Although it is extremely difficult to make predictions about the implications for jobs of the introduction of new technology with any great precision or conviction, the probable direction of future trends may be ascertained from the Department of Industry's projections that microelectronic technology will result in job losses of between 240,000 and 400,000 in the decade up to 1990.

The impact of new technology on jobs in the service sector has also been difficult to gauge, partly due to the overall expansion in the numbers

Table 3.10   *Female part-time employment in Great Britain*

| Year | Female employees | | | % part-time |
	Full-time	Part-time	All	
	1000s	1000s	1000s	
1951	5752	754	6506	11.6
1961	5351	1892	7243	26.1
1971	5166	3152	8318	37.9
1981	5304	3781	9085	41.6
1988	5883	4418	10301	42.9

Source: Employment Gazette

employed, and, in many cases, a dramatic increase in the volume of business in this sector. Also, while the introduction of word processors and computers have rendered some tasks obsolete, most organizations have tended to re-deploy staff to undertake different or new tasks, thereby enhancing the quality of service they can offer. Again, however, it seems likely that the effects experienced so far have been of a small scale compared to what is to follow. The hitherto continually rising employment levels of certain sectors, such as banking, finance and insurance, are levelling off. Also the indications are that the office technology revolution is still in its early stages. Similarly, the distributive trades are beginning to see the effects of new point-of-sale technology and pricing systems, often incorporating the use of lasers.

The difficulty of quantifying in terms of job loss the future effects of the introduction of new technology in manufacturing and, particularly, in service industries is matched by the difficulty of predicting the numbers and types of jobs which will be created in order for that same technology to be implemented. It has been suggested by research at the Institute of Employment Research at Warwick University that employment will grow by 0.5 per cent per annum up to 1995. The Cambridge Econometrics group forecast employment growing from 24.6 million in 1988 to 25.2 million in 1995 and to 25.9 million by 2000 (*Labour Market Quarterly*, March 1988). These predictions are necessarily dependent on factors such as the ability of British firms to maintain or increase their share of world markets.

Part-time employment

A significant trend accompanying the greater participation of females in the labour market and the growth of the service sector has been the increase in part-time employment. In the United Kingdom the Department of Employment definition of a part-time employee is a person normally working for not more than 30 hours a week. Table 3.10 shows that since 1951, while there has been no significant change in the number of females working full-time, the number of part-timers has increased six-fold. Thus, whereas in 1951, 11.6 per cent of female employees were part-time, by 1987 that figure had risen to 43.9 per cent. From an employer's viewpoint the main reasons given for the increase in demand for part-time workers are that they allow flexibility, in that they can be taken on or laid off to complement fluctuations in product demand, and that they reduce labour costs. An OECD report on part-time employment noted that for such workers an employer may not have to pay National Insurance contributions or sick pay and may be able to pay a lower rate for the job (OECD 1983: 43–52). Studies have shown that in Britain the rapid rise in female part-time employment in the latter half of the 1970s was accompanied by a considerable rise in the proportion of those workers who were not covered by employment legislation.

Temporary workers

One of the effects of the intensifed competition associated with the recession and the growth of global markets has been a sustained pressure on manufacturing firms in Britain to introduce more 'flexible' forms of organization. This has led some researchers, notably Atkinson (1984) of the Institute of Manpower Studies to make a distinction between 'core' and 'periphery' workers. 'Core' workers have good working conditions and security of employment, as long as they are 'flexible' in their willingness to perform whatever tasks are required. These tasks may cross over previously strictly demarcated working domains. 'Peripheral' workers, on the other hand, are hired, often on temporary, short-term contracts, and, while probably receiving equivalent pay rates to the 'core' workers, are denied sick pay, holiday pay and fringe benefits. They may not be rehired at the end of their contracts and may, therefore, provide flexibility to the employer in allowing the size of the labour force to be adjusted to suit fluctuations in demand. Workers employed under these conditions may be found in all occupations, from unskilled labourers to computer programmers.

Atkinson highlights several ways in which 'the flexible firm' can reduce the size of its 'core' labour force, all of which have become more prevalent in the last few years. The upsurge of part-time working and the dramatic increases in the numbers on publicly subsidized schemes, such as the Youth Training Scheme, have already been outlined. The sub-contracting of tasks for which permanent employees were previously used is becoming more widespread (Harris 1987). Although services such as catering and cleaning readily lend themselves to this change, sub-contracting is also being used to accommodate requirements for increased production. Indeed, part of the rise in the numbers of self-employed, up by a third since 1979, may be accounted for by employees being made redundant, and then setting up in

Table 3.11   National estimates: types of home-based work: England and Wales

	All	Single employer	Two or more clients
Home-based workers (excluding transport, construction and family workers)	658,250	342,830	315,420
Work done at home	251,040	113,850	137,190
Working from home as a base	407,210	228,980	178,230
Manufacturing work done at home	72,290	44,600	27,690
Non-manufacturing work	585,970	298,230	287,740
Child-minding or related work (at or from home)	13,980	13,150	830
Other types of work:	571,990	285,080	286,910
Done at home	171,180	62,670	109,500
Working from home as a base	400,810	223,400	177,400

NB Due to rounding, there are small discrepancies between totals for a category and the sub-divisions of it.

Source: Department of Employment

their previous jobs providing a sub-contracted service to their former employer.

The recruitment of temporary workers from private employment agencies has for many years been a feature of the UK labour market. Formerly, the bulk of this recruitment centred on the use of temporary clerical or secretarial workers to provide cover for the absence of permanent staff due to sickness or holidays. Recently, however, employment agencies have become more important in providing workers for a wide range of skills. As a result there is now a much greater number of agencies specializing in specific skill requirements, such as computer programmers and systems analysts, engineers and technologists.

Although no record is kept of the numbers of workers on temporary or short-term contracts, research by, amongst others, the Institute for Manpower Studies at Sussex University and the Labour Market Studies Group at Leicester University, has shown that there has been an increase in this type of employment in many large firms. The impetus for this development has come from the uncertainty about future manpower requirements generated by the traumatic effect of the recession and a growing awareness of the likely impact of new technology on jobs.

Another form of employment which relies on labour which is marginal to the permanent, or core workforce, is homework or outwork. Estimates of the numbers involved in this type of work depend greatly on how it is defined. On the basis of two national surveys carried out in 1980 and 1981, Hakim has suggested that the total number is 1.68 million, which is reduced to 658,000 if transport, construction and family workers are excluded (*Employment Gazette*, January 1984: 8–12). Rather surprisingly only 72,000 of those were involved in manufacturing homework (table 3.11). Even if the definition is restricted to work which is actually done at home, only 29 per cent of outworkers are in manufacturing. Recent growth in homeworking has been largely among service-sector occupations, related to new technology (*Personnel Management*, September 1984: 39–43).

Just how far we can attribute all these developments to the pressures of international competition is highly debatable (Pollert 1987). Work by the Labour Market Studies Group at Leicester University (Ashton, Maguire and Spilsbury 1990) suggests that some limited gains in 'flexibility' have been achieved in manufacturing industry but that the major growth of part-time work is due to industrial concentration in the service sector. A third factor has been the political pressure on the public sector to privatize the delivery of services and the attempt by the Thatcher administration to deregulate the labour market. This process has gone much further in Britain than in Canada. However, whatever form this core/periphery development may take, the overall result has been a vast increase in the proportion of workers who have no security of employment, and who are not protected by employment legislation.

The youth labour market

As we have seen, the majority of British youths continue to leave school at 16 and seek a job. The percentage of early school-leavers has changed very little over the last decade, yet during that time the demand for the labour of relatively unqualified youths has changed considerably. Whereas ten years ago the vast majority of school-leavers entered jobs, by 1986 this had been reduced to 15 per cent. The conventional explanation argues that the demand for youth labour is a product of fluctuations in the business cycle, with employers reducing their demand for youths during the downturn and increasing it during an upswing. When the Labour Market Studies Group examined this explanation using the Labour Force Survey data, it proved to be inadequate as a general explanation of what happened during the recession. Although it provided a partial explanation for the rise of male youth unemployment, female youth unemployment was found to be largely attributable to the displacement of young females by older (usually married) women.

Their results indicate that over the last decade, there has been an overall contraction in the demand for the labour of young people aged 16 and 17. This has been especially significant for those with minimal educational qualifications. The reduction in job opportunities as a result of this contraction is over and above that created by the recession of 1979–82 (Ashton, Maguire and Spilsbury 1990).

There are a number of processes of change which were found to be causing this contraction in the demand for youth labour:

1 The decline of the labour-intensive industries such as textiles, hosiery and footwear which have traditionally relied upon the labour of school-leavers.

2 The impact of new technology in manufacturing industry. Many firms which survived the recession, especially those in the engineering industry, invested in new technology. This technology enabled them to increase output substantially without taking on additional labour. Thus, many of the apprenticeships which previously provided a major source of employment for 16-year-old males were lost for ever. In addition, the new technology required specific skills which, together with employers' attempts to enhance the commitment of the labour force to the firm, led to higher educational qualifications for recruits being required.

In view of the changes in (1) and (2) above, it is unlikely that manufacturing industry will ever again seek to recruit large numbers of 16-year-old school-leavers.

3 In the commercial sector, the intensification of competition, together with the introduction of new information technology, is starting to reduce the demand for routine clerical workers. At the same time, employers' attempts to match fluctuations in demand for services with labour supply are leading to a growth of part-time jobs.
4 In hotels, catering and retail distribution, a process of increasing industrial concentration is reducing the demand for the full-time labour of youths. The progressive absorption or displacement of smaller independent businesses by the large corporations is resulting in a substantial change in the demand for labour. As such corporations rationalize their use of labour, full-time jobs which traditionally provided employment for large numbers of school-leavers are being replaced by part-time jobs. The organization is then able to adjust the supply of labour in accordance with fluctuations in the demand for labour. This is another change which is unlikely to be reversed.
5 The Youth Training Scheme, together with its predecessor, YOP, has been influential in increasing the proportion of 16-to-19-year-olds in the composition of the labour forces in construction and banking during the recession. However, in other parts of the labour market it has not succeeded in creating access for young people to jobs from which they have traditionally been excluded, e.g. operative jobs in capital-intensive industries.

The major effect of government schemes has been to counteract the displacement of youths by married women in the sales, cashier and waitress-type jobs in the service sector.

In the short term the problem of an over-supply of unqualified youths will be reduced by the decline in the numbers of 16-year-olds entering the market, but after 1995 those numbers will once again increase. Overall, the results suggest that an advanced industrial society such as Britain no longer requires the labour of relatively unqualified 16-year-olds in large numbers. Apart from the part-time jobs in the service sector, the areas of job growth have been in the professional, scientific, administrative and technical occupations. However, because of the requirement for high-level educational qualifications for these jobs, 16-year-old youths are excluded from competing for them.

Conclusions

In examining the changes which have been taking place in the British labour market we have noted a number which are common to all advanced industrial societies. These include the shift from employment in manufacturing to employment in service industries, the increasing participation of females in the labour market, the growth of part-time employment, and the impact of new technology. Other changes such as the decline of union membership and the continuance of high levels of unemployment are changes common to a limited number of countries. The low qualification levels of new entrants is a feature of the labour force peculiar to Britain. Clearly, there are no simple causes for these characteristics. The fact that some are common to all industrial societies suggests that there are changes in the structure of international markets which are propelling them. Others, such as the high levels of unemployment and the decline of union membership, are only found in a few industrial societies and so other explanations have to be sought.

The implications of all this for the transition from school have been profound. The recession triggered a virtual collapse in the demand for the labour of unqualified 16-year-olds. The traditional pathways into the labour market provided by the apprenticeship were undermined. In their place the government offered first a one-year, then a two-year training scheme. For those making the transition in the more affluent areas, the disruption was significant, while for those attempting to make the transition in the more deprived areas the disruption was dramatic, with many being forced into the ranks of the long-term unemployed or the sub-employed. Thus, what we have witnessed in Britain is a far more severe disruption to the transitional pathways than occurred in Canada.

Note

1 Revised version of paper presented at a workshop on the Comparative Analysis of British and Canadian Youth Labour Markets, 29 September–2 October 1988, Banff, Alberta.

References

Ashton, D. N. (1986). *Unemployment under Capitalism*. Brighton, Wheatsheaf.
Ashton, D. N., Maguire, M. and Spilsbury, M. (1990). *Restructuring the Labour Market: The Implications for Youth*. London, Macmillan.

Atkinson, J. (1984). 'Manpower strategies for flexible organizations', *Personnel Management*, August.

Bell, C. and Howieson, C. (1988). 'The view from the hutch: educational guinea pigs speak about TVEI', in D. Raffe (ed.) *Education and the Youth Labour Market*. Lewes, Falmer.

Bynner, J. (1987). 'The vanishing teenage worker: education prospects'. Inaugural lecture, Open University, Milton Keynes.

Chandler, A. D. (1976). 'The development of modern management structure in US and UK', in L. Hanna (ed.) *Management Strategy and Business Development*. London, Macmillan.

Finn, D. (1987). *Training without Jobs: New Deals and Broken Promises*. London, Macmillan.

Gill, C. (1985). *Work, Unemployment and the New Technology*, Cambridge, Polity Press.

Goldthorpe, J. and Payne, C. (1986). 'Trends in intergenerational mobility in England and Wales 1972–1983', *Sociology*, 20, 1: 1–24.

Harris, C. C. (1987). *Redundancy and Recession in South Wales*. Oxford, Blackwell.

Hobsbawm, E. J. (1968). *Industry and Empire*. London, Weidenfeld and Nicholson.

Makeham, P. (1980). *Youth Unemployment*, Research Paper No. 10, London, Department of Employment.

Northcott, J. and Rogers, P. (1984). *Microelectronics in British Industry*. PSI (No. 625). London.

OECD (1983). *Employment Outlook*. Paris, Organization for Economic Co-operation and Development.

OECD (1985). *The Integration of Women into the Economy*. Paris, Organization for Economic Co-operation and Development.

Pollert, A. (1987). 'The flexible firm: a model in search of reality or a policy in search of practice?'. Warwick Papers in Industrial Relations, University of Warwick.

Raffe, D. (1987a). 'The context of YTS: an analysis of its strategy and development', *British Journal of Education and Work*, 1, 1: 1–31.

Raffe, D. (1987). 'Youth unemployment in the United Kingdom', in Brown P. and Ashton, D. N. (eds.) *Education, Unemployment and Labour Markets*. Lewes, Falmer, 218–47.

Rajan, A. and Pearson, R. (1986). *UK Occupation and Employment Trends to 1990*. London, Butterworth.

Spilsbury, M., Maguire, M. J. and Ashton, D. N. (1986). 'The distribution and growth of the self-employed using data from the Labour Force Survey, 1979–84, Working Paper 12, Labour Market Studies, University of Leicester.

Spilsbury, M., Hoskins, M., Ashton, D. N. and Maguire, M. J. (1987). 'A note on the trade union membership patterns of young adults', *British Journal of Industrial Relations*, 25, 2: 267–74.

4

Education as preparation for work in Canada: structure, policy and student response

Jane Gaskell

Introduction: the Canadian context

Education and training policies in Canada have to be understood in the context of the historical development of federalism in the country. Canada consists of ten provinces and two federally controlled territories. Education is under provincial jurisdiction and the constitution makes it clear that provinces have the right to legislate in relation to education. While there are communalities among provinces, Canada is basically made up of ten education systems. The Council of ministers provides a forum for the discussion of national educational issues, but the provinces are determined to protect their jurisdiction from incursions by the federal government. Any number of substantive educational issues have turned into debates about provincial and federal jurisdiction, instead of about educational policy.

Each province devolves some responsibility for fiscal and curriculum policy to locally elected school boards. Several provinces have more than one school board for each geographical area – Catholic and Protestant, French language and English language. Within school boards, schools retain some local autonomy, although, advocates of decentralization have argued, not nearly enough. And schools themselves are loosely tied to many school-board directives. Principals can shape the ethos of a school, and teachers can 'shut the classroom door' and teach in widely different ways. The result is that the state cannot dictate classroom practice in any simple way.

Privately funded schools are relatively unimportant in Canada. Only 5 per cent of elementary and secondary pupils are enrolled in private schools.

The constitutional federal responsibility for managing the national economy and the labour market provides the federal government with its main justification for involvement in education and training. It is only at the level of post-secondary education and job training that this responsibility has been exercised to any substantial degree. The federal government provides block funding to the provinces for post secondary educational programmes, so that most policy issues remain under provincial control. Only in the area of short term job training does the federal government, through the Department of Employment and Immigration (CEIC), provide funding and dictate policy directly in relation to educational programmes. The Canadian Jobs Strategy is at present the rubric under which these policies are administered. Only preparation for work that lasts less than one year can be funded in this way.

One consequence of the exclusive provincial jurisdiction over elementary and secondary schooling has been the absence of a significant and sustained national political debate over the goals, the standards and the processes of public schooling. In their 1976 report, the OECD examiners concluded that:

Canadian education policy may be one of the least 'politicized' in the world . . . reforms in education are almost totally pragmatic or so generally conceived, and rely so heavily on the United States, British or French models, more or less adapted to Canadian conditions, that the opportunity for party political conflict is for all practical purposes, excluded.

(OECD 1976)

More recently, the McDonald Commission on the economic union and development prospects for Canada stated:

Given the importance of this sector (education) to Canada's future, relevant data and analyses are very scarce . . . little information about programs or students is available at the national level. Curricula vary from province to province, and small attempt had been made to define interprovincial differences or to relate the efficacy of the programs to varying circumstances. Educational institutions and local boards continually conduct evaluations of courses, curricula, and programs, but little of this material is aggregated at the national level.

(Royal Commission on Economic and Development Prospects for Canada 1985)

As all this suggests, policy change in public schools in Canada comes from local innovation and dispersion, as much as from provincial and federal policy initiatives. Local responses to local political and economic conditions remain important, and consistency across the country is unlikely. Provinces differ in the resources they have available, in which political party governs, in political culture and traditions. Regional disparities in wealth are enormous. And the economic structure of a Newfoundland outport where fishing and fish-processing provide most of the jobs has quite a different impact on education from the economic structure of Toronto where a very diverse economy is based largely in an expanding service sector.

The political structure clearly limits the ability of the state to intervene and bring educational structures into line with economic, or even labour market, needs, much as this is urged and discussed. Even when provinces do bring in new policies, translating the policy into changed practice in the classroom is far from a simple matter. Often policy change remains at the level of rhetoric. This limits the ability of Canadian governments to use the educational system as a tool of economic policy, as the British government has done.

At the same time, educational fashions, political shifts and economic exigencies can bring about similar trends across the country. What is commonly experienced is a fiscal crisis that has led governments to reduce spending on education, and to justify educational expenditures in terms of economic outcomes. Reliance on the private sector has increased. Changes in technology, in the organization of the world economy, and in the structure of the economy are experienced by all school districts, but in varying ways, depending on the local economic base. Attempts to 'rationalize' and 'standardize' do create some uniformity, but always within jealously guarded limits.

It is in this context that I will discuss the Canadian educational scene. This paper is divided into three sections. The first will briefly outline the structure of the Canadian educational system through secondary schooling, stressing the curriculum that is taught, and the debate it has engendered. The second section will begin to explore the way students respond to the school, taking into account the cultural norms they have adopted, as well as the economic and educational environment in which they exist. The final section will discuss the way specific vocational content is taught and received in Canadian secondary schools.

The structure of Canadian schooling: streaming and curriculum

Public schooling in Canada begins in the elementary grades which go from kindergarten (or junior kindergarten in Ontario, while kindergarten is not compulsory in some provinces) through to grade 6, 7 or 8. Children begin junior kindergarten at age four or kindergarten at age five. They would complete grade six by the age of 12, and move on to junior high school, or complete grade 7 or 8 at 13 or 14 and move on to a secondary school. Virtually all students complete elementary schooling.

The curriculum in the elementary school is based largely in language and mathematics, with social studies, science, music, art and physical education also having their place. Students tend to be taught several subjects by the same teacher, a structure which allows integration of content from one area to another, and encourages a 'child-centred' pedagogy. There is virtually no explicitly vocational content in the elementary curriculum, although 'relevance' to children's lives is stressed in curriculum guides. Curriculum guidelines are arrived at by ministries of education, through advisory committees that represent government officials, teachers, and often the interested public. Curriculum is translated into practice by teachers in their own classrooms, with some supervision from principals, curriculum specialists at the provincial and local level, and other teachers. The process is a fairly loose one, especially when, as is almost always the case, testing is controlled by the teacher themselves.

Formal streaming is not part of the elementary school system. Grouping is generally done within a single classroom; so that there will be a fast reading group and a slower one, a group for the mathematically able and one for those who are having problems. There are no standardized, government mandated examinations upon the completion of elementary school, although elementary-school achievement tends to be associated with placement in secondary programmes. All students move on to secondary schooling after the same grade.

The streaming that does take place in elementary schools is among schools in different neighbourhoods. Because students attend schools in their own neighbourhood, they attend schools populated by others of similar social-class backgrounds. A whole tradition of community studies, from Middletown (Lynd and Lynd 1929) to Crestwood Heights (Seeley, Sim and Loosely, 1956) to Hamilton High (Grant 1988), have shown the dramatic effects that neighbourhood composition has on the curriculum and social relations of schooling. In recent years the streaming has been exacerbated by the introduction of French immersion programmes, to which many professional middle class families send their children (Olsen and Burns 1983).

The length and organization of secondary schooling varies substantially across the country. Some provinces provide junior high schools for grades 6, 7, 8, and/or 9. In Quebec students attend secondary schools until grade 11, at which point they leave for two years at a CEGEP (college d'enseignement général et professionel) before they are eligible for university. Most provinces keep students in secondary school through grade 12 before they can go to university or community-college programmes. In Ontario, grade 13 is in the process of being phased out.

Canadian secondary schools are overwhelmingly comprehensive schools based in local neighbourhoods, whatever their precise differences. As a result, the processes whereby they stream students and put them on trajectories into the labour market are fairly similar across the country. I will discuss these under two headings, 'dropouts' from the school, and curriculum differentiation within the school.

Retention rates and dropouts

Streaming of students at the secondary level is evident in the length of time young people stay in school. Schools in wealthier neighbourhoods retain their students in school for longer and send more of them on to university.

Students who fail to complete secondary schooling enter the labour-market destined for low-level jobs.

Legally students must stay in school until they are 15 or 16. However, retention rates are comparatively high in Canada, and a substantial proportion of students stay on well beyond the official leaving age (Krahn, chapter 2 of this volume). In 1984, for example, 93 per cent of Canadian 16-year-olds, and 67 per cent of 17-year-olds were attending elementary and secondary schools. Many are working for pay at the same time. The actual rate of dropping out is very hard to estimate, given the way provincial governments collect and analyse their educational statistics. An Ontario commission on dropouts estimated a dropout rate of 30 per cent (Radwanski, 1988); a British Columbia Royal Commission estimated 40 per cent (Sullivan 1988), but a more careful study of school records in Ontario estimated a rate of closer to 15 per cent.

The assumption of all this research is that young people should continue with their high-school education until they reach the 12th grade, usually at 17 years of age. The norm is to complete high school. Those who do not are labelled as 'dropouts', the language itself revealing the way the issue is seen. Dropouts are a problem, a failure of the system, and a disappointment to family and friends. Dropouts are a concern for educators and policy makers.

The dropout problem has been of intermittent concern to Canadian educators. It was a major concern in the 1950s as schooling expanded and human-capital theory shaped the thinking of policy-makers, but it lost its prominence in the 1970s as the problems of an 'overeducated' and underemployed workforce took prominence. Recently more concern has been surfacing, as the economic imperatives of having a well-educated labour force reach the political agenda.

Recently the federal government has called attention to the problem of functional illiteracy and the economic drain it constitutes. Ontario has commissioned several studies on dropouts and has some experimental programmes designed to keep students in school by paying them, setting up alternative programmes, and integrating secondary education with work experience. Ontario's Radwanski report on dropouts calls for a less streamed, but increasingly 'back to basics' curriculum for all students. BC's Royal Commission calls for a more diversified programme for students in grades 11 and 12. It is likely that, whatever new initiatives are suggested, they will continue to be directed towards changing the secondary-school curriculum and encouraging students to complete grade 12, not towards developing any alternative mechanism of job preparation outside the regular secondary-school system.

The educational implications of the 'dropout problem' or the 'literacy problem' are not self evident. In general, one can detect some tension between those who want to tackle the problem through more 'relevance' and often more vocational content in the secondary school, and those concerned about academic standards who urge a more narrowly academic curriculum and a more selective school system.

Concern to keep dropouts in school is matched by concern about the falling standards that are produced by the educational changes that keep them in. Although increasing retention rates would seem to signal higher levels of achievement among young people, there has been concern in Canada, as in other Western countries, about 'standards', about whether high-school graduation continues to mean as much as it used to, and whether expectations for achievement have been adjusted downwards as more young people stay in school and expect to graduate. Public-opinion polls suggest the public thinks the quality of education is declining.

The rhetoric of educational reform is directed at touching all these bases, despite their contradictions. It is the organization of knowledge within the secondary system that becomes the issue, and the streaming of students into vocational and practical or academic and abstracted programmes that is controversial. It is to these structural issues that we now turn.

The organization of academic and vocational knowledge in secondary schooling

Streaming of students takes place within the Canadian secondary school through a process of differentiation of courses. Different kinds of courses have different value and different links to labour-market positions. Different kinds of students take different courses. The courses they take reflect the position they and/or their teachers anticipate they will occupy in the labour market.

The high-school curriculum in Canada looks much like the 'smorgasbord' or 'cafeteria' model that has been extensively described in the US (Powell, Farrar and Cohen 1985; Boyer, 1987). A very wide range of courses is available for credit towards a high-school diploma. Students are required to take some core subjects, usually English, mathematics, social studies and science. The requirements are more extensive in the earlier grades, and quite minimal in the final two years of secondary school. Students elect courses to fill out their programme and, while each school will differ somewhat in its offerings, the range is wide. It includes courses that are vocational in their orientation (e.g. carpentry, cafeteria, electronics, marketing, accounting, home economics, typing, and several forms of work experience), courses that are considered more academic (history, geography, calculus, French, physics, computer science), and courses in fine arts, personal development and physical education (music, painting, drama, community recreation, photography, guidance). All of these are offered in most large high schools, although some schools have a wider range of elective courses than others and some specialize in particular areas, offering special programmes in vocational or arts fields. In most provinces there is some provision for locally developed courses which allow individual schools or teachers to develop a specialized programme and teach it to their students. These courses will be taught at varying levels of difficulty, with varying kinds of prerequisites for entry. The diversity of courses offered in Canadian high schools is somewhat less than in the US, but it remains very substantial.

The historical roots of the comprehensive secondary school curriculum can be traced back to the nineteenth century. The first publicly supported Canadian secondary schools offered a variety of useful subjects for the local bourgeoisie (accounting, penmanship, surveying) alongside Latin and the more traditional subjects. Most students would pick up a smattering of different kinds of courses, and the ability so closely to serve the interests of a local community ensured the political base for the expansion of publicly supported education (Gidney and Lawr, 1979). Despite attempts by some school officials to adhere more closely to a classical model of secondary schooling and separate the academic from the vocational (and the girls from the boys), a pragmatic collection of course offerings persisted in the curriculum of the grammar school (Royce, 1975; Jackson and Gaskell, 1987).

In the early twentieth century the introduction of subjects of use to the working class occasioned much debate. Typing, manual arts, some technical subjects and home economics were eventually added to the curriculum, but they were clearly separated from academic courses, labelled vocational, and seen as appropriate for students destined for, in the case of technical or industrial courses, working-class or, in the case of clerical and domestic science courses, female jobs. These vocational offerings expanded through the first half of the twentieth century, as enrolments increased dramatically. But the traditional academic curriculum held its place of prominence, increasingly clearly demarcated from vocational courses.

Until the late 1960s students continued to be clearly streamed into vocational or academic programs. Each had its specified course requirements, examinations and diploma. In the early 1970s, major reforms took place. Overt streaming, mandated by the school, disappeared and was replaced by a system where students streamed themselves through their selection of courses. The number of required courses was reduced, standardized examinations disappeared and the number of electives any student could choose increased. Students were allowed to put together a much greater variety of individualized programmes.

This lack of visible streaming has a variety of advantages in terms of equity and flexibility. Some of the early studies of the change in the 1970s stressed how pleased students were to feel they were responsible for their course choices, instead of having them imposed by the school. The result was that students felt much more in control of their own school careers and would tend to blame themselves for selecting the wrong courses, instead of blaming teachers or the school for inadequate instruction (Fleming 1974). The clear labelling of students as superior or inferior diminished. (Laxer, Traub and Wayne 1974).

But streaming did not disappear. It merely became more difficult to describe and assess. Statistics on the kinds of courses students take are hard to collect and report. They are not listed on diplomas and are not aggregated at a national level, even if they are collected provincially. The streaming is not hidden from the view of students themselves who are fairly clear about their relative position, nor from post-secondary institutions who deny entry to students who have not taken appropriate courses. But they have become less obvious to parents and employers, and confusion can mean some students fail to get the kind of preparation they need as they put together their course of studies. No standardized examination system compares the results of different students, or different courses, or different schools.

This system has persisted, although there have been recent attempts to cut back on the diversity allowed to students. Today the process of streaming in the secondary school has a somewhat different character in different provinces. It is more disguised in some provinces than in others by the comprehensive system of course electives. Ontario, the most industrialized and wealthy province, has the most clearly streamed system. Ontario schools offer courses at different levels – labelled gifted, academic, general, basic, etc., and numbered hierarchically from 1 to 6. Students tend to see themselves as in one stream or another, although they do not have to take all their courses at the same level. Although vocational courses will tend to be offered at the lower levels of difficulty, and the more discipline-based academic electives are available at the advanced levels, most kinds of courses are available at different levels. Students can take their required courses at whatever level of difficulty they deem appropriate. In order to be eligible for university, students need a required number of 'academic', i.e. higher-level (5 or above), credits.

In British Columbia, to provide a contrasting example, the process is more subtle. Few courses are officially streamed. Only a few are labelled 'modified', signalling a lower level of difficulty. Other courses are offered to all students who decide to enrol at a particular grade level – e.g. algebra 11, English 10, history 12. Differences in students' programmes arise through the type of course they select, rather than the level of difficulty that is officially attributed to it. The more academic students will take more mathematics, science, language and history courses. The less academic students will take more vocational electives, more business mathematics, home economics, media studies and human biology, to illustrate with just a few examples. Post-secondary institutions set up their own regulations about which high-school courses will count for admission, and as a result secondary schools need to be closely in touch with the post-secondary sector in order to advise students about what courses to take. Vocational courses do not count for university entrance, even in areas like commerce and home economics, where the university does offer programmes. To be eligible for university entrance, students must take a fairly extensive range of prescribed academic courses.

Recently, reflecting the more conservative politics of the 1980s, provincial governments of all political stripes have begun to revert back towards the model of the 1950s and 60s. There are proposals to increase the requirements for high school graduation, to reinstitute a system of provincial examinations, and to stream students more clearly into distinct and laddered programmes.

Political concern about monitoring standards has led to a new emphasis on standardized examinations. The past few years have seen a reintroduction of grade 12 examinations in Alberta, British Columbia, Saskatchewan, Quebec and New Brunswick, and an increased emphasis on standardized testing and accountability starting in the elementary grades.

Concern about standards has also led to a large number of provincial curriculum reviews, leading in many cases to changed requirements for graduation, 'clarification' of goals and attention to core-curriculum content. The Council of Ministers summarizes,

> The trend towards greater prescription is evident in the specifying of core curriculum, the defining of essential learnings, and an increase in the number of compulsory courses at the secondary school level. At least five provinces have introduced stricter requirements for the secondary school diploma by making more courses compulsory, and four have specified core curriculum. Alberta and Saskatchewan have in addition identified what they term 'essential learnings'.
>
> (Council of Ministers 1986)

The emphasis on science and technology in the schools comes directly from concerns that the country's ability to compete in the international environment will increasingly depend on scientific competence. A study by the Science Council of Canada in 1984 called for reforms in science teaching from the earliest grades. Emphasis on putting computers into the curriculum has also been felt across the country, with new courses, new machines and new demands on teachers. The place of computer courses on the vocational/academic divide is still being negotiated, and often different computer courses are offered for academic and vocational purposes.

The attempts to change the curriculum seem most intense at the rhetorical level. Translating the initiatives into changed practice in the classroom is another matter. However, it is clear that students are being encouraged to take more maths and science, and that requirements for graduation are designed to increase the number of academic courses students take.

The emphasis on increasing academic standards and at the same time making school relevent and attractive for all students creates contradictions which tend to be resolved by streaming, by having both but separating them out. The separation of the vocational and the academic gets increasingly built into the school system, entrenching a hierarchy of kinds of knowledge appropriate for students destined for different places in the labour market. It is in this sense that schooling becomes increasingly tied to economic imperatives in Canada, as more students stay in school, and more elaborated and differentiated programmes are developed to deal with the students who are there.

Students' responses to school: vocational orientations

Canadian students respond to school in ways that reflect both the structure that confronts them, and the culture they have learned. They respond in ways that are varied and individualized, but shaped by the social, economic, cultural and educational world they know.

It is clear that middle-class youth are more satisfied with their experiences in school than working-class youth. They stay in school longer, get better grades while they are there and express more positive opinions of the school environment.

Working-class youth are the educational 'problem', the unknown quantity, the disaffected group for whom educational solutions should be found. It is working-class youth who have been the focus of my research (Gaskell, 1985a, 1985b). The research was carried out in British Columbia, not in a sample of representative schools, but in a few schools in working-class neighbourhoods.

My research suggests that working-class youth in Canada are very conscious of the economic uses of completing secondary school and going on to post-secondary schooling, especially university. They buy into an individualistic, competitive ethic that promises mobility on the basis of success in school, even when they are not at all interested in what they are being taught. The result is a commitment to schooling based not on its intrinsic interest and value, but on its economic purposes.

The typical exchange with students in my research notes went something like this:

> STUDENT: It's important to finish
> INTERVIEWER: Why?
> STUDENT: Because then you can find a better job.

or

> I: What about your friends who have dropped out of school?
> S: They've got mostly restaurant jobs. That's all they can get. They don't have the education.

The dominant ideology in Canada has as one of its major tenets the notion that anyone can get ahead if they do well at school. School is the avenue of social mobility, the way upwards economically. The immediate experience these students have of the world confirms the distinctions that education promises. High-paying professional and managerial jobs require university education. Waitressing and sales jobs which pay low wages and are easily available require few educational credentials. At a gross level the relationship between education and occupation is incontrovertible.

Students are aware of the social processes that set high-school graduates clearly apart from and above the dropouts. As Krahn has shown, the possession of a secondary-school diploma makes a substantial difference to earnings, to both the male and female students, though female earnings are substantially lower.

At the level of university education, there are some very close linkages between schooling and access to jobs. Students cannot become physicians without attending university, and then attending medical school, for example. This close credentialling linkage is reflected in the tendency for those going on to post-secondary schooling to be most sure of the economic benefits of their education. The belief that university education is a passport out of unemployment and work troubles is widespread:

Hopefully, with a university education, jobs will come easier.

My parents just think don't get involved in politics (to solve economic problems) . . . who cares what they are doing. Just go about your everyday things and get into university.

The role of high-school courses in regulating entry to sales and office jobs is less clear. Indeed, much of the literature suggests that educational credentials are not very important to employers in discriminating among potential employees, as in Britain (Blackburn and Mann 1979; Maguire and Ashton 1981). But students continue to stress the value of a high school diploma in the immediate post-high-school labour market.

When you go out to find a job, people ask you 'have you graduated from high school? You need that.'

If I was going to apply for a job and didn't have a high-school diploma and the guy beside me did, I feel he will get the job before I will.

People that I knew who had a high-school education said it was important. After that you can decide what you want to do.

It is not just the diploma, but also the marks that students feel matter economically.

INTERVIEWER: Do you care about your marks?
STUDENT: Yes, a lot of people are scared of failing so they try to do their best. They don't want to fail, to repeat it.

This student is concerned about her marks because she equates good marks with getting her 'dogwood', i.e., her diploma. Others say that the marks themselves are important to employers.

STUDENT: In grade 11 or 12 the marks are going to be on your diploma and the kind of job you get in the future is going to depend on your marks.
STUDENT: If you see an F on the transcript, it doesn't look so good.
INTERVIEWER: To whom?
STUDENT: At the university if you want to get in, or the employer. They look at the comments. They look at your attendance.

STUDENT: If you apply for a job, first of all they will look back on your high school record.

STUDENT: If you get Bs and As . . . OK. If you go apply for a job they think you will do a good job, but if you have C, C-, or F or E or something, they are going to say what is this – I don't want this.

These students see their high-school record as a way of providing information to the employer about their capabilities and interests. Marks are important because 'they go on your transcript, right?' School credentials are important even for low-level jobs because they signal capability, hard work and commitment.

What is striking about the students' talk is the emphasis they put on getting diplomas and marks, and the lack of emphasis that they put on knowing something or learning anything that will actually be useful on the job. This holds for academic as well as vocational courses. While they believe that what is on paper will be used by employers in a way that will make a difference for their chances in the labour market, they rarely believe that what they actually know will make a difference to how well they can do on the job. While they affirm the general value of what they learn in school in an abstract way, its practical uses are few.

If you don't have school and someone asked you a question, you wouldn't know what they are talking about, right?

It's like knowing a little bit of electronics, drafting and such . . . that will come in handy . . . and typing . . . everyone should take some of that.

I sure have learned a lot and it is all gathered up in my brain some place and I think it is worthwhile.

But most students see little direct relevance for what they learn in school.

Some of the accounting helps. That's about it . . . and also being able to speak in sentences or whatever . . . like adding and subtracting. All this algebra garbage . . . I think it is a waste of time . . . you'll never use it unless you're a scientist.

I don't think it's useful. Right now in English we have to like everything you read, you have to analyse and decide on what the author was trying to say and all that. I don't think I'll use that when I get out of school. I just read the book. I liked it. I'm not going to be analysing chapters or anything like that.

Like social studies and science . . . I don't think they are very useful unless you are going into that specific job or something . . . like in grade 10, I don't think social studies had anything to do with us.

I worked at the switchboard at the other place . . . that helped because I learned to talk to people . . . but the rest . . . no not really. Not at all.

In other words, school matters for economic success, these students say, but it matters in terms of marks and credentials, not in terms of what they learn. It matters as a sign of their willingness to work hard, but not as a sign of intelligence, understanding or knowledge. Their disillusionment with the content of schooling is striking. Even so they are willing to co-operate, rather than give up, in the expectation of economic advantage.

Specific vocationalism (or 'occupationalism') in the secondary school

Most of the courses taught in secondary school in Canada do not have content that is job related. However, as was outlined above, some courses do purport to prepare students for specific places in the labour market, and some purport to prepare them specifically for the workplace, rather than for further education. These specifically vocational courses have long been part of the secondary school and have an importance they do not have in Britain, where this level of vocational training has been more available in apprentice-ships, in government training schemes and on the job. These vocational courses are important in articulating school and work in a variety of working-class jobs, especially clerical work.

As has been pointed out, there are few elaborated and publicly differen-tiated vocational programmes in the secondary school. What exists instead is a series of course 'choices'. Streaming is hidden in an individualized system of course electives. The secondary-school curriculum is by and large not closely linked to any particular labour market but is seen as generalized social and intellectual preparation for work and further education.

Vocational programmes in the high school constitute an attempt to make the logic of the labour market more immediate and persuasive to students and to base the rationale for education in skill acquisition rather than credentialling. The arguments for vocational classes have been that they will keep students in school and they will render students more manageable in class. Arguments about the economic benefits for industry have been articulated by those outside schools, but inside the walls of the school the most persuasive case for vocationalism has been attendance and discipline (Oakes 1985; Hogan 1985; Lazerson and Grubb 1974).

The appeal of vocational programmes in the high school lies in their promise of 'relevance' and economic advantage to students. Teachers are confronted with a substantial number of students who want to graduate from high school, because they feel they will get better jobs, but who find school 'boring' and 'useless'. One widespread response of school systems, going back to the turn of the century, has been to teach courses that have specific relevance for particular kinds of jobs, courses that have come to be known as vocational.

Any link between the kind of high-school programme students have taken and their ability to compete in a particular labour market depends not on specific credentials, but on the development of interests, contacts or skills that link students with specific job opportunities. There are a few high-school programmes that promise to develop such skills and interests for a specific place in the workforce.

The lack of credentialling in the school restricts the provision of vocational education in any area where workers have been able to insist on control of training. Skilled blue-collar trades are only introduced in the secondary school. Industrial education emphasizes tool use, technological literacy and avocational projects. Specific job training is the province of the community college or the employer or the union. Apprenticeships have never been well developed, in any case, and Canada has relied to a remarkable extent on immigration to provide skilled labourers.

Business education has been the most consistently vocational subject taught in the public high school. Business courses have been included in the public-school curriculum since the mid-nineteenth century, when book-keeping and penmanship were part of what every student learned (Rogers and Tyack 1982). In the early twentieth century, typewriting and shorthand were introduced into the public school shortly after they were introduced into the office, and commercial subjects were expanded and separated out from the academic mainstream to constitute a distinct vocational pro-gramme. This programme has remained surprisingly unchanged to the present day, although 'commercial' education first became 'business' education and now 'business studies', 'bookkeeping' is now called 'account-ing', and 'business law' has become 'general business'. Most Canadian high schools today offer courses in typing, office procedures, accounting, business communications, office machines, and shorthand.

The peculiar relationship between high-school business preparation and office jobs is accounted for by the feminization of office work at the turn of the century when preparation for the office was already firmly entrenched in the public-school curriculum. Employers were reluctant to train and promote women on the job, as they were seen as temporary workers in whom investment was wasted. Private business schools sprang up to prepare employees for the expanding office jobs. Public high schools, anxious for public legitimacy and an expanded clientele, added the practical subjects of stenography, typing, secretarial practice to their curriculum. The resulting availability of pre-entry training for office jobs kept wages down, made women attractive employees and kept the supply of office workers up. Wolf and Rosenfeld (1978) have pointed out that lack of on-the-job training and extensive pre-entry training are characteristics of female work in general.

Business education courses instruct students in skills that are directly related to office jobs – typing, bookkeeping, office procedures, shorthand, business communications, office machines and business law. Secretarial jobs require the ability to type and to format a letter. Clerks who deal with financial statements need to know what an 'asset' is, and how it differs from a 'liability'. The courses build on this connection between what is needed at work and what is taught in school to make schooling meaningful to students and to promise concrete payoffs to course-taking in the labour market.

Business education has not been a marginal enterprise in the school system. In 1970, the Royal Commission on the Status of Women (1970) estimated that a quarter of all female secondary school students were enrolled in commercial courses. A 1977 report suggested that 45 per cent of Ontario secondary-school girls were in commercial courses (Synge, 1977). The importance of business courses reflects the importance of clerical work. In 1981 clerical workers comprised one out of every five Canadian workers, making it the largest major occupational group. A third of all women work in the clerical sector.

One thing that becomes clear when talking to students about their reasons for taking business courses is that this specific vocational logic is only part of what attracts them. Within the high school a streaming process occurs, whereby 'academic' courses are more difficult and 'vocational' courses are easier to pass.

Students' interview comments drive the point home. Here are some responses to the question, 'Why did you take business classes?'

I thought it would be easy and it wouldn't be all that much homework.

You just go along in the book and you know it is pretty fun. You do just basic mathematics. It is quite easy.

My sister took it and said it was easy, so I took it.

Because I thought it was easy . . . all they do is type letters . . . I like typing letters. I think a lot of people took it for an elective because it's quite easy to pass.

The counsellor encourages this approach, advising students to take courses they can pass. He says his 'bias' is 'trying to keep as many doors open as I can, so if a kid is choosing between taking the business math, and algebra 11, if there's any chance of making algebra 11, then I'll say . . . I suggest you take algebra 11 . . . simply because it leaves that option open.' The option he refers to is the option to go to university. The door he wants to open is the one to professional or managerial work through post-secondary schooling. Vocational courses clearly become the second-class route for students who are destined for a lower place on the occupational ladder.

The teachers adapt the content of their courses to the level of student they expect. 'We have to keep lowering our expectations in order to let the kids get some success and in order to let them feel good about themselves.' Demanding a lot is described as a mistake by the teachers. 'If you start doing that, you start fighting with your colleagues and hating the kids . . . so you just say they are nice kids, we'll give them some self-confidence. Maybe they can get out there and life will teach them.' The result is that vocational classrooms become part of a process of streaming in the high school, a process which separates out the less successful students. Vocational courses have lower status with students and, a good deal of evidence suggests, with employers who prefer academic students. Vocational courses then are part of a complex pattern of streaming in the high school, a pattern which reproduces the inequality of academic and manual work within the school, devaluing whatever is taught in vocational classrooms.

A large number of students take business courses then, not because of their specific job relevance, but because they constitute an easier way to achieve a high-school graduation diploma, or to achieve higher marks than they would get in other courses. As was pointed out earlier, this desire to graduate with a good record is based on assumptions about the value of school credentials in the labour market. But it means that the specific vocational relevance of the courses becomes less important than their more general relevance as 'a credit.'

A majority of the students did agree however that part of their motivation for taking business courses was 'because I thought it would help me get a job.' Vocational courses will help students in the labour market if they teach specific vocational skills that employers want and that academic students do not have. It would be wrong to see the connection between course-taking and vocational preparation as necessarily a very direct one. Many students take the course 'in case' they want an office job. They want to be able to 'fall back on' office work. Many plan to go on to further schooling rather than going directly to work and did not look to the courses for direct job preparation so much as to try the area out. But in some way or another the vocational uses of the courses did figure in most students' approach to them.

In the interviews, students expressed job-related reasons for taking business courses as follows:

Because I want to be an accountant when I grow up.

Because I want to go into fashion merchandising and you have to know how to keep books.

Because I wanted to go into business . . . because I wanted to know what it was like . . . you know . . . to do the paperwork.

Like if I go into an office, I will know the basic things – what I am doing.'

Their talk can be summed up by saying that they believe business courses give them knowledge about the office that is useful and will be recognized by employers when they decide whom to hire. The advantage they will have is not one that is enforced through licensing, but one that depends on a shared understanding that what is taught in high-school courses is valued on the job.

Gender divisions are much more marked in vocational classrooms than in academic ones. When students think about what skills will be vocationally relevant, they think about it in light of a labour market that is gender segregated. Young women who want to continue their education take typing and office procedures in order to get summer jobs. Young women oriented toward the labour market see clerical jobs as better than the alternatives of waitressing and sales.

You grow up knowing secretarial is girls' work, it is hard to change.

Mostly it is secretarial kind of work and I guess guys don't feel comfortable typing and filing, stuff like that, because there are not many male secretaries. They get the impression that when they take typing courses, they'll get laughed at or something.

> INTERVIEWER: What kinds of students take business courses?
> FEMALE STUDENT: Most girls . . . because like my Mom, she wanted me to get into business.
> INTERVIEWER: Why?
> FEMALE STUDENT: Because that's mostly what girls do.

Given the labour market division, social pressure makes it difficult for individuals to break the gender barrier.

> INTERVIEWER: How is it for boys in office practice?
> FEMALE STUDENT: I think it's really tough because they get called sissy and things like that.
> MALE STUDENT: At first it was pretty difficult . . . the only guy in the class . . . I was shocked . . . I was self-conscious about it. That's about it. Nobody bothered me about it.

Stereotypes get reinforced by the students' immediate experience of gender divisions in the school. Vocational classes thereby strengthen and reproduce the general ideology of what constitutes 'male-ness' and 'femaleness'.

Students take business courses as an easy way to a high-school credential; they also take them because they offer something specific and valuable in the way of job preparation. The courses offer skills directly articulated to the labour market, skills for which students themselves can see a payoff. Vocational relevance becomes a bonus for students who want meaning and relevance in their schooling, and for teachers who want a motivational device. But the process of selecting students for vocational classes recreates in the school the labour-market divisions that exist in the adult world of work.

My recent work suggests that the close linkage between high-school preparation and office jobs is breaking down, as the number of office jobs decreases, and technology reorganizes skills and training. Business courses are becoming more oriented towards 'life skills' for students who want a relatively easy route to a diploma, and less oriented to the specific skills that are necessary in an office. The specific skill of typing, which used to set apart girls who had taken business courses and make them particularly attractive to employers, is now more widely available through the necessity of 'keyboarding' for computers. College programmes are becoming the ones that try to impart job-specific skills.

Increasingly what is emphasized in vocational programmes in the high school is a general orientation towards being a good worker, developing the attitudes and values that employers prefer. More work experience is being added to the curriculum, but the only employers who will place students are non-unionized employers in low-skill areas. Students may work in the school cafeteria, in the school store, or for a few weeks in an office or a bank. The emphasis remains on learning about work. While there has been a good deal of discussion of how to introduce more vocationally oriented courses and content into the secondary school, high-school education by and large remains general preparation, not oriented towards any particular segment of the labour market. Graduates remain unskilled in any particular occupation, even if some of them graduate with a fairly clear idea of where they want to go to get work.

In various ways provincial governments have moved to strengthen programmes that bring school and work closer together. Enrolment in various kinds of work experience programmes outside the high school seem to be increasing rapidly.

Ontario has been particularly active in developing 'co-op' programmes with a substantial out-of-school component. The programme was approved by the province in 1979 and has expanded rapidly until the ministry estimates 22,000 students are involved in the programme in 1986–7. Special provincial incentive funds are available to initiate and expand co-operative education and transition to employment programmes for school leavers. Ontario has also organized a 'linkages' programme which allows secondary school students to earn credit towards advanced vocational training, particularly apprenticeships, while they are in high school. A World of Work curriculum has been developed for use in schools in combination with out-of-school work experiences. Prince Edward Island, Alberta, Quebec, British Columbia and Saskatchewan have all in different ways affirmed the importance of preparation for work in the secondary curriculum in the last few years.

However, this direction stands in some contrast with the new emphasis on academics. The comprehensive structure of schooling allows academic and vocational programmes to coexist. Firmer streaming of students into academic and vocational programmes may resolve some of the difficulties. The schools' ability to resist most outside initiatives at a level of practical policy further reduces the potential for conflict. But at a time when the resources available to schools are declining, increased tension can be predicted around these contrasting directions.

The Canadian experience: distinctive and the same

Within the Canadian context one comes to take for granted the shape and content of the relations between the labour market and the educational system. In a comparative framework, one sees what is distinctive and can begin to point to the impact of Canada's particular history and political arrangements in shaping these connections.

One of the major functions of education, for students, for employers, and for the state, is the preparation of young people for the workplace. Whatever the form of the education, academic or vocational, located in high schools, colleges or apprenticeships, it is linked closely to labour market preparation. The interesting questions then are the form of the linkages. The fact of streaming, of separating students out in such a way that they are prepared to enter different segments of the labour market, is universal. The mechanisms vary and will have different consequences for young people, for the class structure, for gender relations, for the productivity of the economy, and for the flexibility of labour in the face of technological change and the reorganization of global capital.

All of these questions cannot be answered here but, in raising them, this kind of comparative work probably performs its most important role. In concluding this essay I will reflect on only three of the conceptual issues that emerged as I reflected on the Canadian experience in light of the British one: the role of specific and general vocational preparation, the responses of the state, and the responses of students.

Vocational and academic education

The distinction between vocational and academic courses is fundamental to the organization of the educational system. In the Canadian system vocational courses are offered throughout all levels of education: in the secondary school, in the college and in higher education. The provision of vocational training outside these three systems is relatively under-developed. There is little on-the-job training offered directly by employers, as many government documents lament. The new initiatives the federal government has undertaken under the Canadian Jobs Strategy have been primarily directed at public institutions, even as they call for more private initiatives. The Canadian tradition has been to offer job training primarily through the public educational system. Canadian students are urged to stay in school and get more education, rather than being urged to take particular forms of job-specific training.

This is in contrast to the new initiatives in Britain, where government-sponsored job training initiatives have developed rapidly outside the secondary-school system, the further-education system, or the universities. An alternative system, directed at disadvantaged youth, has developed independently.

The contrast is not a complete and clean one, of course. The Canadian state does attempt to privatize some training, and some of the job-entry schemes sponsored by the federal government bear a distinct resemblance to British programmes for school leavers. The further-education system in Britain has expanded in response to state initiatives for unemployed youth, and TVEI has introduced a variety of vocational schemes into secondary education.

However, we can ask what difference the educational, institutional location of job training might make. Locating vocational courses within the structure of the secondary school does have an impact on what is taught, who teaches it and how students respond to it. Any school subject tends to be seen as part of the general education of youth, and to be subject to the pressures of any school subject . . . to compete for resources, students and status. There is pressure for these courses to be articulated in some way to the intellectual and democratic goals that justify the school system.

At the same time, the processes of differentiation within the school are powerful, and many have pointed to the way the school environment deadens and trivializes the most interesting content. Students treat vocational courses as just more school, to be endured because one needs a credential, and this is the easiest way to get a credential.

Within the vocational curriculum, the issue that arises within both the British context and the Canadian one is how much of the relevant content is social ('life skills'), how much is reading and writing, and how much is specifically job related. In both countries, there is pressure to move from specific job-skill training to a more generalized notion of preparing a well-behaved, and preferably literate worker. And notions of the generic good worker in schools or elsewhere continue to be based in class and gender inequality.

What remains at the basis of both systems is the distinction between the academic and the vocational, the intellectual and the social, instead of a recognition of their interrelations. Even in the comprehensive Canadian system the social processes within the school separate out the academic students from the vocational ones, giving the latter a diminished social and economic status, as well as a lesser claim on intellectual development. In the more clearly differentiated British system, the narrowly vocational gets increasingly distinguished from the broader academic goals of public schooling.

The separation of the vocational and the academic is neither necessary nor helpful, in terms of educational goals or economic prosperity. Employers need broadly educated workers, with the ability to understand what they are doing and to make reasonable judgements (Livingstone, Hart and McLean 1982). The close links between technical skills, social skills and intellectual skills are reflected in the demands that vocational preparation include 'life skills', and the role that academic education plays in regulating entry to higher-paying jobs. Students are quite cognizant of the vocational purposes of even academic courses, and of the way social relations, as much as intellectual achievement, are at the basis of doing well in school. Vocational courses make the economic purposes of education explicit but do so in a way that narrows the intellectual purposes, and therefore the general intellectual and social development of students. Academic teachers ignore vocational goals only by ignoring the actual structure of labour markets and credentialling.

State responses

Thinking about the directions in which the Canadian school system is moving draws attention to the contradictions that are part of the process, and the limited ability business, labour or politicians have to make the school system an instrument of economic policy. In Canada there are calls for closer links between school and work, for more work-study programmes, for increased attention to on-the-job training. At the same time there are calls for higher academic standards, for a more academic high-school programme, and for more examinations.

Education has been the focus of economic restructuring at several points in Canadian history. After World War I, federal legislation funded vocational and technical education, but the control remained provincial, and the form of the provision was left to local initiative. After World War II, the expansion of post-secondary education was also funded by the federal government, but the forms of new post-secondary institutions were left to the provincial control.

There are still attempts to find educational solutions for economic problems, but the lack of a co-ordinated political thrust, along with an historical tradition of letting the school system pragmatically adapt to local pressures, has left the school system remarkably untouched by changing economic and political conditions. The secondary-school system has continued to absorb a variety of new initiatives but has retained its basic shape and content over the past twenty years. Students are streamed, vocationalism is an important part of that streaming process, the introduction of new programmes has increased the variety of options available in the school system and thereby increased the streaming, but no clear new directions have emerged.

Outside the secondary school, the marked change has been the increase in community-college programmes. Vocationalism has emerged in publicly funded colleges, not in the secondary school, and not in private or public job-training schemes. The government attempted increasingly to privatize the provision of job training, but the college system is also solidly entrenched and has absorbed the new government initiatives largely inside its walls.

To change the basic institutional patterns that have evolved would take a co-ordinated and consistent political intervention over a period of time. This seems unlikely in the Canadian context. Local institutions are likely to continue to adapt pragmatically to local political pressure and educational wisdom. The concerted centralized efforts to change educational provision which have occurred in Britain seem unlikely in Canada.

Student responses

The ways that students make sense of the school system, and of their economic prospects, can be understood only in the light of the assumptions they make about the world, and the actual structure of their lives, at school, at work, and in their families. The understandings they create in turn shape the world as they live it, and shape the world as teachers, politicians, parents and the next generation also experience it. Such is the nature of 'structuration' as Giddens (1985) calls it, the creation and recreation of institutions by the everyday activities of those who exist within them. It is important to pay attention, not just to state responses, but also to the responses of youth.

Canadian youth culture has often been described as a rather quiescent one, rarely challenging of authority relations, of institutions as they are structured. There seems to be little 'oppositional' culture, little class-based youth culture. Much of the British research on youth culture has ignored young women, so the visible contrasts may more safely be drawn between British young men and Canadian young men. But the picture of Canadian youth that emerges from several studies is of young people who adapt pragmatically to conditions as they find them, accept the social norms of individual competition and mobility, and strive to make a better life for themselves (Gaskell and Lazerson 1980; Brake 1985).

Cultural change may occur. The recent increase in visible minority immigrant groups may have an impact on Canadian youth culture that has not yet been explored. A much greater diversity of responses can be expected, as students who do not speak English at home become the majority in many large urban school systems.

But culture cannot be treated independently of economic and educational context. The opportunity structure shapes cultural responses, as well as being shaped by them. This interactive process is what makes exploring comparative institutional contexts so important, for policy but also for social theory. The Canadian youth response is likely to remain somewhat less 'oppositional' than the British response, and as a result the pressure for centralized interventions instead of local adaptations will remain smaller.

References

Blackburn, R. and Mann, M. (1979). *The Working Class in the Labour Market*. London, Macmillan.
Boyer, E. (1987). *High School: A Report on Secondary Education in America*. New York, Harper & Row.
Brake, Michael (1985). *Comparative Youth Culture*. London, Routledge & Kegan Paul.
Council of Ministers of Education (1986). Report to the 40th Session International Conference on Education, Geneva.
Fleming, W. G. (1974). *The Individualized System: Findings from Five Studies. High School Studies*. Toronto, Ontario Institute for Studies in Education.

Gaskell, J. (1985a). 'Course enrolment in the high school: the perspective of working class females', *Sociology of Education* 58, 1: 48–59.

Gaskell, J. (1985b). 'Explorations in vocationalism: through the eyes of high school students'. In Mason, G. (ed.) *Transitions to Work*. Winnipeg, Institute for Social and Economic Research.

Gaskell, J. (1986). 'The changing organisation of business education in the high school: teachers respond to school and work', *Curriculum Inquiry*, 16, 4: 417–37.

Gaskell, J. and Lazerson, M. (1980). 'Between school and work: perspectives of working class youth', *Interchange*, 11 (3): 80–96.

Giddens, A. (1985). *The Constitution of Society: Outline of the Theory of Structuration*. Berkeley, University of California Press.

Gidney, R. D. and Lawr, D. A. (1979). 'Egerton Ryerson and the Origins of the Ontario Secondary School', *The Canadian Historical Review*, LX, 4: 442–65.

Grant, G. (1988). *The World We Created at Hamilton High*. Cambridge, MA, Harvard University Press.

Hogan, D. (1985). *Class and Reform: School and Society in Chicago 1880–1930*. Philadelphia, University of Pennsylvania Press.

Jackson, N. and Gaskell, J. (1987). 'White collar vocationalism: the rise of commercial education in Ontario and British Columbia, 1870–1920', *Curriculum Inquiry*, 17, 2, 177–201.

Laxer, G., Traub, R. and Wayne, K. (1974). *Student Social and Achievement Patterns as Related to Secondary School Organizational Structures*. Toronto, Ontario Institute for Studies in Education.

Lazerson, M. and Grubb, N. (1974). *American Education and Vocationalism: A Documentary History 1870–1970*. New York, Teachers College Press.

Livingstone, D. W., Hart, D. J., and McLean, L. D. (1982). *Public Attitudes Toward Education in Ontario*. Toronto, OISE.

Lynd, R. S., and Lynd, H. M. (1929). *Middletown: A Study in Modern American Culture*. New York, Harcourt Brace & World.

Maguire, M. and Ashton, D. (1981). 'Employers' perceptions and use of educational qualifications', *Educational Analysis* 3, 2: 25–36.

Oakes, J. (1985). *Keeping Track: How Schools Structure Inequality*. New Haven, Yale University Press.

OECD Examiner's Report (1976). *Review of National Policies for Education: Canada*. Paris, Organization for Economic Co-operation and Development.

Olson, P. and Burns, George (1983). 'Politics, class and happenstance: French immersion in a Canadian context', *Interchange*, 14, 1: 1–17.

Powell, A., Farrar, E. and Cohen, D. (1985). *The Shopping Mall High School: Winners and Losers in the Educational Marketplace*. Boston, Houghton Mifflin.

Radwanski, G. (1988). *Ontario Study of the Relevance of Education and the Issue of Dropouts*. Toronto, Ministry of Education.

Rogers, D. and Tyack, D. (1982). 'Work, youth and schooling: mapping critical research areas'. In Kantor, H. and Tyack, D. *Work, Youth and Schooling*. Stanford, Stanford University Press.

Royal Commission on the Economic and Development Prospects for Canada. (1985). Vol. 2 Ottawa, Supply and Services.

Royal Commission on the Status of Women (1970). *Status of Women in Canada*. Ottawa, Information Canada.

Royce, M. (1975). 'Arguments over the education of girls – their admission to grammar schools in this province', *Ontario History*, 67: 1–13.

Seeley, J. R., Sim, R. A., and Loosely, E. W. (1956). *Crestwood Heights: A Study of the Culture of Suburban Life*. New York, Basic Books.

Statistics Canada (1981). *Women in the Labour Force: 1978–1979*. Ottawa, Ministry of
Labour.

Sullivan, B. (1988). *A Legacy for Learners*. Royal Commission on Education. Victoria:
Ministry of Education.

Synge, J. (1977). 'The sex factor in social selection processes in Canadian education.'
In Carlton, R., Solley, L. C. and MacKinnon, N.J., *Education Change and Society*.
Toronto, Gage Publishing Ltd.

Wolf, W. C. and Rosenfeld, R. (1978). 'Sex structure of occupations and job mobility.'
Social Forces, 56, 3; 823–44.

5

Schooling and employment in the United Kingdom[1]

Phillip Brown

In advanced industrial societies the educational system has been respon-sible for the socialization and selection of future generations of worker/citizens. It is therefore not surprising to find, with the onset of world recession and the rapid increase in youth unemployment during the 1970s and early 1980s, that the organization and 'products' of schooling have been brought into question.

In most Western capitalist societies, nation states have responded to their changing economic fortunes by increasing the vocational relevance of schooling because the school has been blamed, at least in part, for the increase in youth unemployment. However, whereas the OECD (1985) report *Education in Modern Society* concluded that: 'the essentially moral – and certainly ambitious – objective that each child should be educated to the limits of his or her ability appears to have survived the economic thunder' (p. 11), this cannot be said for education in the UK. The reasons for this, however, are not primarily economic, but political. Whereas many countries have attempted to make the school curriculum more vocationally relevant, in England and Wales the relationship between education and industry has become inextricably part of a political debate about the future of comprehen-sive schooling. Those opposed to post-war reforms in education have not been slow to exploit the disquiet expressed by employers about the products of education, to support a powerful (and largely successful) lobby which has undermined the ideological foundation of post-war liberal democratic reforms. As a consequence major changes are taking place in the educational system, which amount to a 'third wave' in its socio-historical development.

The 'third wave' can be characterized in terms of the rise of the 'paren-tocracy', involving a move away from a form of educational organization based upon 'age, aptitude and ability' to one where the education a child receives must conform to the *wealth and wishes of parents* (Brown 1988, 1989). Therefore, although the main focus of this paper will be upon what has been described as the New Vocationalism (Ranson *et al.* 1986; Bates *et al.* 1984), it cannot be divorced from its political, social, and cultural context, because although similar vocational initiatives may be well established in Canada, their consequences for the individuals involved and, for the future of the educational system, may be very different.

This paper is divided into three sections. The first will provide a brief account of the educational system in England and Wales and will also describe some of the changes which may take place as a result of the Education Reform Bill (HMSO 1987).[2] The second will examine the changing political context of the debate about education and economic efficiency, and in the third we consider the classroom context of the new vocationalism. The latter will be based on the research findings of a recent study conducted by the author in urban South Wales.

The education system in England and Wales

The structure of education in England and Wales today is largely the product of the 1944 Education Act, despite a number of important amendments, including those which will result from the recent Education Reform Bill (see Simon 1988; Maclure 1988).

The 1944 Act established a continuity of educational provision from 'primary education' (5–11 years), to 'secondary education' (11–16) and to further education (16–18), although the latter is not compulsory. The Act also established a Ministry of Education (which has since become the Department of Education and Science (DES)). The Secretary of State for Education was made responsible for the education of people in England and Wales, and the Local Education Authorities (LEAs) which were a product of the 1902 Education Act were required to carry out their part 'under his control and direction'. In reality the Act gave the LEAs considerable powers to organize the local system of education, and headteachers considerable control over the curriculum. Indeed, until the publication of the Education Reform Bill in 1987, which will centralize educational decision-making and impose a core curriculum on all state-maintained schools, religious instruc-tion was the only subject the school had a statutory duty to teach.

Primary education (5–11 years of age) is non-selective and apart from a significant shift from a subject- to child-centred pedagogy in the 1960s, there have been few organizational changes. However, secondary education (11–16 years of age) has undergone some important structural change and is likely to do so again in the near future.

In the 1944 Education Act the LEAs were not legally bound to organize secondary education in a common format, although it was assumed that secondary education would take the form of a 'tripartite' system. Academically able pupils would enter the 'grammar' schools; other able children with a special aptitude for technical subjects would enter the 'technical grammar' schools, and the masses, whom it was believed would be best served by receiving a practical and concrete education, would attend the 'secondary modern' schools. Despite being called a 'tripartite' system, in practice, most of the LEAs opened few, if any, technical schools.

Selection to the different schools depended upon pupil performance in what is now the largely discredited 11+ examination, although a small number of LEAs still use it. The 11+ examination was heavily influenced by psychological evidence which was used to prove that a child's educational potential could be predicted by the age of 11 and categorized with the aid of the 11+ examination into one of three different 'types' of mind which corresponded to the three types of school. Therefore, because secondary education was available to all and educational ability could be assessed at an early age, it was assumed that equality of educational potential would be achieved, and because pupils had different aptitudes (i.e. practical vs. academic) it was also assumed that 'parity of esteem' would exist between the different types of school.

The conclusion reached during the 1950s was, however, that the tripartite system failed to provide equality of opportunity or parity of esteem (Banks 1955). The secondary-modern pupil was seen as a failure, and a growing body of social-science research revealed that the 11+ was a poor predictor of 'educability', and that the tripartite system was leading to the underachievement of many pupils from a working-class background. The failure of the tripartite system to generate equality of educational opportunity was particularly worrying in the early 1960s, because a shortage of skilled labour power was placing increasing demands on the educational system to tap the 'pool of ability' which was known to exist among the working classes (see page 92). A further indictment of the tripartite system came from middle-class parents who were acutely aware that failing the 11+ was a life sentence, particularly if one could not afford to send one's child to a private school.

These criticisms of the tripartite system culminated in a concerted attempt to move towards a system of comprehensive education. This shift was a gradual process and even in 1986 there remained 155 grammar schools concentrated in a few LEAs, alongside over 4,000 comprehensives. The *ad hoc* and piecemeal growth of the comprehensives was fuelled in 1965 when the DES issued circular 10/65 'The Organization of Secondary Education'. This circular asked LEAs to submit plans for comprehensive reorganization, although it contained few specific details about the way the local comprehensive systems should be organized. The lack of specific detail encouraged a number of different interpretations of the circular which was later reflected in the variety of comprehensive schools which emerged (see Benn and Simon 1972; Ball 1981). It is worth noting, however, that prior to

Table 5.1

	1975	1986
School/further education	37	45
Government scheme (YTS)	–	26
Unemployment	2	10
In employment	61	19

Source: Department of Education and Science, *Statistical Bulletin*, 2/1987.

the publication of Circular 10/65, 71 per cent of all LEAs either had or intended to establish some form of comprehensive education (Simon and Rubinstein 1969).

The expansion of comprehensive education did not lead to the abolition of private schools. In 1986 85 per cent of pupils in maintained schools were in comprehensive schools, but the proportion of pupils in independent (private) schools increased from 5.8 per cent in 1976 to 6.9 per cent in 1986 (*CSO* 1988). However, this figure hides the fact that in 1986 there were 18 per cent of 16-to-19-year-olds in private schools, and this proportion is likely to increase further as a result of recent attempts to expose schools to free-market competition.

At the end of compulsory schooling which currently stands at 16 years of age, there are four options available: to enter employment, to go on a government Youth Training Scheme (YTS) which lasts for two years, to remain in school for further academic study until the age of 18 in order to get the qualifications which are required to enter higher education (although many schools with provision for 16-to-18-year-olds are now offering more vocational courses and certificates), and, finally, to study for academic or vocational qualifications in a college of further education. The option of becoming unemployed is no longer available because school leavers who refuse one of these options cannot claim financial support from the state until the age of 18. The transition from school is discussed in other chapters (see chapters 3 and 8), but it is worth noting here that, prior to the massive increase in youth unemployment in the late 1970s, over 60 per cent of 16-year-olds left school and entered employment (see table 5.1). By 1986, however, only 19 per cent found work and 45 per cent remained in school or were studying in a college of further education. Unlike Canada (Gaskell *et al.* 1987) and many other Western capitalist societies therefore, the proportion of 17- and 18-year-olds in full-time education is still relatively low. In Canada, for example, 72 per cent of young people were in some form of full-time or part-time education in 1981, whilst the figure for the UK was 30 per cent (OECD 1985: 45). The situation in higher education is much the same. In 1985–6 28 per cent of 19-to-20-year-olds were continuing their education, divided evenly between non-advanced (mainly part-time and in colleges of further education) and higher education (mainly full-time in universities and polytechnics) (DES *Statistical Bulletin*, 1/88). Hence there were 14 per cent of 19-to-20-year-olds in higher education (2 per cent part-time) of which women accounted for 41 per cent, compared to only 35 per cent in 1970 (*CSO* 1988).

The Education Reform Bill

In the 1980s there has been a concerted attack on comprehensive education from the 'New Right', the media and a number of influential industrialists. The comprehensive school has been blamed for causing a decline in educational and moral standards and for failing to meet the needs of industry. The latter is discussed in the next section. In the limited space which remains here, I want briefly to note some of the main implications of the Education Reform Bill (HMSO 1987) which attempts both to centralize educational decision-making by dramatically reducing the powers of the LEAs, and to expose schools to the rigours of the free market in the belief that it will raise standards in all schools.

The most important features of the Bill in terms of the structure of the education system are 'open enrolment' and 'opting out'. The former is particularly damaging to the planning of local educational systems because the secondary-school population is declining and the number of pupils which any school can admit is to be set at the 1979 level. This was a year when the school population was much higher than it is now. The government has argued that open enrolment is necessary to give parents more 'choice' of school, but it seems inevitable that it will result in the closure of those schools which do not perform well in the free market. The 'opting out' proposal is that the governing body of schools can apply to 'opt out' of local-authority control and into central state control by becoming grant-maintained schools. Such schools would then receive direct funding from the Department of Education and Science instead of the LEA, generating what Mrs Thatcher has called 'state independent schools'! Only a simple majority of school governors is required in order to be able to apply to the Secretary of State to become a grant-maintained school. This decision must then be put to the parents of pupils attending the school at that time. Again, provided that a simple majority is achieved, and that the Secretary of State (who has the final say) is in agreement, the school will receive direct-grant status. This policy Mrs Thatcher believes will create a new system of education involving three types of school which would give a wider choice of public provision for those who are not satisfied with the current system.

Simon (1988) has noted that the main thrust of the Education Reform Bill is towards 'destabilizing locally controlled "systems" and, concomitantly, pushing the whole structure of schooling towards a degree, at least, of privatization, so establishing a base which could be further exploited later' (p. 48). What Simon is hinting at here is the possibility of moving towards the introduction of educational vouchers and an 'independent education for all' (Hillgate Group 1986).

There are two further aspects of the Education Reform Bill which require a brief mention (for a full discussion see Simon 1988). First, the government's intention to introduce the formal testing and assessment of pupils at the age of 7, 11, 14, and 16. This represents part of the attempt to provide parents with the necessary consumer information to decide to which school to send their child. Formal testing and the imposition of a 'core curriculum' is also seen as a way of increasing standards, because as Mrs Thatcher has asserted, even those schools which wish to stay under local-authority control 'are going to have a core curriculum and they are going to have it because some schools have failed with children' (*Independent* 14 September 1987). But, as Simon has correctly pointed out, while the right want a *variety* of schools they also demand a 'strict *uniformity* in the curriculum where, they now claim, there is too much "variety"' (emphasis in original, p. 17). Therefore, despite the rhetoric of 'choice' and 'individual freedom', in practice the educational system is becoming *more* centrally controlled. The Education Reform Bill is estimated to give the Secretary of State for Education over 175 new powers.

Second, the government is attempting to tighten the bond between the products of schooling and the needs of industry. Following the introduction of the Technical and Vocational Education Initiative (TVEI) in 1983, Kenneth Baker, the Secretary of State for Education, unveiled his reforming agenda for education with a pilot network of twenty centrally funded City Technology Colleges (CTCs) (*Guardian* 8 October 1987; DES 1986). The intention of the CTCs, like the TVEI (see p. 94), is to seek to develop the 'qualities of enterprise, self-reliance and responsibility, and secure the highest possible standards of achievement' (ibid). It is the political context of the 'new vocationalism' to which I now want to turn.

Education and economic efficiency: the political context

In the post-war period the vast majority of pupils from a working-class background left school at 15 or 16 years of age and entered employment. There was little demand for further education among these young workers, and training (when provided) was largely reserved for those (usually male) school-leavers who had found an apprenticeship.

Researchers who had examined this transition from 'school to work' presented evidence to show that, for the vast majority, the transition from school to work was fairly 'smooth' and 'unproblematic'. It was also found to be a welcomed release from school and the trapping of childhood, despite the fact that most of the jobs undertaken offered little opportunity for career advancement or intellectual challenge. Today most people would no doubt welcome a return to the time when all school-leavers got a job. But even during the 1950s and 1960s the buoyant demand for young workers led some commentators to question the reproduction of working-class children into working-class jobs because able pupils were leaving school and taking jobs which did little to fulfil the growing demand for more highly skilled and qualified workers which demands entry into further and higher education.

The implications of this argument for the educational system were immense. Economic growth and Britain's future prosperity were seen to depend upon an expansion of educational opportunities, particularly for the disadvantaged. This argument, I will suggest, provided the basis for a political consensus and well served (at least in the short term) the interests of those who were advocating greater equality of educational opportunity as a key goal of the Welfare State.

Rising unemployment during the 1970s, which culminated in the virtual collapse of the youth labour market in the early 1980s, however, has led to a fundamental challenge to post-war arguments about education and economic growth and the implications for the educational system have been equally profound. There have been cuts in educational expenditure, a shift from an academic to vocational education (at least for the working class) and an attempt to expose the educational system to free-market competition. There can be no doubt that economic conditions have had a profound impact on the way the educational system is perceived and evaluated. Nevertheless, in this section, I want to argue that despite the close relationship between economic conditions and educational change, the reforms which are currently taking place within the educational system cannot be simply 'read off' from changing economic circumstances. In Britain the attempts to blame the school for a failure to meet the needs of industry has become part of a broader New Right assault on the ideals of comprehensive education. Therefore, without some knowledge of the political context within which the debate about education and the economy has been conducted, it is impossible to make sense of the changes which are currently taking place. What the discussions in this section also highlight is the fact that despite the limited potential for the educational system to 'compensate for society', the shift to vocationalism does not signal the abandonment of educational solutions to social and economic problems, only a change in educational production methods and design.

Since the establishment of universal elementary education in 1870, the relationship between education and economic growth has provided a major lever for educational change (Williams 1961). In the period 1945–73 there was a major expansion of education, particularly for those between the ages of 11 and 16 years of age. This expansion was part of post-war reconstruction which was fuelled by sustained economic growth. Liberal democratic policies dominated both Labour and Conservative politics during this period. Both parties accepted (albeit for somewhat different reasons) that a major investment in education was the best way of sustaining industrial competitiveness and that opportunities for educational and economic advancement should be expanded to allow the most able and talented to rise above the rest, regardless of social background. The latter was premised on a belief that most jobs were placing a much greater demand on the skills of the workforce, and that the technological revolution was demanding that society be led by the most able and talented rather than those with the most 'cultural capital'. The pursuit of the dual objectives of increasing social justice and economic efficiency culminated in the transition from selective to comprehensive education and various compensatory education programmes, in the hope that talented children from socially disadvantaged backgrounds would be able to respond to new educational opportunities and fuel the British economy.

The contradictions which underlie the objectives of increasing social justice and the management of human resources in the interest of economic efficiency were temporarily submerged by the perceived need to invest in human capital. The increase in unemployment and Britain's accelerated economic decline, following the 1973 oil crisis and 'three-day week' which resulted from industrial action by the National Union of Mineworkers, led to an abrupt end of the post-war political settlement. The Black Papers (see Cox and Boyson 1977) on education which were produced by the radical right gained increasing support for their vitriolic attack on comprehensive reorganization. Critics of comprehensive education were quick to seize upon the criticisms from a growing number of industrialists who identified Britain's failing economic performance, and the right-wing press were more than willing to launch a sustained attack on comprehensive education for causing a decline in educational and moral standards.

In response to the criticisms levelled again comprehensive reorganization, a 'Great Debate' on education was launched by the Labour prime minister, James Callaghan, in 1976. This debate covered a range of issues, of which the relationship between school and work was central. He acknowledged the concerns of industrialists that the 'more participatory style' of modern schools could allow pupils to choose unbalanced or not particularly profitable courses to study or to opt 'in numbers insufficient for the country's needs for scientific and technological subjects' (Hopkins 1978: 102). Callaghan nevertheless drew back from asserting that the organization of education and the distribution of educational opportunities should be subordinated to the 'needs of industry'. Instead he reasserted the claim that the goals of education were 'to equip children to the best of their ability for a lively, constructive place in society and also to fit them for a job of work. Not one or the other, but both' (Callaghan, quoted in Hopkins 1978: 117).

The launch of the Great Debate and the regional conferences which followed did little to quell the growing concern and criticism being levelled against the comprehensive system (Brown 1989). Indeed it set the stage for a more penetrating attack on post-war educational reforms, and from this point on it has been the New Right who have defined the educational agenda, because, whilst Britain's economic prosperity was seen to depend on the schools' ability to tap the pool of able working-class children in the 1960s, by the late 1970s such efforts were identified as a source of social and economic liability. Moreover, the concern about the schools' failure to meet the needs of industry was fuelled by the virtual collapse of the youth labour market in the early 1980s, and the 'Waste of the nation's resources and the demoralization of youth, potentially leading to a variety of anti-social behaviour' (Atkinson and Rees 1982: 1). Fears about society's failure to fulfil the aspirations of school leavers were also expressed by a senior civil servant in the DES:

> We are in a period of considerable social change. There may be social unrest, but we can cope with the Toxteths. But, if we have a highly educated and idle population we may possibly anticipate more serious social conflict. *People must be educated once again to know their place.*
> (quoted in Ranson 1984, emphasis added)

The New Right's critique of education has not questioned the school's potential for shaping pupil aspirations, or for providing solutions to Britain's economic and social problems. What they have criticized is the fact that its organization and content have been subordinated to liberal democratic principles of equality of educational opportunity rather than the 'national interest' (sic). Therefore a faith in the school's ability to provide solutions to such problems has not been questioned. There is nothing wrong with investing in human capital (although it is believed that this should be organized through the operation of the free market rather than through a state monopoly of education) but that the education pupils receive must correspond to the requirements of their future occupational roles. The Right have argued that the comprehensive school has given the wrong medicine, in the wrong dosage, to the wrong children, and that this explained why a disproportionate number of school leavers are unemployed, and why so many of them were also so unprepared for the world of work. As a result of this diagnosis the Thatcher government (partly under the guise of falling rolls) has performed major surgery on the educational budget. There have also been efforts to remedy the apparent mismatch between the 'needs' of industry and the products of schools, by restructuring the secondary-school curriculum. Initiatives have included improving occupational information for school leavers, improving communication between teachers and employers, which in some instances has involved teachers' spending time in industry and, in a small number of cases, employers in schools. The major thrust, however, has been towards making the school curriculum more vocationally relevant with the launch of the Technical and Vocational Education Initiative (TVEI). This initiative was launched to the surprise of nearly all in the educational world by the Prime Minister, Margaret Thatcher, in November 1982. More recently Kenneth Baker, the Secretary of State for Education, has also announced the introduction of City Technology Colleges (CTCs) about which I will say more in a moment.

There were 14 LEAs involved in the TVEI in England and Wales in September 1983, and it is now operating in schools throughout the country. According to the Manpower Services Commission (MSC) the main purpose of TVEI is to make the school curriculum more relevant to the world of work, and it is intended to be available, on a voluntary basis, to all pupils between the ages of 14 and 18 years old, regardless of sex or educational attainment (MSC 1985). However, it is evident from speeches by leading Conservative reformers, such as Lord Young and Norman Tebbit, that they are particularly interested in developing new forms of technical and vocational education for non-academic pupils or, as Norman Tebbit has put it, 'for those who do not fancy the rich and academic diet, we are providing them with a rather more nourishing technical diet' (quoted in McCulloch 1986: 44.)

In 1987, 103 TVEI pilot projects were operating in over 700 schools and colleges, involving 80,000 young people (MSC 1987). In a recent government White Paper *Working Together – Education and Training* it was announced that from 1987 the TVEI would be extended into a national scheme which will influence the curriculum of all 14-to-18-year-olds, providing young people with access to a 'broad, balanced, practical and relevant curriculum' (MSC 1987: 19).

Much of what has been written about the 'new vocationalism' has focused on the changing orientation from an academic curriculum to one based on vocational relevance, at least for the working class. Equally significant, however, is the way in which vocational initiatives have been used to break the power of the LEAs to control educational change. The monies made available for the TVEI, for example, were administered by the MSC rather than the DES, and the former made it known that, if their vocational initiatives were blocked, they would seriously consider establishing their own vocational schools over which the LEA would have no authority. The lure of new financial resources at a time of government cut-backs in education was enough to overcome any reservations which the vast majority of LEAs expressed about the TVEI. Despite this, the threat of independent vocational schools has become a reality, but not under the auspices of the MSC. They are the CTCs which were announced by Kenneth Baker:

> Their purpose will be to provide a broadly-based secondary education with a strong technological element thereby offering a wider choice of secondary school to parents in certain cities and a surer preparation for adult and working life for their children.
>
> (DES 1986)

These schools will be independent from LEAs and, despite falling rolls, they will directly compete with existing schools catering for 11-to-18-year-olds. It was intended to fund the CTCs largely through contributions from local industry and businesses, but many companies have refused to get involved with the CTCs (Chitty 1987) because they would undermine the high quality of many local schools. Kenneth Baker envisaged 20 CTCs each taking between 750 to 1,000 pupils, but it is unclear how many will ultimately open, although the first was opened in Solihull in 1988. Solihull is a Conservative stronghold and the multi-national company, Hanson Trust, has invested £1 million to ensure that at least one CTC approximates to Baker's original formulation. (For a detailed discussion of the TVEI and CTCs see Chitty 1987; Gleeson 1987.) In summary, it can be suggested that the TVEI is already being used to make the school curriculum more vocationally relevant to the less academic working-class pupil (see page 104) and the CTCs will have the effect of 'creaming off' working-class children who show academic promise, and to serve the lower middle classes who cannot afford to pay for private schooling. Therefore, rather than expand good-quality education for all, we are getting more differentiation in and between schools which will extend existing educational inequalities. Moreover, the new vocationalism, has been used as a way of softening up the educational establishment for the more far-reaching policies contained in the Education Reform Bill (HMSO 1987). The comparative lesson to be drawn from this discussion is that, although vocational programmes have been developed in many countries in recent times, the specific initiatives deployed in Britain and their likely consequences demand that we attend to the political, cultural and historical context in which they are rooted. This is an issue to which I will return but, before doing so, I want to move from the political to the classroom context of the new vocationalism.

Class, classrooms and pupil preoccupations

In the UK the question of how pupils respond to school has been part of a broader question concerning social-class difference in educational behaviour and performance. The latter has consistently led to attempts to explain the underachievement of working-class pupils and why many pupils from a working-class background leave school at the age of 16. Until the publication of Paul Willis's *Learning to Labour* (1977), almost without exception pupil responses were defined in terms of a byproduct of the schools' organization and teacher-selection processes which were believed to disadvantage working-class pupils. Willis' study alternatively emphasized the *cultural* context of schooling. He recognized that pupils are not 'empty vessels to be filled' but deployed within the school the collective cultural resources from the neighbourhoods where they live. Willis therefore argued that pupil responses to school were primarily the product of collective cultural processes rather than the sorting and selection processes of the school. The relative merits and weaknesses of these explanations have been dealt with elsewhere (see Brown 1987). What is of relevance to the present discussion is that, by breaking free of choosing between what I have called the 'process of educational differentiation' (where pupil responses to school are explained in terms of the schools' sifting, sorting and selection processes) and the 'process of cultural differentiation' (which emphasizes not the schools' but the pupils' selection processes), it is possible to develop a conceptual framework which may help us to explain some of the similarities and differences which are to be found among pupil responses in

Britain and Canada. This can be achieved by highlighting the interrelation-ship between identities and institutions (Abrams 1982) about which I will say more in the conclusion.

Another recent development in the way we have attempted to explain pupil responses has arisen as a result of feminist writers who have correctly criticized (male) sociologists for failing to account for gender differences in pupil responses (Byrne 1978; Acker 1981). With these class and gender issues in mind, I conducted a study of pupil responses to school in an urban industrial region of Middleport, South Wales (see Brown 1987).

The Middleport study of schooling and unemployment was based on data collected from three coeducational comprehensive schools, two in working-class catchment areas, and the third in a middle-class area. 451 question-naires were completed by 16-year-old pupils from the three schools. The information gathered from these questionnaires was used to identify the range of pupil response to schooling and their occupational aspirations and expectations. I also observed classroom lessons and participated in informal lunch-time activities in the youth wing by working in the school 'tuck-shop'. A number of interviews were also conducted with different groups of pupils in all three schools.

The conclusion of this study was similar to the findings of Jane Gaskell's Canadian research (1985; 1987), namely, that pupil responses to school were closely related to future occupational aspirations, and therefore pupil responses to school were primarily *instrumental*. In other words, their reasons for making an effort in school depended upon the school's perceived value as a distributor of 'badges of ability' (credentials) which would open doors to desired occupations. Yet in the Middleport study, although the dominant response to school was of an instrumental nature, regardless of social class background or gender, it was equally clear that the dominant form of instrumentalism was different among working and middle-class pupils. Among the middle-class pupils we found a 'normative instrumental' orientation. This type of instrumentalism was 'normative' because the pursuit of qualifications was accompanied by a degree of intrinsic interest in some of the academic elements of the school curriculum. For them what was learnt at school, even if it did not directly relate to their occupational interests, was viewed as a necessary prelude to the acquisition of knowledge which was both 'required' and 'desired'. Such pupils were more attuned to the formal culture of the school since the types of employment they aspired to were perceived to be 'knowledge' based. It is this characteristic of their future employment which acted to bring these pupils closer to the normative aspects of the formal culture of the school.

> PAUL: You have to get maths and English well, I did my maths [O level] last year and English. Those are important subjects because it gives you a sort of . . . I mean they're . . . important because you've got to have them. Other than that, I suppose the sciences you know . . . I mean they're indirectly what I want to do. The others are just subjects

really, but I still enjoy what I do, well most of it anyway . . . a lot . . . well as far as I'm concerned they're just extra O-levels . . . they're not going to actually help you – it's just a pass to get in, so that's why you do it.

To stand any sort of chance of getting a job whether or not you're good at what you do, you need qualifications before you can get a chance to do what you want to do . . . there are few subjects that help you in the end for what you want to do, but on the whole, you do the subjects just to say you're up to a certain standard, that's all they prove really.

Among the working class pupils an 'alienated instrumental' orientation was the dominant response. Their instrumentalism can be regarded as 'alienated' because their involvement in the formal context of schooling was fairly limited. They did not identify with the school's perceived aim, with what teachers 'stand for' or the majority of what was taught in classroom lessons. The only elements of interest and perceived 'relevance' that did exist for them were on the practical rather than the academic side of the curriculum, elements which were assigned a lower priority and status by the vast majority of teachers.

> JANE: Well, I suppose maths [is important] in some ways, but all this Pythagoras and all that jazz, I don't think that's worth it, you know. I used to be allright in maths when I used to work. I used to do loads of things then, count loads of votes up, but all the rest then, I think it's dull. As long as you can count and take away and divide and times, you know. It's stupid doing all these . . . what do you call it? . . . all this complicated stuff.

> MARK: History, with history now, say somebody wants to be a motor mechanic say, I can't see where history comes into it, you know, I can't really see what history has got to do with school, you know . . . with learnin', 'cos history is . . . it . . . just deals with the past.

> MARTIN: We got maths lessons, they're puttin in like, all different things, like algebra, cross-sections and trigonometry and all that, but like me, I want to be a welder, won't need none of it. Might have something like adding up, to measure a piece of metal to which you're going to weld to it. But you don't need nothin' like statistics like, things like that . . . like science, you don't want to know all the different things.

These 'ordinary' working-class pupils 'made an effort' because they believed that modest levels of endeavour and attainment (usually leading to less academic qualifications) would help them 'get on' in working-class terms. The study was conducted in a neighbourhood which was like many other traditional working-class communities (Jackson 1968; Willmott 1966; Jenkins 1983). In such communities 'getting on' usually meant boys being able to find an apprenticeship and girls entering low-level clerical or personal-service occupations. Hence these pupils were less attuned to the formal culture of the school, since the types of employment they aspired to were perceived to be 'practically' based. It was this characteristic of their future employment which acted to alienate these pupils from much of which was taught in school and led them to question the overly academic curriculum which paid scant attention to the individual's ability to *do* the job. The alienated instrumentalism of the ordinary kids also helps us to understand why these pupils have had little reason to stay in full-time education beyond the compulsory school-leaving age. Their occupational aspirations have largely been met without academic success. For the male school-leavers in particular 'getting on' required entry to an apprenticeship which would incorporate day-release for further technical education and on-the-job craft training. To stay on for additional years of full-time education would considerably reduce their chances of entering an apprenticeship because salary was commonly based upon the trainee's age. For the female 'ordinary' kids there was less of an institutionalized route from school to work and once they had left full-time study their chances of receiving further education and training whilst in employment were relatively small (Cockburn 1987).

The impact of unemployment

The collapse of job opportunities for school leavers in the early 1980s has had a serious impact on pupil responses to school. This is particularly true of those pupils with an instrumental orientation. Nevertheless it would appear that unemployment is affecting working- and middle-class responses to school in different ways. Among middle-class pupils, whose instrumental orientation is likely to be 'normative', unemployment appears to have led them to attach an even greater instrumental importance to school work. Getting qualifications has become more rather than less important as more and more school leavers chase fewer jobs. Moreover, access to higher education is also perceived to have become more competitive, therefore getting the best possible examination results appears to be the best insurance policy for the future, no matter what:

> JANE: It's hard enough to get a job as it is, there's no point in not getting qualifications, because you think you're not goin' to get a job. You got to, um try hard . . . there's so much competition you've just got to do the best you can, you have got a chance then . . . to get a job or go to university.
> PETER: It depends what you want to do really. I think if you work now, if you want to go to the sixth form or if you want to leave school, but if you want to leave school, there's not much chance of getting a job. There's no work about anyway, and if you want to do somethin' later in life, you've got to stay here [in school].

The impact of unemployment on working-class pupils, who are more likely to adopt an alienated instrumental orientation, has proved to be far more worrying for the school. Whereas they were previously willing to 'make an effort' in order to 'get on' in working-class terms, they have increasingly questioned its value and purpose, as the jobs they want have vanished. Moreover, because the academic curriculum held little interest or relevance for the ordinary kids, teachers have found it difficult to encourage pupils to work in school for intrinsic reasons:

AMY: All the teachers are the same, they say 'oh you should get this, you could pass in this', but they're no good to you, when you're leaving'. I don't see the point in havin' 'em . . . people these days have got qualifications but they still haven't got jobs.

SUE: It all depends what job you want.

AMY: But, you know, they don't get you anywhere. It's good to have them though.

PB: Why do you think it's good to 'ave 'em then?

AMY: Well like, you know, if someone went for a job and they didn't have qualifications, it's obvious the other one . . . they'd go for the ones with qualifications. But half the time they just don't bother about them, they ask for them mind ya . . .

The teachers I spoke to in Middleport also acknowledged that most of what is taught in comprehensive schools has always been irrelevant to the future lives of working-class school-leavers. However, despite considerable bouts of boredom, low levels of academic endeavour and attainment exhibited by the ordinary kids, and a sense of futility among many of the school staff, teachers were able and willing to justify what they were doing on the grounds that modest levels of academic achievement appeared to provide access to the sorts of jobs their pupils wanted. This rationale for a far-from-satisfactory situation can no longer be sustained, and the realization of this fact is seriously affecting teachers' morale, and forcing teachers to find new ways of justifying their day-to-day practices both to themselves and to their pupils. The decline in the job opportunities for ordinary kids has therefore presented the teaching profession with a dual problem. First, how to ensure the compliance of the ordinary kids without which day-to-day institutional practices would be impossible. Second, even if order can be maintained, teachers confront a crisis in *morale*, given that maintaining social order becomes an end in itself rather than a means of imparting school knowledge.

Evidence from Middleport suggests that teachers, given a lack of alternative resources, will continue to bolster the unstable foundations on which the compliance of the ordinary kids is grounded. However, teachers are well aware that the effort–qualifications–jobs motivational sequence is losing its hold:

JANET: When I first started here . . . um . . . I used to be able to say if you get this qualification in typin' or office practice or whatever, it's going to stand you in good stead for a job. I mean I can't say that now, they'd just laugh if I said that. They know different . . . em . . . I think employment was a big motivator.

This problem, coupled with the prevailing climate of government cutbacks and falling school rolls, along with the financial incentives offered to local education authorities and schools, has made TVEI an all-too-inviting innovation (Watts 1983; Bates 1984). The TVEI offers teachers the opportunity of bolstering their own sense of purpose and pupil compliance by placing less emphasis on the value of qualifications which can be traded in the market for jobs, and more upon the *direct* relevance of school learning to employment. This emphasis upon the extrinsic value of school *learning*, rather than school certificates, is seen as providing the opportunity for making the move to increase the *practical* content of the curriculum more *intrinsically* meaningful and interesting.

But if more involvement in practical endeavour is the carrot dangled in front of the ordinary kids, there is also a stick. The most worrying aspect of recent attempts to reform the educational system involves a shift from relatively impersonal and objective (although academic) systems of educational assessment to one where the school increasingly emphasizes the personality package (Fromm 1962) where pupils' subjective attributes are assessed on a highly subjective basis. It is the whole person which is now on show and at stake in the market for jobs. It is the personality package which must be sold in the market-place. This trend, epitomized by the growing popularity of 'pupil profiles', emphasizes – as the kids do themselves – that it is not only 'what you know' which gets one a job. The school's attempt to maintain the compliance of large numbers of working-class pupils has therefore involved an attempt to *formalize* the informal elements of recruitment practices into the school's brief.

However, such changes continue to tie the teacher's authority closely to the exchange value of school learning for jobs, and to set limits upon that authority consistent with the ordinary kids' previous orientation to the school. It also serves to highlight serious contradictions in the school's attempt to win the compliance of large numbers of working-class pupils. The success of some of the ordinary kids' social inferiors in the school (i.e. the dropouts) in getting jobs on the basis of 'who you know' provides them with evidence that, if it is a question of getting 'any' job, then it is not who you are or what you know, but whom you know, which is of crucial importance. So long as the school does not have control of the social networks of working-class people, it will fail to formalize the extensive use of informal recruitment practice on the basis of 'whom you know'. What this conclusion also highlights is the contradiction between the criteria which the school assumes will be used when young people are selected for employment, and the characteristics actually required by employers. They are frequently not those positively valued within the school (Lavercombe and Fleming 1981; Ashton and Maguire 1986).

Moreover, the more teachers are forced to emphasize the personality package of pupils as a factor in job acquisition, the more pupils are likely to believe that the only reason for compliance is because the teacher has the power to define the pupils. Compliance is a matter of doing what you are told under threat of not getting the good school reference necessary to help find employment. A further threat to the ordinary kids' compliance results from the ambivalence evident among these pupils about whether occupational opportunities should be based upon the possession of appropriate formal qualifications, or on proven ability to *do* the job.

Moves to make the school curriculum more vocationally relevant, by teaching pupils more of what they need to know to do the job, may both heighten their desire to enter 'appropriate' employment and cause them to view the discrepancy between an ability to do the job, and the need for increasing numbers of academic qualifications to get the job, as manifestly unjust. For example, some of the 'swots' (academic pupils) have been forced to 'trade down' and apply for jobs once the preserve of the ordinary kids. This is not only sensed by the ordinary kids as an illegitimate use of qualifications achieved by extraordinary activity at school, but one which leads them to think that 'making an effort' to achieve some qualifications is futile, because they know that there will always be someone better qualified who is likely to get the job, irrespective of ability to do the job.

However, I am not suggesting that the vast majority of teachers have got involved in the TVEI because they see their role as agents of social control. There is a genuine concern that the educational system has been failing many of its pupils in more ways than one for far too long, and that TVEI does hold the potential for progressive educational reform such as a new pedagogy of experiential learning and problem-solving against traditional or academic learning (Ranson, *et al.* 1986; Blackman 1987). There is also a genuine belief that greater involvement in technical and vocational education may be in the best interests of *their* pupils, in the hope that it is they who will get a job. Yet a consequence of teachers' having to work within the constraints of the 'chalk face' and attempting to resolve their personal and professional troubles, is that the question of school-leaver 'employability' is not defined as it should be, as relative to the *demand* for labour, but as a personal trouble which can only be overcome at the expense of other teachers' equally deserving (or undeserving) pupils. In the short term the TVEI may help to maintain some degree of interest in 'practical' school subjects. However, the contradictions between what the ordinary kids want from school and present labour-market realities in many parts of the UK cannot be resolved on a diet of technical studies, despite its being more palatable.

Conclusion

In this conclusion I want to briefly make three comparative points:

Education as a secular religion

Despite the economic problems and high rates of unemployment which both societies have experienced and the fact that the educational system has been, at least in part, blamed for youth unemployment, the potential for education to make a major contribution to economic development has *not* been questioned. The school has continued to be perceived as a powerful means of shaping the individual in the interests of national policy (Spring 1980). What have been questioned, however, are the contents and products of schooling. The school curriculum has been defined as unnecessarily abstract and academic for a large proportion of pupils who are seen to be leaving school ill prepared for their future economic roles.

In both the UK and Canada this has led to a more utilitarian view of education, manifest in the increasing emphasis on vocationalism. The problems which have emerged between education and industry have therefore been defined in both countries as a *technical* problem, and the vocational solutions adopted to overcome them represents a fine tuning of 'human capital' theory, rather than its rejection.

'Reality' and research has *not* dented the faith which nation states are willing to invest in the efficacy of the educational system to overcome indigenous economic and social problems. This faith in the educational system is not peculiar to the UK and Canada, and in part it reflects the limited control which nation states have over international competition and the pace of technological innovation. The educational system is relatively easy to manipulate, but it is far more difficult to 'create' jobs, or control international competition. Moreover, in the UK any interference with the operation of the labour market is politically unacceptable to its right-wing government unless designed to remove any remaining impediments to the free play of market forces.

Britain's radical departure

In the UK and Canada, vocational education and training have become the latest vogue in educational reform, in response to similar economic conditions. However, such similarities hide an emerging divergence in educational policies which can be understood only in terms of the political, social and historical context of the educational systems in the two countries. For although the new vocationalism has been introduced into a comprehensive system in both countries, in Canada vocational tracks have existed for much longer, and in Britain the new vocationalism has (as noted on p. 92) been incorporated into a larger debate about the relative merits of selective versus comprehensive education and a state monopoly of education versus a privatized education system. Britain's radical departure raises some interesting questions about how the educational system can best meet the changing demands of the economy in the 1990s. Here it will be argued that Canada will be in a much stronger position that the UK to meet these changing demands.

In Britain the Thatcher government is engaged in a major educational experiment which does not end with the Education Reform Bill. Further changes such as more privatization in education through the introduction of educational vouchers may yet become a reality (Brown 1989). In earlier sections it has been noted that these changes represent a move away from an education based on 'age, aptitude and ability' as enshrined in the 1944 Education Act, to one in which the education a child receives must conform to the *wealth* and *wishes* of parents: that is, from the ideology of meritocracy (Young 1961) to what I have called the ideology of parentocracy.

Although it is too early to assess the consequences of the 'parentocracy', in the milder form it will take following the Education Reform Bill, a likely consequence will be an increasing class polarization in educational opportunities and performance. The middle classes who have traditionally placed considerable importance on academic achievement, and who have the means to purchase educational advantages for their children, will capitalize on the educational system, whilst the working classes who have traditionally questioned the value of academic study and have little disposable income to pay for a 'good' education will be forced to seek their schooling in those schools which do not fare well in the free market.

An important comparative question is therefore whether the 'rise of the parentocracy' will remain peculiarly British or whether other nation states, such as Canada, will follow Britain's lead? The different political cultures in the two countries (Ashton 1988) make it difficult to believe that Canada will abandon a system of comprehensive education, although in the USA the educational parentocracy may also become a reality (see Shor 1986; Botstein 1988). Moreover, the hidden injuries of the parentocracy are not far from the surface and are likely to come into focus within the next few years. The fact that the job prospects confronting school-leavers in the early 1990s will be very different from those a decade earlier is one important reason for this. Demographic changes will result in a significant decline in the number of school-leavers (by one-third over the next decade), and this is already being accompanied by a change in the demand for youth labour as a result of economic restructuring. The importance of the latter has been noted by Ashton, Maguire and Spilsbury (1988): 'The overall effect on labour forces has been an increase in the demand for more highly qualified recruits and a reduction in the demand for unqualified 16 year olds.' In Canada similar trends are occurring (Ashton 1988) but, given that the Canadians are maintaining a more open and meritocratic system, offering far greater opportunities for higher and adult education, they are in a much better position to respond to the changing economic demands for a more highly educated and flexible workforce. The moves taken by some market-economy countries to provide a good general education to all has been recently recognized by the International Labour Organization (ILO 1986):

Schools are beginning to defer the time at which a choice must be made between predominantly academic and predominantly vocational pursuits, thus maintaining flexibility and promoting the general education that is necessary for all forms of work (p. 17).

In contrast, the recent reforms of education in the UK are leading to the reverse trend towards early selection and specialization. This will result from the introduction of formal national tests for all students at the ages of 7, 11, 14 and 16. There has also been considerable reluctance to move away from the narrow specialization into academic or vocational tracks at the age of 14, which a number of recent studies have recommended. Therefore, whereas the Canadian educational system will continue to justify the importance of *contest mobility*, the UK will revert to a system of *sponsored mobility* (Hopper 1971) which will make it extremely difficult to educate the labour force of the 1990s, despite the existence of CTCs which will be used to 'cream off' some working-class pupils who show early signs of 'educability' (sic).

The stark reality of the class interests and politics of greed which has infested British society will arguably result in problems for the educational system in the UK similar to those which the ILO (1986) have identified among *developing* rather than developed nations such as Canada:

> formal education and training systems are not geared to producing graduates with the requisite skills and knowledge for the world of work; far too many youths, particularly women and the poor, have inadequate access to education and training; a mismatch frequently exists between the skills taught and the skills needed for work; and training systems have not succeeded in adopting their teaching methodology or curricula to the requirements of the labour market (p. 16).

The issue of youth training in the UK and Canada is dealt with in other chapters in this volume. The argument here is that the recent educational reforms in the UK will not alleviate a mismatch between education and industry, but in the changing conditions of the 1990s they seem certain to cause one.

The instrumental pupil

There is empirical evidence that *instrumental* attitudes to education are dominant among older pupils in both the UK and Canada (see page 96). However, it is equally evident that the nature of that instrumentalism may vary particularly among the working classes in the two countries. In Canada the type of instrumentalism found by Gaskell is more typically found among the middle classes in Britain. The instrumentalism found among the British working class does not involve a drive for academic achievement and has not typically led to an expectation of continuing full-time education beyond the age of 16. This finding raises two comparatively interesting questions, first, how to explain these different types of instrumentalism, and secondly, how to explain the tendency for Canadian working-class youth to remain in education beyond the age of 16, and for those in the UK to leave at the earliest opportunity?

In seeking an answer to both questions the most fruitful line of enquiry seems to me, at least, to be found through studies of historical sociology. Philip Abrams (1982: 26) has noted that historical sociology is not:

> a matter of imposing grand schemes of evolutionary development on the relationship of the past to the present. Nor is it merely a matter of recognizing the historical background to the present. It is the attempt to understand the relationship of personal activity and experience on the one hand and social organization on the other as something that is continuously constructed in time.

It is by contextualizing individuals and social groups with purposes, expectations and motives, in their historical, institutional and political context that we can provide a sociological account of the similarities and differences which exist between pupil responses to school in the UK and Canada. It is the interplay between the pupils' collective understandings of being in school, which depend upon class, gender and racial differences, and the institutional structures of opportunities in both school and the youth labour market which hold the key to explaining differences in pupil responses in the two societies.

The attitudes, values and conduct of working-class pupils in both societies are not wholly invented *de novo* by them, they draw upon a fund of experience built into their lives outside the school and built up historically within working-class communities in general' (Giddens 1986: 299).

Hence, the different education and labour-market experiences of working-class people in the UK and Canada is an important contributory factor, giving rise to different class cultural understandings of schooling. The lack of a well-developed sense of class consciousness among the Canadian working class certainly helps to explain the lack of a class cultural resistance to school (Tanner 1978) which have been identified in a number of British studies.

A recognition of the school's role in framing the life chances of pupils is equally important, however, because it avoids the tendency for 'cultural' accounts to drift into forms of voluntaristic explanation which underplay the significance of the school (and local labour market) to determine life chances. David Ashton's study of the youth labour market in England and Canada found that the opportunity structure facing each new generation of school and college leavers is strikingly different in the two societies (Ashton 1988: 3).

In Canada, for example, there are few job opportunities for 16-year-olds, but far more opportunities for entering higher education. In contrast, in the UK the system of apprentice training has offered employment opportunities (particularly for males) at the age of 16 and has discouraged remaining in full-time study because apprentice wages are usually age related. There are also far fewer opportunities for young adults in the UK to enter what remains an élitist system of higher education.

Finally, I would like to suggest that a comparative study of pupil responses to school can provide a valuable contribution to our understanding of intra-national and international variations in educational behaviour. But if this is to be achieved, we will need to reject explanations which rely on the 'process of educational differentiation' (where pupil responses to school are explained in terms of the opportunity structure confronting pupils) and the 'process of cultural differentiation' (which emphasizes not the structure of constraints but the collective aspirations and expectations of pupils), because they are equally one-sided.

The way forward is not to jettison what has gone before in favour of yet another 'new' sociology of education, but to suggest that the attempt to explain comparative educational responses needs to begin by examining the inter-relationship between educational and cultural processes in each society.

Notes

1 I would like to thank John Bynner for his comments on an earlier draft of this paper.
2 Education in Scotland is organized somewhat differently and due to limitations on space it will not be described in this paper (see Raffe 1984; 1988; Gray, *et al.* 1983)

References

Abrams, P. (1982). *Historical sociology*. London, Open Books.

Acker, S. (1981). 'No-women's-land: British Sociology of Education 1960–1979', *Sociological Review*, 29, 1: 77–104.

Ashton, D. N. (1988). 'Sources of variation in labour market segmentation: a comparison of youth labour markets in Canada and Britain, *Work, Employment and Society*, 2, 1: 1–24.

Ashton, D. and Maguire, M. J. (1986). 'The structure of the youth labour market: some implications for educational policy', paper prepared for Economics and Education Management, A National Seminar.

Ashton, D., Maguire, M. J. and Spilsbury, M. (1988). 'Restructuring the labour market: the implications for education and training', Working Paper, International Centre for Management and Labour Market Studies, University of Leicester.

Atkinson, P. and Rees T. L. (1982). 'Youth unemployment and state intervention', in Rees, T. L. and Atkinson, P. (eds.) *Youth Unemployment and State Intervention*. London, Routledge & Kegan Paul.

Ball, S. (1981). *Beachside Comprehensive*. Cambridge, Cambridge University Press.

Banks, O. (1955). *Parity and Prestige in English Secondary Education*. London, Routledge & Kegan Paul.

Bates, I. (1984). 'From vocational guidance to life skills: historical perspectives on careers education' in Bates, I. *et al. Schooling for the Dole?* London, Macmillan.

Bates, I. *et al.* (1984) *Schooling for the Dole?* London, Macmillan.

Benn, C. and Simon, B. (1972). *Half Way There* (2nd edn), Harmondsworth, Penguin.

Blackman, S. J. (1987). 'The labour market in school: new vocationalism and socially ascribed discrimination', in Brown, P. and Ashton, D. N. (eds.) *Education, Unemployment and Labour Markets*. Basingstoke, Falmer Press.

Botstein, L. (1988). 'Education reform in the Reagan Era: false paths, broken promises', *Social Policy*, 18, 4: 3–11.

Brown, P. (1987). *Schooling Ordinary Kids*. London, Tavistock.

(1988) 'Education and the working class: a cause for concern', in Lander, N. and Brown, P. (eds.) *Education: In Search of a Future*. Basingstoke, Falmer Press.

(1989). 'Education', in Brown, P. and Sparks, R. (eds) *Beyond Thatcherism: Social Policy, Politics and Society*. Milton Keynes, Open University Press.

Byrne, E. M. (1978). *Women and Education*. London, Tavistock.

Central Statistical Office (1988). *Social Trends*. London, HMSO.

Chitty, C. (1981). 'City technology colleges' in Chitty, C. (ed.) *Aspects of Vocationalism*, Post-16 Education Centre, Institute of Education, University of London.

Chitty, C. (ed.) (1987). *Aspects of Vocationalism*, Post 16 Education Centre, Institute of Education, University of London.

Cockburn, C. (1987). *Two-Track Training: Sex Inequalities and the YTS*. London, Macmillan.

Cox, C. B. and Boyson, R. (eds.) *Black paper 1977*. London, Temple Smith.

DES (1986). *City Technology Colleges: A New Choice of School*. London, Department of Education and Science.

(1988) *Statistical Bulletin*, 1/88. London, Department of Education and Science.

Fromm, E. (1962). 'Personality and the market place', in Nosow, S. and Form, W. H. (eds), *Man, Work and Society*. New York, Basic Books.

Gaskell, J. (1985). 'Explorations in vocationalism: through the eyes of high school students', in Mason, E. (ed.) *Transitions to Work*. Winnipeg, Institute for Social and Economic Research.

Gaskell, J. (1987). 'Education and the labour market: the logic of vocationalism' in Wotherspoon (ed.) *A Sociology of Education: Readings in the Political Economy of Canadian Schooling*. Toronto, Methuen.

Gaskell, J., Jother, K., and Rubenson, K. (1987). *Education and the Economy: The Canadian Case*. Centre for Policy Studies in Education, University of British Columbia.

Giddens, A. (1986). *The Constitution of Society*. Cambridge, Polity Press.

Gleeson, D. (ed.) (1987). *T.V.E.I. and Secondary Education: A Critical Appraisal*. Milton Keynes, Open University Press.

Gray, J., McPherson, A. F. and Raffe, D. (1983). *Reconstructions of Secondary Education: Theory, Myth and Practice since the War*. London, Routledge & Kegan Paul.

HMSO (1987). Education Reform Bill. London, HMSO.

Hillgate Group (1986). *Whose Schools? A Radical Manifesto*. London, Claridge Press.

Hopkins, A. (1978). *The School Debate*. Harmondsworth, Penguin.

Hopper, E. (1971). 'Notes on stratification, education and mobility in industrial societies', in Hopper, E. (ed.) *Readings in the Theory of Educational Systems*. London, Hutchinson.

ILO (1986). *Youth*, Geneva, International Labour Organization.

Jackson, B. (1968). *Working Class Community*, London, Routledge & Kegan Paul.

Jenkins, R. (1983). *Lads, Citizens and Ordinary Kids*. London, Routledge & Kegan Paul.

Lavercombe, S. and Fleming, D. (1981). 'Attitudes and duration of unemployment among sixteen year old school leavers', *British Journal of Guidance and Counselling*, 9, 1: 36–45.

Maclure, S. (1988). *Education Re-formed: A Guide to the Education Reform Act 1988.* Sevenoaks, Hodder & Stoughton.

McCulloch, A. (1986). 'Policy, politics and education: the TVEI', *Journal of Education Policy*, 1, 1: 35–52.

MSC (1985). *TVEI Review 1985.* Sheffield, Manpower Services Commission.

OECD (1985). *Education in Modern Society.* Paris, Organization for Economic Co-operation and Development.

Raffe, D. (ed.) (1984) *Fourteen to Eighteen: The Changing Pattern of Schooling in Scotland.* Aberdeen: Aberdeen University Press.

Raffe, D. (ed.) (1988). *Education, Youth and the Labour Market.* Basingstoke, Falmer Press.

Ranson, S. (1984). 'Towards a tertiary tripartism: new codes of social control and the 17+', in Broadfoot, P. (ed.) *Selection, Certification and Control.* Basingstoke, Falmer Press.

Ranson, S., Taylor, B. and Brighouse, T. (eds) (1986). *The Revolution in Education and Training.* Harlow, Longman.

Shor, I. (1986). *Culture Wars: School and Society in the Conservative Restoration 1969–1984.* London, Routledge & Kegan Paul.

Simon, B. (1988). *Bending The Rules: The Baker 'Reform' of Education.* London, Lawrence and Wishart.

Simon, B. and Rubinstein,· D. (1969). *The Evolution of The Comprehensive School.* London, Routledge & Kegan Paul.

Spring, J. (1980). *Educating the Worker-Citizen.* New York, Longman.

Tanner, J. (1978). 'Youth culture and the Canadian high school: an empirical analysis', *Canadian Journal of Sociology*, 3, 1: 89–102.

Watts, A. G. (1983). *Education, Unemployment and the Future of Work.* Milton Keynes, Open University Press.

Williams, R. (1961). *The Long Revolution.* Harmondsworth, Penguin.

Willis, P. (1977). *Learning to Labour.* Farnborough, Saxon House.

Willmott, P. (1966). *Adolescent Boys of East London.* London, Routledge & Kegan Paul.

Young, M. (1961). *The Rise of the Meritocracy.* Harmondsworth, Penguin.

6

Reluctant rebels: a case study of Edmonton high-school dropouts[1]

Julian Tanner

Introduction

High-school dropouts are a subject of recurring concern in North American society. The manifest source of this anxiety resides in the perceived social, economic and personal costs incurred when large numbers of young people fail to complete their secondary education. There is, however, a further factor that, in a very important sense, helps to shape and define the dropout problem.

Public education in North America may be characterized in terms of the emphasis that it places upon mass participation. Under the auspices of a folk norm of contest mobility, the North American young are encouraged to stay in school and contend for élite status (Turner 1960). However, the fact that large numbers of adolescents seemingly voluntarily withdraw themselves from the competitive arena of high school suggests that student compliance with this folk norm cannot be relied upon.

As a result, dropouts are viewed as rejectors of the goals and values of education. They are also a visible reminder of the failings of an allegedly meritocratic educational system. High rates of attrition from the school system, particularly when associated with distinctive class or racial groupings, make it hard to maintain the fiction that variations in educational performance are a function of individual motivations and efforts only. Substantial dropout rates, therefore, highlight the persisting connections between social origins, educational achievement and class destinations and reinforce the suspicion that those same social origins are in some way responsible for the subsequent rejection of schooling.

For the better part of four decades social scientists, largely employing quantitative methods, have tried to unravel the causal relationship between social origins and educational achievement that the dropout problem might be seen as epitomizing. Typically they have found it easier to describe the enduring patterns of educational inequality than to explain them. Hence the influence of class background in the school system, for example, has been documented but not, by and large, accounted for.

One reaction to this impasse has been a resurgence of interest in qualitative research methods. The ethnographic case study has been advocated in some quarters as the most appropriate method for explaining the process whereby the inequalities of class get reproduced from generation to generation, and the role that the educational system might play in this.

One centre of the ethnographic revival has been the United Kingdom, where the research strategy has been directed towards the perennial problem of working-class underachievement. Observational studies carried out by David Hargreaves (1967) and Colin Lacey (1970) in the 1960s explored the linkages between school failure and anti-school peer cultures in expediting the mass exodus of (male) working-class pupils from secondary-modern and grammar schools respectively. Their formulation – derived from American sub-cultural theory – conceptualized anti-school peer cultures as a response to school failure.

More recent British ethnographic explorations have, however, reversed this causal ordering. Paul Corrigan (1979) in *Schooling the Smash Street Kids* and Paul Willis in *Learning to Labour* (1977) assign the male working-class school counter-culture a crucial role in determining working-class educational underachievement. Willis' research, in particular, has become very influential, and it is upon his highly original thesis that I wish to concentrate.[2]

Willis's focus is upon the process of school rejection and how this results in working-class males getting working-class jobs. His analysis is a deliberate antidote to those structural accounts of schooling that depict educational failure as something that is imposed upon working-class adolescents. Such accounts, says Willis, are unduly mechanistic and deterministic and ignore the issue of how working-class adolescents experience school and how their orientations to it affect their educational performance. More especially, structuralists understate the active contribution that the working-class young make to their own working-class futures. Why is it, Willis asks, that working-class males seemingly choose unskilled jobs despite their participation in an educational system that provides opportunities for them to escape that fate?

The answer that he offers directs attention towards the school counter-culture that the 'lads' are involved in. Based on values and prior expectations derived from the broader working-class culture (and not, therefore, a reaction to subsequent failure within school), the anti-school peer group encourages the lads to deride book learning, contemptuously dismiss white-collar jobs and celebrate the masculinist culture of manual labour. Their participation in the school counter-culture prepares the lads for the kinds of menial work that they end up getting upon leaving school. But – and this is the crucial issue – this preparation is experienced, not as oppression, but as freedom, autonomy and independence. Willis's point is that working-class boys end up in working-class jobs not primarily because of the efforts of the educational system to foist inferior economic status upon them but because of their own resistance to schooling.

The rationale for discussing Willis's account of working-class school rejection in England is that it provides the starting point for our own examination of high school dropouts in Edmonton, Alberta, Canada. Although it was not designed as a test nor a replication of the British study, it has, none the less, been informed by it. Most previous work on dropouts in the United States and Canada has been of a quantitative nature and has tended to concern itself with a limited range of issues – principally the demographic and social characteristics of those adolescents most prone to dropping out (Friesen 1967; Ekstrom *et al.* 1986; Rumberger 1987).

By contrast, the present study appropriates Willis's concern with process and examines why and how some adolescents choose to quit high school before completion of their grade 12 education. Willis's formulation of the issue is particularly apt for our purposes because dropouts are, on the face of it, students who have rejected school as much as they have been rejected by it and, as the virtual lumpenproletariat of the North American educational system, potentially engaged in the kind of cultural repudiation of schooling detailed by Willis. Our inquiry into high-school dropouts concentrates upon the school and work experiences of mainly, though not exclusively, white adolescents. We mention this because the well-above average dropout rates experienced by young native people in Canada are not addressed in this paper. Questions surrounding the distinctive problems that racial minorities encounter in Canada's educational system are beyond the scope of the present inquiry.

The research was undertaken in Edmonton, Alberta, a Western Canadian provincial capital with a population of approximately 600,000. Throughout the 1970s, the local economy had flourished, thanks to a booming oil and gas industry. However, recession and plummeting oil prices in the 1980s transformed this boom to bust. By May of 1985, when we had completed our interviewing, the unemployment rate in Alberta for young people aged between 15 and 19 was 20.1 per cent. Previous research tells us that the rates of joblessness are likely to be even higher for high-school dropouts. It is against this boom-to-bust backcloth that our investigation of dropouts took place.

Methods

The sample was composed of 162 young people living in Edmonton who had left school without completing grade 12. Our goal was to interview a

Table 6.1 Sample composition

	%	
Personal contact	27.0	(43)
High-school counsellor	17.0	(27)
Job clubs	14.0	(23)
Social-service agency	11.0	(17)
Hostels/shelters	9.0	(15)
Alberta Vocational College	7.0	(12)
Belmont Correctional Centre	6.0	(10)
Alberta College	6.0	(9)
Probation officer	3.0	(5)
Northern Alberta Institute of Technology	0.6	(1)
	100.0	(162)

wide range of early school-leavers in order to capture the diversity of their experiences. An attempt was made to include in the sample both employed and unemployed dropouts, males and females, and individuals who had contact with social-service agencies as well as those who did not. The respondents were reached by referrals from employers, other individuals already in the sample, social-service agencies (including a correction centre), school counsellors, employment centres, and government-sponsored 'job clubs' (job search and on-the-job learning programmes).

The composition of the sample, and its sources, is detailed in table 6.1.

Table 6.2 presents some of the more important background characteristics of the sample, slightly more than half of whom were males. The youngest sample member was 15 and the oldest was 26, with 85 per cent of the group aged 17–23. On average, both males and females were 20 years of age at the time of the interview, and had been out of school for almost three years. Over 90 per cent of the sample had completed Grade 9, but female sample members were somewhat more likely than their male counterparts to have completed Grade 11.

A greater proportion of the male sample members (65 per cent compared to 48 per cent) were unemployed when interviewed. The occupational distributions of parents of the sample members show a moderate proportion of respondents coming from families of higher occupational status. Despite this, it is clear that unemployment is part of the typical family experiences of many of these respondents. Only 25 per cent were from families that had never experienced unemployment in the past.

Although we have no definitive way of knowing how representative our sample is of the total dropout population in Edmonton – the appropriate information is not collected by the Edmonton Public School Board – the overall profile of our sample is not very different from that detailed in another recent Canadian study of dropouts in Ontario (Radwanski 1987). The one divergence is that we do record a slightly higher proportion of

Table 6.2   Characteristics of high school dropouts (n = 162)

Mean age:			
Male	20 years		
Female	20 years		
Sex:		%	
Male		51 (n = 82)	
Female		49 (n = 80)	
		100	
Employment Status:		*Male*	*Female*
		%	%
Employed		34 (29)	52 (42)
Unemployed		65 (53)	48 (38)
		100 (82)	100 (80)
Highest grade completed in high school:		*Male*	*Female*
		%	%
Grade 7		1	0
Grade 8		6	9
Grade 9		30	16
Grade 10		35	32
Grade 11		28	44
		100	100
Mean length of time out of school:			
Male	2.7 years		
Female	2.6 years		
Parents' Occupations:		*Father*	*Mother*
		%	%
Managerial/professional		28	28
Clerical/sales/service		15	40
Manual		48	5
Self-employed		8	21
Housewife		0	5
		100	100
		(n = 110)	(n = 131)
Percentage from families where members have experienced unemployment:		75%	(n = 142)

Note: Percentages reported in tables in this report may not add to 100 per cent due to rounding.

respondents from managerial and professional backgrounds than the Ontario study (28 compared with 22 per cent).

The interviews were semi-structured and, with the respondents' permission, tape-recorded; they ranged in length from 30 minutes to over an hour. Trained interviewers used an interview schedule developed around nine salient topics, including evaluations of schooling, labour-market experiences and major life goals, with lead questions and probes designed to allow respondents to document their situations fully. The bulk of the interviews were conducted in such public places as libraries, coffee shops and shopping malls. The taped interviews were subsequently transcribed and their content analysed and coded by the principal researchers and interviewers.

The fact that the interviews were tape-recorded encouraged open-ended discussion between interviewer and interviewee. Although all of the major topic areas were covered in each interview, the comprehensives of the coverage varied according to the amount of importance that the respondent seemed to attach to it. One consequence of this is that in a number of instances a specific question was not asked; or, if it was, the respondent chose not to answer it. Hence, there are variations in the number of responses to each question.

Findings: school and work experiences

We began our investigation by asking respondents why they had left school. Their responses to this open-ended question quickly confirmed the findings of previous research (e.g. Ekstrom *et al.* 1986; Friesen 1967) – namely, that by their own admission, young people have varied motives for dropping out. Content analysis of the interview transcripts allowed for the coding of up to three reasons per respondent.

Some respondents offered no clear rationale for their decision to quit school, or emphasized essentially situational factors. As one middle-class male put it:

> Well, actually I just left on a whim I guess, I just, never even thought of it before, about quitting school, I just went to school one day and I had lunch and then I came back to school and uh, I went to my locker and I thought about, ah, maybe not going back to class that day and then I just took off and never went back. I never opened my locker, left all the books there . . .

Others gave many reasons for their decision, stressing the interactive effects of different factors.

Nevertheless, the overall picture is clear enough: school-based reasons are the most important self-reported explanation of dropping-out for all groups of adolescents. Neither gender nor class background modified this rank ordering, although we did find that more females than males (27 compared with 15 per cent) cited the quality of family relationship as a reason for leaving.

The features of respondents' school experiences that caused them to quit were not themselves of a piece. They objected to particular teachers, teachers in general, specific subjects, the irrelevance of the curriculum as a whole (as one male respondent put it: 'I'm never going to go to Spain or use

Table 6.3   Reason for dropping out of school by sex

Reason	Male		Female	
	%		%	
School	61	(105)	58	(98)
Family/friends	15	(25)	27	(46)
Jobs/money	19	(32)	15	(24)
Deviance	6	(10)	1	(2)
	100		100	
Total reasons*	172		170	

Note: * Up to three responses were coded for each sample member who answered the question.

what I learnt about Spain or Europe or nothin'. I'm never going to be there so why should I know about it?'); they complained about childish and unfriendly peers, they reported poor grades and revealed learning difficulties; all these reasons and more were coded as falling under the broad rubric of school-based reasons for leaving.

In addition, some respondents made it clear that their decision to leave school was not entirely a voluntary one – that rather than dropping-out of school they felt that they had, in fact, been kicked out. Usually this was because of their attendance record ('I missed 98 classes in 2½ months and they finally said, "If you're not going to come then you might as well go home."')'; in some cases (male) students had been expelled for hitting teachers.

The responsibility for encouraging marginal students to leave or stay in school fell to school counsellors. Previous research in the sociology of education has shown how schools categorize and process students, thereby preparing them for different occupational futures; usually the focus is upon the streaming or tracking system (Hargreaves 1967; Polk and Schafer 1972). Cicourel and Kitsuse, however, look specifically at the role of school counsellors (The Educational Decision-Makers, 1963). They investigate the ways in which counsellors construct categories of good and bad students and what the consequences are of the confirmation of those labels. We can extend this argument by suggesting that counsellors help to filter poorly committed students out of high school.

Over the past several years the Edmonton Public School Board has changed its policy with regard to recalcitrant school attenders. Those students with poor attendance records are warned that continuance of this pattern of behaviour will result in their being asked to leave school completely. This aggressive 'shape up or ship out' strategy means that high-school counsellors, under guidelines from the school board, often play a very pro-active role in accelerating some students' transition from school to labour market:

INTERVIEWER: . . . why did you leave school?
R: Well, I was kinda forced out, like they have a new policy for absences

and stuff and they gave me more absences than I had so they said I better leave.

Well, in grade 9 I got kicked out . . . actually. I didn't get kicked out but I kept on leaving the school for long periods of time and then finally I just got kicked out.

Likewise, although the next respondent claimed that the decision to leave school was of his own making, it is quite evident that he was strongly encouraged to do so:

INTERVIEWER: How did you decide to quit, was it your own decision or someone elses?
R: It was my decision.
INTERVIEWER: You didn't talk to a counsellor or anything about quitting?
R: Well, I talked to my co-ordinator about it and she and I never got along and she said 'Great, if you've been skipping you may as well leave for good.'[3]

It cannot therefore be assumed that dropping out of school is always a truly voluntary decision: the choice involved is sometimes more illusory than real, and schools play a more vigorous role in this outcome than is commonly recognized.

But regardless of the appropriate weighting of coercion and choice in the decision-making process, the fact remains that accounts of respondents dropping out which emphasize negative encounters with teachers, the irrelevance of the curriculum and mind-numbing boredom are indicative of school rejection. The message conveyed is one of generalized discontent. Something of this embryonic opposition to schooling is captured in the following exchanges. Asked why she quit school, this working-class female replied:

Well, mostly, I was pregnant, number one, I never really did like high school, oh, I don't know, I just never did like the system, they made you feel like a kid and I was really rebellious.

The same question brought the following answers from male respondents:

'Cause I don't like – I didn't – it was getting to the point where I just wanted to go to work. I was tired – I was tired of going to school, I didn't like the teachers or nothin so . . . I just quit.

Well, I – I had no interest eh, I just figured uh, I knew what I wanted to do and I figured school was just a waste of time.

It didn't interest me. I thought there was something else out there I was missing and I wanted to work. I've always felt that I was a little more mature than my peers.

I didn't really do that well in school. I really didn't care too much about school. I didn't want to go to school, I just wanted to get out and work.

I got bored with it. I wanted to get out and work.

I found it very boring after a while . . . I just wanted to go to work.

As these responses make clear, a general dislike of school is often linked to a desire for work. The prospective attractions of a job (adult status and adult wages), combined with the known drudgery of the classroom, are clearly factors that encourage early leaving.[4]

However, intimations that some adolescents quit school because they repudiate its underlying cultural and value system does not mean that all dropouts share this motivation, even though they might use the same vocabulary when describing school. Terms like boredom or dislike can be shorthand expressions for deep-rooted and wide-ranging objections to schooling, but this is not necessarily the case. The same language was also used to voice quite specific and, indeed, particular objections to school: respondents 'disliked' the English teacher (but not the maths teacher); hated maths (but not English), and so on. Hence, while some respondents quit because of a thoroughgoing estrangement from school culture, others left for more idiosyncratic reasons.

Thus, although it is the case that school experiences provide the majority of respondents with the motivation for dropping out, it does not axiomatically follow that all are engaged in the sort of class-based resistance to schooling outlined by Willis. In fact, what impressed us most about our respondents was not the magnitude of their opposition to, or alienation from, school but the very opposite; given that dropouts, by definition, are the Canadian educational system's most estranged clients, it was surprising to find how favourably that system was perceived and how qualified and muted many of their criticisms really were. Let us elaborate.

Dropping out of high school was a fundamentally ambiguous experience for most respondents. One question that we asked them was whether they felt, in retrospect, that leaving school had been a good or a bad thing. Roughly equal proportions answered 'good', 'bad' or 'both good and bad'. There were no significant class or gender differences to this pattern of response. On the one hand, respondents saw dropping-out as a viable short-term solution to the various problems that they were encountering in school; some, indeed, saw it as being virtually the only option available to them, given the circumstances of their lives. Others were even prepared to suggest that the decision to leave school qualified, at least in retrospect, as a cathartic experience. On the other hand, these short-term benefits were more than tempered by respondents' awareness that their early departure from the high-school system would likely pose problems for them in the not too distant future. The essential dualism that underpins respondents' feelings about the correctness of the decision to leave school could be summed up as short-term gain for long-term pain:

> Well, at first I thought it was a good thing because I was going to be moving on to something. Right now, I don't know.

> I wouldn't say it was either good or bad. I would say that it was, ah, an experience that would have to be lived. I can't say that it's an enlightening experience neither. There was good and bad parts about it. I did have a good job, I was making money, but on the other hand, I missed being with my peers a lot, so I can't really say it was good or bad.

> Well, it's got its pros and cons. If I would have stuck it out and got my diploma, I don't know what I might have done. I might have gone to university, but I don't know that I would have got high enough marks. The one benefit of leaving school was that it was kinda a learning experience 'cause I understand what it was like to go out into the workforce. And it turned out that I didn't like it that much. I couldn't picture myself doing that for the rest of my life – working a blue-collar level.

This last respondent was not alone in feeling that his time as a dropout had taught him a few of the economic and social facts of life, not least of which was the limited nature of unskilled blue-collar employment. Similar sentiments were expressed by another young dropout in his assessment of the early leaving experience:

> Well, it was bad because I lost some years. But it was good too because then I knew exactly what education was and when I went out to fill out the applications for jobs, you know. Some jobs you have to have high school and you just don't find a good job without a high school diploma . . .

> Q: So you feel that by quitting school you got to find out . . . what?
> A: Yeah. I learned a few things. I learned about how hard work is, like a real tough job. Like I never really knew. I thought you know, construction and stuff like that would be – wouldn't be too bad, but then it gets to you. It's hard.

These, and similar comments, leave little doubt that many respondents, male and female, from middle-class and working-class backgrounds, have retained at least a lingering commitment to an educational system that they have dropped out of. The reasons for this are not hard to find and have already been alluded to. First of all, respondents realized that the completion of grade 12 would improve their chances in the labour market: without it, they were likely to be ghettoized in a very narrow range of low-paying, menial and often part-time jobs. As one middle-class male put it: 'There's not really anything out there other than working at something like McDonalds, which I . . . see . . . I don't like working for slave wages so that's why I won't work there.'[5] Others, like this working-class male, noted the disparity between the quantity and quality of jobs available to dropouts: 'There isn't that many great jobs, but there is a lot of work.' Many of them felt that as dropouts they had been exploited mercilessly by unscrupulous bosses who knew that they were in no position to challenge the wages and conditions on offer. Second, many respondents felt that completion of grade 12 signified to employers that a young person had, as one informant put it, 'staying power'. Regardless of what had (or had not) been learnt in the process of twelve years of schooling, a grade-12 diploma was used by employers as a predictor of worker stability and reliability: 'If you go to a job and they see you don't have a diploma, they think you're a quitter' (working-class male). In essence, their labour-market experiences forced them, for the first time, to confront the stigma of being a dropout:

> When you're a high school dropout, a lot of the businesses really don't want to hire you 'cause they don't think you're intelligent enough the way you are. Um, like if I wasn't intelligent in finding work. They don't realize that just because you've dropped out of school, it doesn't really mean that you're not capable of doing the job [male].

Respondents' cognizance of the likely career path of a high-school dropout caused them to re-evaluate the merits of an educational system that they had previously dismissed.

These reluctant rebels may not like school, but they do recognize its importance as a means of escaping dead-end jobs and improving their life chances; as one male respondent put it, 'A lot of jobs in the paper, if you got the trade, man, boom, you get the job.'[6] This fundamental belief in the efficacy of credentials doubtless explains why such a surprisingly large number of respondents were still receptive to the idea of more education in the future. When asked 'Would you like to get more education?', 70 per cent answered positively, 24 per cent said 'Maybe' and only 6 per cent were certain that they had been through enough school. Once again, this was a pattern of response that did not vary significantly by sex or social class background.

A related question, however, reveals that for a large minority of dropouts, high school is perceived as a barrier to their pragmatic educational aspirations. We asked our informants if they would go back to school (table 6.4).

The modal response is the one of interest here: some 38 per cent agreed with the basic sentiment, but then qualified it by saying 'not to high school'. Respondents were clearly more hesitant about returning to high school than they were about acquiring more education. This is particularly the case with respondents from professional backgrounds – 47 per cent (14 out of 30) of whom were disinclined to complete their education at high school. Some of these dropouts entertained ideas of higher education, while others were interested in trade-related or similar vocational types of training. Some

Table 6.4   Desire to go back to school

	%
No	12
Maybe/not sure	19
Yes	32
Yes, but not to high school	38

wanted to get their grade 12 diploma by correspondence courses; and quite a few preferred institutions such as Alberta Vocational College and Alberta College that offer high-school programmes to adult students. These preferences are a further commentary on the nature of adolescents' antipathy to schooling. They suggest that the focus of discontent is often the ambience or social climate of the high school.

In some instances, the reference point was the school's authoritarian atmosphere. They resented being treated like 'kids', denied the freedom and autonomy which they felt, as individuals on the brink of adulthood, they deserved. As one complainant put it: 'It's so phoney in high school . . . you are not treated like an adult because you are not yet an adult, but they're not willing to treat you like it if you're going to act like one.'[7]

Once again, complaints of this sort suggest a questioning of the school's moral authority. But what is more difficult to gauge is whether it is class or age that generates the reaction: are teachers negatively assessed as representatives of middle-class authority, or more generally and simply as adult authority figures unreasonably controlling the freedom and autonomy of the young? Respondents' comments provided no definitive answer to this question. However, the large numbers of middle-class dropouts who want to complete their education at institutions other than high school does suggest that it is the general expectation of student compliance with teacher authority that is the source of the problem.

Moreover, respondents who spoke with bitterness about the quality of social relationships within their schools were not necessarily indicting either the adult authority structure or individual teachers: they were also referring to the prevailing peer culture. In this regard, the major focus of complaint was the immaturity of fellow students or the exclusionary nature of the dominant peer groups. This is how one female respondent explained her decision to leave school, one of the more affluent and prestigious ones in Edmonton:

> Ah, 'cause I wasn't enjoying myself, I wasn't having fun there, I didn't really fit into that kind of group 'cause at 'Mac' people were one way or the other. The major people that I knew there were very rich and very full of themselves. If you weren't part of this group and didn't know these people, they wouldn't speak to you. They're all snobs, I was shocked because they were all so snotty. There's just no way you can get in with them unless all of a sudden you come into a lot of money.

They judge you by what you wear and how you talk and what your parents do for a living and I felt I didn't have to justify anyone. I didn't appreciate them at all.

This male was even more specific when asked why he quit:

Well, I was having a few problems with, uh, not only the teachers in the school, it was, uh, the kids in the school. Like I was brought up religiously; and, uh, kids were always, you know, 'Come on let's go smoke dope'.

In light of the emphasis that ethnographers such as Willis place upon involvement in an anti-school peer culture as a determinant of early leaving, it is somewhat ironic to find some of our Canadian dropouts explaining that they left school because they were either denied access to the dominant peer culture or disapproved of its focal concerns.

Aspirations for the future

Investigating, in retrospect, dropouts' educational experiences and judgements about the propriety of early school leaving have revealed them to be still sensitive to the instrumental, if not moral, appeal of schooling. That high-school dropouts have not cut their ties to the dominant economic and normative order is similarly evident when we examine their aspirations for their adult lives. We did this with the aid of a general question about their major life goals and a specific one about the kind of jobs they would like to have in five to ten years' time.

Presented in table 6.5 is information about the occupational aspirations of our male and female respondents.

Both groups display very high levels of occupational ambition, bearing in mind the unfavourable circumstances under which they have made their entry into the labour market. Among the females, fully 40 per cent (27 out of 68) harbour a desire for professional jobs – a figure that increases to 53 per cent for those from professional backgrounds. For the males, skilled trades were the preferred occupational destination of 39 per cent of respondents, while another 21 per cent aspired to join the professional ranks. Class background had no discernible impact upon male aspirations.

It matters little, for the present argument, that these aspirations are hopelessly unrealistic and will, in most cases, go unrealized. What is more significant is that our respondents see upward mobility as both possible and desirable. Neither the absence of a grade 12 diploma nor generally desultory prior labour-market experiences have done much to suppress our respondents' job goals. There is little evidence, at this stage of their post-high-school careers, that this group of adolescents has settled for a lifetime of subordinate positions in the occupational hierarchy. Very few of the males, for instance, envisaged unskilled blue-collar futures.

Table 6.5 Kind of job wanted in five to ten years' time by sex

	Female		Male	
		%		%
Professional	27	(40)	16	(21)
Skilled trades	8	(12)	29	(39)
White collar	20	(29)	8	(11)
Unskilled manual	3	(4)	4	(5)
Sport or entertainment	7	(10)	9	(12)
Self-employed	3	(4)	8	(11)

A concomitant of this point is that we found no eagerness on the part of male respondents (or female ones, for that matter) to invert the prevailing mental/manual labour hierarchy or celebrate, and anticipate, the supposed virtues of unskilled manual labour (cf. Willis). Jobs – past, present, future – tended to be judged primarily in terms of how secure and well paid they were, on the one hand, and how much interest they could provide, on the other. These criteria informed their preferences for the skilled trades, and similarly justified their rejection of all forms of unskilled labour, particularly the sorts that they had most personal experience with – such as fast-food restaurants and telephone soliciting.

The definition of a skilled trade as a good job is fuelled by an additional factor that is not evident from the information presented in table 6.5 An important reason why males favoured the trades was that they saw them as furthering their not inconsiderable entrepreneurial ambitions. Their preferences for a skilled trade were quite often fused with the long-term goal of establishing their own small business. Becoming a mechanic, for instance, was thus seen as the preliminary step towards owning and operating a body shop. This desire for their own business also reveals a strong streak of individualism, as can be seen in the comments of this would-be self-employed trucker (he's currently a fork-lift truck driver):

> R: Well, if you have the smarts, I think the thing to do is to start your own business, you know. The old capitalist's method of making money.
> INTERVIEWER: You think that's the way to do it?
> R: That's the only way it'll get any better you know, if someone starts using their head and thinks up an idea that makes money.
> INTERVIEWER: Be a little entrepreneur or something?
> R: Yeah, cause right now – I can't see anything really – really good out there, you know.
> INTERVIEWER: Working for somebody else?
> R: Yeah, like I want to get my own truck eventually, eh? I want to be a lease operator. I've heard that there's not much money in it but you

Table 6.6   Major goals in life by sex

Goal	Male		Female	
	%		%	
Money/material possessions	14	(20)	10	(13)
Travel	4	(5)	4	(5)
Family (get married/have family)	10	(14)	18	(24)
Education/skills/training for a trade	16	(23)	16	(21)
Happiness (in general)	6	(8)	8	(10)
Work (to get a job/a good job)	17	(24)	15	(19)
Specific occupational goal	26	(36)	24	(31)
To help others	4	(5)	2	(3)
Other	3	(4)	1	(1)
To be successful (unspecified)	1	(1)	1	(1)
To get place to live on own	–	–	2	(2)
Total number of goals[1]	141		130	

Note: [1] Up to three goals were coded for each sample member who answered the questions.

know, I'm not really interested in making big bucks, I just – I got white line fever, eh?
INTERVIEWER: You want to set your own hours kind of thing, I guess.
R: Yeah, I want to be on my own out on the road, eh?

This belief in self-employment as a means of personal upward mobility has, of course, been recorded in other research on work aspirations in North America. Eli Chinoy (1955) noted its presence in his study of American auto workers in the early 1950s; and Gavin Mackenzie (1973) found further evidence of it among the skilled American craftsmen that he investigated in the late 1960s. Like previous generations of workers, our respondents see in self-employment possibilities for job satisfaction, dignity and freedom not available in other work situations. The very existence of such entrepreneurial ambitions might also be seen as a further measure of the extent to which our respondents endorse conventional success goals – despite, of course, being in a very poor position to realize them.

We had anticipated different patterns of aspirations for our male and female respondents. Not only do female school-leavers have to find paid employment, they also have to negotiate a set of domestic expectations that young males, by and large, do not have to confront. Girls and young women have been brought up to believe that they will assume prime responsibility for family matters – housework and child-care and so on – and that these duties take precedence over careers outside the home. However, an examination of respondents' life goals reveals that female ambitions are roughly similar to those of the males (table 6.6).

That is, the young women in our sample identify work, alongside marriage and children, as being at the centre of their adult lives. Although they are slightly more inclined than the males to envisage having a family of their own, this traditional domestic goal is not necessarily going to be pursued at the expense of success in the job world. It is, of course, entirely possible that these work ambitions will be displaced by domestic ones over time. But for the moment, the orientations to work of our female respondents are not significantly different from those of the males in the sample.

Our respondents were heavily committed to the 'work ethic' and wanted jobs that would provide an optimum balance of intrinsic and extrinsic rewards. They desired jobs that were both interesting *and* well paid. They saw the labour market as a hierarchical one – there were good and bad jobs, with the latter overwhelmingly composed of service-sector and unskilled manual occupations, and therefore to be avoided if at all possible. Their aspirations for satisfying work and frustration with many of the jobs available to them is perhaps best summed up by the working-class female who stated that 'I would rather take unemployment to *any* job but I would rather have a *good* job than be on unemployment, for sure.' They would like work to be a central life interest (Dubin 1956); they construed it to be a significant part of human activity, a prime source of creativity and self-expression. This optimistic conception of work's liberating capacities again contrast with the essentially pessimistic frame of reference through which Willis's 'lads' interpret the future work world.

Our sample of high-school dropouts have fallen out of grace with a system that, in the final resort, many of them still believe in. They adhere to an essentially vocational view of education; they accept that the acquisition of qualifications is how you get on in the world, and that the opportunities provided by the educational system are available to all with sufficient talent and motivation. Nor do they reject the priority that capitalist society places upon non-manual employment. In fact, the manual/non-manual distinction – so important to Willis's 'lads' in ideologically evaluating jobs – is, in all important respects, irrelevant to our respondents. Non-manual jobs are neither favoured nor rejected for reasons of prestige; instead, they are preferred because they are seen as offering better material rewards and more inherently satisfying work tasks.

Conclusions

When we began this project, we anticipated a straightforward connection between the dropout problem and school rejection. Drawing on recent ethnographic research, we hypothesized that dropouts from Edmonton high schools would hold views of school and work that would parallel those found among working-class early-leavers in Britain. The results of our investigation do not, by and large, support this proposition.

While our respondents did not, needless to say, like school very much, and invariably experienced it in terms of conflict of one sort or another, it would be an exaggeration to claim that their discordant sentiments have the hallmark qualities of an alternative value system, opposed to the one sponsored by the high school. There is insufficient rejection of qualifications, abandonment of individual ambitions or solidaristic affirmation of manual labour by our respondents to justify the argument that dropouts are adolescents who have necessarily inverted the formal culture of the high school.

The dropout label connotes distinctive patterns and value configurations on the part of those so defined. It implies that dropouts inhabit a qualitatively different world than non-dropouts. The findings from the present research challenge the accuracy of this portrayal of dropouts; in fact, the label itself may conceal fundamental similarities between those adolescents who stay in school and those who do not.

Dropouts and non-dropouts share a common commitment to getting a good job. This goal encourages a new universal pragmatic interpretation of the purposes of education. The dispute that dropouts have with the prevailing educational system has to do with the institutional means of achieving dominant success goals. By definition, they are, by and large, less tolerant of high school than are other adolescents. But this intolerance should not obscure the fact that many of them leave school despite their commitment to education, pragmatically defined, not because they saw it as worthless.

Part of the reason why the dropouts that we studied are less resistant to schooling than the working-leavers observed by Willis in Hammerton has to do with differences between British and Canadian educational systems of the sort identified by Ralph Turner (1960) and discussed at the beginning of this paper.

The highly selective British educational system, in essence, prepares working-class and middle-class adolescents for very different labour markets: middle-class adolescents are groomed for university and white-collar positions, working-class adolescents for a variety of low-skilled jobs (Parkin 1972: 62). Although this strategy is fairly successful in encouraging working-class adolescents to tailor their aspirations to their likely destination in the occupational order, it also induces resentment among them; they feel conscripted into a system of schooling that offers them little in return for their compliance. As a result, leaving school as soon as possible is a widespread expedient among British working-class adolescents.

This contrasts with the North American situation where decisions about ultimate destination in the occupational order are delayed as long as possible, and where the prevailing achievement ethic enjoins individuals from all strata of society to strive for common success goals.[8] Most high school-students have internalized these aspirations and accept that educational qualifications are the means of reaching them. Consequently, staying in school and completing secondary education are the norm among North American adolescents, and the reason why our respondents are aware of, and sensitive to, the pejorative overtones of the dropout label.

These differences between Canadian and British educational systems undoubtedly have a real impact upon how adolescents in the two societies make the transition from school to work; at the same time, though, we must not lose sight of the fact that the cross-cultural comparisons that we are making are based on the assumption that a class-based resistance to schooling is normative among working-class adolescents in Britain. It is from this benchmark of resistance that, in large measure, our dropouts are judged to be 'reluctant rebels'. However, research carried out since Willis observed the 'lads' suggests that, even in Britain, the amount of resistance to schooling exhibited by working-class adolescents has been overstated.

On the basis of a case study of adolescents in school and work in South Wales, Phil Brown persuasively argues that the pattern of school resistance identified by Willis is by no means characteristic of all working-class adolescents.

In fact, he suggests that it is a minority response associated with the 'rough' working class whose behaviour in school is disavowed, not only by middle-class teachers, but also by their more numerous 'respectable' working-class peers (Brown 1987). Most of the working-class adolescents in his case study, whom he refers to as 'ordinary kids', had the same sort of pragmatic instrumental approach to schooling that we are suggesting is common among all strata of adolescents in Canada.

The findings from a recent Willis-inspired ethnography in the United States give added credibility to Brown's criticism that Willis has concentrated his intellectual resources upon but one form of working-class accommodation to school and work. Jay Macleod (1987) observed and participated in the activities of two similarly placed groups of working-class males living in the same depressed inner-city neighbourhood. One group, the 'Hallway hangers', rejected the dominant success goals of American society and restricted their job ambitions to the sorts of unskilled jobs that they felt they were likely to get (a process that was not, incidentally, accompanied by an evident disdain for white-collar work).

But the other group, the 'Brothers', did buy into the 'American Dream' and its underlying achievement ideology; they believed that working hard in school was the strategy for getting a good job, defined conventionally in terms of money and prestige. Macleod then tries to explain why and how two similarly located groups of adolescents respond so differently to their educational and work environments.

The post-Willis research thus suggests that, on both sides of the Atlantic, working-class adolescent responses to schooling are more pluralistic than Willis supposes; it also raises questions about how widespread working-class resistance to schooling is and the circumstances that give rise to that specific mode of adaption highlighted by Willis.

On the basis of the existing research, it seems that Willis is providing a commentary on cultural practices among young working males that are the product of distinctive work and community settings that, in all probability, are irrevocably on the decline. 'Hammerton' is a community based on heavy industry, a cradle of the industrial revolution, a veritable breeding ground of 'traditional proletarianism' (Lockwood 1966). The values and behaviour of the 'lads' obviously derive from, and are shared with, the parent working-class culture. Hence the celebration of 'rough' working-class forms of masculinity and involvement in a class-based school counter-culture dedicated to turning middle-class school culture on its head. In essence, then, Willis observed a class-based resistance to schooling in an industrial and community context most favourable to its manifestation.

But the corollary of this is that communities (in Britain, Canada or elsewhere) that do not share Hammerton's economic and cultural characteristics will be less conducive to that kind of response to schooling. Edmonton, Alberta – with almost no tradition of heavy industry to speak of – is a case in point. Given that heavy manufacturing industry will be less important as both a source of employment and cultural meanings about work in the future, we might predict that the behaviour of the 'lads' will come to be seen as less and less typical of the working class as a whole.

Notes

1 The research described in this paper is part of a collective project involving Tim Hartnagel, Harvey Krahn, Graham Lowe and myself. I am indebted to them for the many and varied contributions that they have made to this paper. I am also very grateful to David Ashton, Jane Gaskell, Sev Isajiw, Aysan Tuzlak and Jerry White for helpful comments that they made on previous drafts of the paper. Thanks are also due to those people who, in addition to Harvey Krahn and myself, conducted the interviews on which the research is based: Marie Carlsberg, Mary-Anne Hendrik, Della Letnes, Les Samuelson, Alice Walter and particularly Lawrence Walter who not only did the lion's share of interviewing but also provided important insights into interpretation of the information received. Finally, I would like to acknowledge Joan Barnes' exemplary typing and editorial skills.

2 One measure of how influential Willis's study is comes from the results of a survey of British sociologists carried out in 1980. Respondents were asked to give examples of sociological works containing a highly regarded explanation. *Learning to Labour* received more citations than any other study – including such acknowledged classics as E. Durkheim's *Suicide*, K. Marx's *Capital*, and M. Weber's *Protestant Spirit and the Rise of Capitalism*, (Heath and Edmondson 1981).

Now this rapturous endorsement might simply be an example of British ethnocentrism; or it might be early recognition of an emergent classic, a sociological study that, because of its sensitivity to action *and* its structural constraints, serves as the model for understanding the behaviour of working-class adolescents in transit through the educational system.

3 This echoes and corroborates a point made by James Rosenbaum (1976). He found that school guidance counsellors managed to direct students in such a way that both they and their parents felt that they had exclusive responsibility for the educational choices made.

4 That said, there was very little evidence indicating (in contrast to Radwanski 1987) that the disenchanted quit school because they held jobs.

5 Respondents' bitterest comments about employers were, in fact, reserved for the

major fast-food chains. An important reason for their hostility was that, as young men and women of the world, they did not regard such workplaces as being part of a truly adult labour market. Working at Burger King or McDonalds meant working at a non-adult job with non-adult co-workers for non-adult wages.

6 This assessment is, of course, absolutely correct: there *is* a fairly strong correlation between the accumulation of credentials and high-paying jobs.

Ironically, though, the kinds of unskilled jobs that our respondents have most experience of – and which they are likely to spend their working lives doing unless they get more qualifications – are ones where formal credentials are less likely to be demanded by employers (Jenkins 1983; Ashton and Maguire 1986, Gaskell 1987).

The priority that our respondents place upon the vocational aspects of education is, we venture to suggest, an important reason why they dislike school: it is not vocational enough! Only 19 per cent of our respondents felt that their schooling had helped them look for work. The negative answers to this question reflect their assessment of the school's ability to furnish them with the skills that will actually enable them to do job tasks better; it is *not* a comment about their perceptions of the import of credentialism (cf. Gaskell, 1987: 263–4).

7 A recent observational study of youth in different communities in the American mid-west has similarly shown that working-class students are particularly sensitive to what they perceive as disrespectful treatment by teachers. Their concern with self-respect and personal dignity manifests itself, as it does in our study, as an objection to being dealt with in a less than adult fashion (Schwartz 1987).

8 The large minority of respondents who in the present study expressed an interest in becoming a rock musician is consistent with an observation made by both Turner (1960) and Parkin (1972) that such fantasy aspirations are more likely to occur in egalitarian educational systems than in selective ones.

References

Ashton, D. and Maguire, M. (1986). 'Young adults in the labour market', Research Paper No. 55. London, Department of Employment.

Brown, P. (1987). *Schooling Ordinary Kids: Inequality in Unemployment and the New Vocationalism*. London, Tavistock.

Chinoy, E. (1955). *Automobile Workers and the American Dream*. Boston, Beacon.

Cicourel, A. and Kitsuse, J. (1963). *The Educational Decision-Makers*. Chicago, Rand-McNally.

Corrigan, P. (1979). *Schooling the Smash Street Kids*. London, Macmillan.

Dubin, R. (1956). Industrial workers' world: a study of the central life interests of industrial workers', *Social Problems* 3: 131–41.

Ekstrom, R., Goertz, M., Pollack, J. and Rock, D. (1986). 'Who drops out of high school and why?' *Teacher's College Record*, 87: 336–73.

Friesen, D. (1967). 'Profile of the potential drop-out', *Alberta Journal of Educational Research*, 13, 4, December.

Gaskell, J. (1987). 'Education and the labour market: the logic of vocationalism' in T. Wotherspoon (ed.) *The Political Economy of Canadian Schooling*. Toronto, Methuen.

Hargreaves, D. (1967). *Social Relations in a Secondary School*. London, Routledge & Kegan Paul.

Heath, A. and Edmondson, R. (1981). 'Oxbridge sociology: the development of centres of excellence': 39–52, in Abrams, P., Deem, R., Finch, J. and Rock, P. (eds.) *Practice and Progress: British Sociology, 1950–1980*. London, Allen & Unwin.

Jenkins, R. (1983). *Lads, Citizens and Ordinary Kids*. London, Routledge & Kegan Paul.

Lacey, C. (1970). *High-Town Grammar*. Manchester, Manchester University Press.

Lockwood, D. (1966). 'Sources of variation in working-class images of society', *Sociological Review*, 14, 249–67.

Mackenzie, G. (1973). *The Aristocracy of Labour*, Cambridge, Cambridge University Press.

Macleod, J. (1987). *'Ain't No Makin' It': Levelled Aspirations in a Low-Income Neighbourhood*, Boulder, Colorado, Waterview Press.

Parkin, F. (1972). *Class Inequality and Political Order*. London, Paladin.

Polk, K. and Schafer, W. (eds.) (1972). *Schools and Delinquency*. Scarborough, Prentice Hall.

Radwanski, G. (1987). *Ontario Study of the Relevance of Education, and the Issue of Drop-Outs*. Ontario, Ministry of Education.

Rosenbaum, J. (1976). *Making Inequality*. New York, John Wiley.

Rumberger, R. (1987). 'High school drop-outs: a review of issues and evidence', *Review of Educational Research*, 57, 2: 101–21.

Schwartz, G. (1987). *Beyond Conformity or Rebellion: Youth and Authority in America*. Chicago, University of Chicago Press.

Turner, R. (1960). 'Sponsored and contest mobility and the school system', *American Sociological Review*, 25, 6, December 1960: 855–67.

Willis, P. (1977). *Learning to Labour*. London, Saxon House.

7

Transitions to work: findings from a longitudinal study of high-school and university graduates in three Canadian cities[1]

Harvey Krahn and Graham Lowe

Introduction

Has the transition from school to work for Canadian youth been affected by the current restructuring of industry? Rapidly rising youth unemployment in the early 1980s was the most obvious sign of such a change. A closer look at the labour market reveals that many organizations introduced new technologies and cut staff in a quest for greater flexibility and efficiency. This may have reduced the number of entry-level positions open to youth. Furthermore, the preceding generation of baby boomers may have created demographic bottlenecks in organizations, thus further reducing recruitment of recent graduates.

Meanwhile the service sector has been expanding. But the creation of service-sector jobs (many of which are part-time, poorly paying and insecure) has not completely offset declining full-time employment in traditional industries. These changes then have been linked to the increase in youth unemployment. They have also prompted speculation that traditional entry-level jobs are disappearing, and that the majority of jobs now open to youth are in service-sector ghettos. In other words the relatively smooth transition to adulthood that characterized most of the post-World-War-II era may have become increasingly difficult.

We begin with the premise that finding a job consistent with one's educational attainment soon after graduation is an essential prerequisite for youth to become fully integrated, contributing adult members of society (Dayton 1981). Without stable and rewarding employment, young people are deprived of an income, of the attendant material and social benefits, and of the opportunity to develop an occupational identity. To the extent that jobless young people are pushed to the margins of society, individual adjustment difficulties and serious social problems may result.

If we can no longer assume an unimpeded progression from school to work, and from dependence on one's parents to independence, careful research is needed to outline the new processes of transition and any resulting social tensions. This paper attempts to map the various pathways followed by Canadian high-school and university graduates into the labour-market during a period of profound economic change. We look in detail at educational choices and labour-market experiences reported by recent high-school and university graduates in three Canadian cities. We also describe some of their educational and work aspirations and attitudes.

The data analyses below are primarily descriptive; this is a first attempt to examine the school – work transition using data from a longitudinal study of 1985 high-school and university graduates in three Canadian cities. However, by asking how gender, other socio-demographic characteristics, educational attainment, and local labour-market conditions play a part, we also begin to address central analytic questions about the nature of transition processes (Hogan and Astone 1986: 110) and the structure of youth labour markets (Ashton 1988: 2).

A key design feature of our study is the comparison of three different urban labour markets which reflect the regionalized nature of Canada's economy. Toronto's economy is booming, while Edmonton's economy, based as it is on the energy industry, is still attempting to recover from the devastating effects of the recession. Sudbury is a smaller, more isolated resource community with an even less diversified local economy. Another important variable is level of education and therefore age of labour-market entry. We compare the labour-market entry experiences of high-school graduates from a range of vocational and academic programmes, and of university graduates from a variety of faculties. Gender is equally central to our analyses. Have, for example, recent economic events accentuated male–female differences in decisions about education and careers, reversing some of the advances made during the last decade towards greater gender equality in the labour market?

Our longitudinal-research design allows a clearer understanding of the dynamic nature of the transition process and of the forces which shape it. Indeed, the concept of 'transition' demands such a longitudinal perspective (Anisef *et al.* 1986: 67; Mason 1985: 27). Cross-sectional studies seldom uncover the complexities of transition processes and do not provide a clear choice between alternative intrepretations of why changes are occurring. For example, two recent multi-national surveys present the sanguine view that young people will in due course 'become fully integrated and productive members of society' (Braungart and Braungart 1986: 377). However, other analysts offer a disturbingly bleak picture in which the institutions which previously bridged the gap between youth and adulthood, school and jobs, have all but collapsed for specific groups (eg: Ashton and Maguire 1986; Roberts *et al*. 1987; Walker and Barton 1986; Brown and Ashton 1987).

It is noteworthy that most of these pessimistic studies are of British origin. There is very little equivalent Canadian research. The significant industrial, labour market, legislative and educational differences between the two countries noted in earlier chapters suggest that transition processes might differ as well. Thus this largely descriptive paper is a Canadian contribution to the growing comparative literature on the sociology of youth, education, and labour markets (Anderson and Blakers 1983; Grootings 1986; Hartmann 1987; Heinz 1987).

With a few notable exceptions, such as studies of educational opportunity (Porter *et al*. 1982) and the links between education and occupational attainment (Anisef *et al*. 1980; 1986), panel research designs have rarely been used to examine school-to-work transition issues in Canada. However, cross-sectional studies have focused on vocationalism (Gaskell 1987), gender segregation (Looker 1985), the high-school dropout problem (Radwanski 1987), specific occupational outcomes (Clark *et al*. 1986; Picot *et al*. 1987), and policy implications (Senate of Canada 1986). The longitudinal results presented here should add to our understanding of these issues.

Research design, response rates and sample attrition

Base-line data (Year 1) were collected in the spring of 1985 from graduating high-school and university students in the cities of Edmonton, Sudbury and Toronto. High-school sample members completed the Year-1 questionnaire in class, while university graduates received theirs through the mail. All follow-up surveys were completed by mail. The first took place in May 1986 (Year 2) and the second was done in May 1987 (Year 3). Thus, this panel study covers a 24-month period following completion of the last year of high school or an undergraduate university degree.

The university sample contains graduates of arts, business, education, engineering and science faculties at the University of Alberta, the University of Toronto, and Laurentian University. Faculties such as law, medicine and dentistry were excluded from the study due to small enrolments and unique labour markets. In Year 1 a systematic sample was generated by choosing every third name on lists of graduands in the designated faculties provided by university registrars. Questionnaires were mailed in April, with follow-up by mail and phone where necessary.

Given the difficulties of obtaining a random sample of graduating high-school students in the three cities, we opted for a strategic sampling design with the school as the sampling unit. We deliberately selected a wide range of high schools (from working-class and middle-class neighbourhoods) with a diversity of programmes and student backgrounds. Once permission had been obtained from school officials, and from parents of eligible students under the age of 18, members of the research team

Table 7.1 Sample sizes and response rates by city, year and education level

	May 1985		May 1986		May 1987	
	Time 1		Time 2		Time 3	
	HS	Univ.	HS	Univ.	HS	Univ.
Edmonton	983	589	665	458	547	421
	[894]	[533][1]	(68%)[2]	(78%)	(56%)[2]	(71%)
					[61%][3]	[79%]
Toronto	754	519	412	358	296	326
	[674]	[433]	(55%)	(69%)	(39%)	(63%)
					[44%]	[75%]
Sudbury	492	227	240	156	187	128
	[338]	[221]	(49%)	(69%)	(38%)	(56%)
					[55%]	[58%]
Total	2,229	1,335	1,317	973	1030	875
	[1,906]	[1.187]	(59%)	(73%)	(46%)	(66%)
					[54%]	[74%]
Total	3,564		2,289		1,905	
	[3,093]		(64%)		(53%)	
					[62%]	

[1] Number of year-1 respondents who provided their name and address for follow-up purposes.
[2] % of total year-1 sample re-interviewed.
[3] % of those year-1 respondents who gave their name and address, signifying willingness to participate in the panel study.

distributed the Year-1 questionnaires in classrooms within the chosen schools.

Prior to undertaking each of the follow-up surveys, newsletters were sent to respondents to keep them informed about the progress of the study and to report preliminary findings. This strategy also allowed the updating of mailing lists. A four-stage data collection procedure was employed in all of the mail surveys (see Heberlein and Baumgartner 1978). The sequence included the initial questionnaire and covering letter, a reminder letter, a second questionnaire package and, where necessary, telephone contact with an offer to send out a third questionnaire. In each year we succeeded in contacting all but a few sample members by mail or phone. Sample attrition was largely due to the unwillingness of some Year-1 sample members to complete subsequent questionnaires.

Sample sizes and response rates are reported in table 7.1. There were 3,564 respondents in Year 1, with a 60/40 split between high-school and university graduates. Almost two-thirds (64 per cent) of the original sample (N = 2,289) responded in Year 2. Attrition further reduced the sample in Year 3 (N = 1,905). The final high-school sample contains 54 per cent of those who gave their name and address on the 1985 questionnaire, compared to 74 per cent for the university sample. This discrepancy reflects different data collection methods in Year 1. The in-class survey used for high-school students ensured a very high initial response rate, with less interested respondents dropping out of the study in subsequent years. Alternatively, use of a mail questionnaire for the university graduates in Year 1 made it easier for those not interested in the study to choose not to participate at the outset. The overall response rate in Year 3 was 62 per cent of those giving contact information in Year 1, and 53 per cent of all those who filled out the Year-1 questionnaire.

A potential source of bias in any panel study is sample attrition. A systematic comparison of Year-1 respondents who subsequently dropped out of the study (in either Year 2 or Year 3) with those who participated in all three years identified several possible sources of bias (Krahn 1988: 11–17). Fewer potential biases were observed in the university sample, where response rates across the 24 months of the study were higher.

Specifically, in both the high-school and university samples, males had a higher attrition rate. Within the high-school sample only, those individuals with previous labour-market experience were somewhat more likely to drop out of the study. On the other hand, more academically oriented high-school youth and those from higher socio-economic backgrounds were more likely to continue to participate. The labour-market experience effect was not observed in the university sub-sample, and the effect of socio-economic background was not as pronounced. However, both samples had a higher attrition rate among members of racial/ethnic minorities (compared with Canadian-born respondents). Finally, as table 7.1 shows, there were marked differences in response rates across the three cities.

In our analyses below, we use only Y1–Y2–Y3 panel data (N = 1,905; high-school = 1,030; university = 875). When commenting on Year-1 results, we make comparison to the complete Time-1 sample where appropriate. Without exception, we reach the same conclusions with both the complete sample and the sub-sample which remained part of the study till Year 3. In short, we find no evidence of attrition significantly affecting relationships within the data presented in this paper.

Plans and reasons for staying in school

When we began this study, we expected that a sizeable number of the high-school graduates and somewhat fewer of the university sample would plan to continue in school. We were surprised, however, at just how many of these young people reported such plans. A very large majority (80.7 per cent) of the high-school sample expected to continue their education in the fall of 1985. And over one-third of the university graduates (36.6 per cent) answered similarly. While we were aware that university and college enrolments in Canada have been increasing steadily for the past few years (Statistics Canada 1987), this very high level of commitment to further education was clearly an unexpected finding.

No gender differences in plans for further education were observed among either the high-school or university graduates in this study. Again this reflects the general university and college enrolment patterns in Canada. But, as we expected, socio-economic background does have an effect. In both the high-school and university samples, those with parents who had attended university were significantly more likely to plan additional schooling.

Escalating post-secondary enrolments and rising youth unemployment in the first part of the 1980s encouraged speculation that the two were causally related, that more Canadian young people were choosing to continue their education because of their experiences in a limited labour market. Bivariate analyses of both the high-school and university results fail to support this hypothesis. Those who had experienced unemployment were actually less likely to plan to return to school in fall, although the relationships were not statistically significant.

More than one-third (41 per cent) of the high-school graduates planning to return to school were expecting to go to university, while 36 per cent were aiming at community colleges or technical schools. One in five planned to return to high school (some to upgrade their marks, others to complete subjects needed for a diploma and, in Ontario, some to take grade 13). Among university graduates with additional education plans, 59 per cent reported that they would be going on to professional or graduate schools. About one-quarter (23 per cent) were planning additional undergraduate training within a university setting. Only 6 per cent said they would be enrolling in a community college or technical school; such plans are clearly not very common.

While no gender effects on plans to return to school were observed, we do find some differences in the type of schooling planned by male and female graduates. Among high-school graduates, females were more likely to plan to go to university (45 versus 37 per cent), while males were more likely to plan to return to high-school (23 versus 17 per cent). Male university graduates were somewhat more likely to be planning graduate studies or training in a professional school (63 versus 56 per cent of female university graduates).

Asked why they planned to return to school, these graduates responded with a wide range of reasons. After grouping these diverse responses into eight basic types (table 7.2), we observe that job or career-related reasons were predominant: 44 per cent of the high-school graduates and 63 per cent of those leaving university gave this type of answer. An additional 19 per cent of the high-school graduates and 9 per cent of university sample members noted that they needed more education to get ahead, to get into university, or something similar – a less direct job-related reason. And another smaller group noted that more education would provide a higher standard of living or more independence. In short, about two-thirds of each group could be interpreted as having job considerations in mind when planning further education. Additional analyses based on the total Year-1

Table 7.2 Reasons for planning to return to school by education level by gender.[1]

Reasons	High-school graduates[2]			University graduates		
	Female[3]	Male	Total	Female	Male	Total
	%	%	%	%	%	%
Get a job/career/better job/more choice/etc.	46.3	42.1	44.2	63.4	62.6	63.1
Need more education to get into university/get ahead/finish high school/etc.	17.7	20.8	19.2	9.7	7.5	8.7
Get more knowledge/ more skills/enjoy school	17.3	14.4	15.9	21.7	23.8	22.7
Get more out of life/ more independence/ higher standard of living	6.6	4.4	5.5	–	0.7	0.3
No jobs available	0.9	1.0	1.0	1.1	1.4	1.2
Something to do/a chance to decide what I want to do with my life	3.8	3.2	3.5	–	–	–
Other (parents want me to/my friends are going/for the social life/etc.)	2.6	3.7	3.1	1.1	0.7	0.9
NR/DK/'I want to'	4.7	10.5	7.6	2.9	3.4	3.1
Total	100.0	100.0	100.0	100.0	100.0	100.0
(n)	(423)	(409)	(832)	(175)	(147)	(322)

[1] Members of the year 1–2–3 panel who said they planned to return to school in fall of 1985.
[2] Differences between high-school and university sample (chi-square test) are statistically significant ($p < .001$).
[3] Differences between female and male respondents (chi-square test) are statistically significant ($p < .05$).

sample (including those who did not participate in follow-up surveys) produced essentially the same results.

Gender differences in the university sample are almost non-existent (table 7.2). In the high-school sample male and female respondents were about equally likely to have job considerations in mind (reasons one and two). However, males were somewhat more inclined to say 'don't know' or to not respond. In short, stereotypes about young men being more career oriented are certainly not supported by these findings.

It is noteworthy that only 1 per cent of both samples answered that they were going on in school because no jobs were available. There is an important difference between this answer and the others discussed above. These young Canadians did not admit to staying in school because jobs were scarce but reported that they were trying to get the skills and credentials necessary to compete for scarce jobs. This is an active, rather than a passive response to a tight labour market. Similarly, only a very small minority of subjects admitted that additional education was a way of passing time, or a response to parental or peer pressures. These results show very clearly how much young Canadians are committed to the belief that higher education is the ticket to career success.

What should high-schools and universities be teaching?

The Year-1 questionnaire included open-ended questions about the most important thing high-schools (for the high-school sample) or universities should be teaching. Without the prompting which forced-choice questions might provide, most of the sample members still had an opinion on this subject and some provided more than one answer. A wide range of opinions was received, but these could be collapsed into three basic categories. Table 7.3 summarizes the distribution of answers, separately for the high-school and the university panel samples. The same analyses for the complete Year-1 sample (results not shown) produced essentially similar results.

Roughly one-third of the answers provided by members of both samples suggested that the role of educational institutions was to provide job or career training. However, comments about the need for a general education, the importance of teaching critical thinking and other 'liberal arts' types of concerns were equally frequent. The university graduates were somewhat more inclined to provide such answers, while high-school graduates were a bit more likely to suggest that high-schools should be teaching social skills, communication skills, and so on.

Members of the university sample (but not the high-school graduates) were also asked a forced-choice question about whether their education had been an adequate preparation for the job market (No, Uncertain, Yes). Slightly more than one-third (37 per cent) answered 'Yes', 33 per cent were uncertain, and 30 per cent said 'No' (results not shown). Criticisms about the labour-market relevance of completed education were more widespread among those planning to return to school in fall, that is, among arts and science graduates. Business, education and engineering graduates who, no doubt, saw a clearer career route leading from their degree (and who were more likely to have a job arranged prior to graduation), were less critical of their education in this respect.

Male graduates were somewhat more likely (41 per cent) than females (34 per cent) to evaluate their university education positively in this regard, although the gender difference was not statistically significant ($p > .05$). However, once again, this difference primarily reflects the concentration of women and men in particular faculties. For example, in the predominantly

Table 7.3 Opinions about the most important thing which high schools and universities should be teaching, by city

City	Job search/ career focus	General education/ critical thinking	Social skills/ other	Total
High school				
Edmonton	34.0%*	32.8%	33.2%	100%
	(229)	(221)	(224)	(674)
Toronto	35.2%	31.5%	33.3%	100%
	(131)	(117)	(124)	(372)
Sudbury	26.6%	30.9%	42.5%	100%
	(62)	(72)	(99)	(233)
Total	33.0%	32.1%	34.9%	100%
	(422)	(410)	(447)	(1279)
University				
Edmonton	33.3%	45.0%	21.7%	100%
	(153)	(207)	(100)	(460)
Toronto	27.9%	41.4%	30.7%	100%
	(109)	(162)	(120)	(391)
Sudbury	35.7%	38.6%	25.7%	100%
	(50)	(54)	(36)	(140)
Total	31.5%	42.7%	25.8%	100%
	(312)	(423)	(256)	(991)

* Percentages based on the total number of answers provided by the year 1–2–3 sample (up to two per person) to this open-ended question (rather than the total number of respondents). Most respondents gave only a single answer (10 per cent of the high-school students and 7 per cent of the university graduates did not answer at all), but 34 per cent of the high-school respondents and 20 per cent of the university sample members gave two answers.

male engineering faculty, 57 per cent of the graduates answered in the affirmative. In contrast, arts graduates (more of whom are female) were the least positive (24 per cent).

Individuals who answered 'no' or 'uncertain' to this question were asked to state the reason for their negative assessment. A majority were critical of the university system: 46 per cent said that their education had not been sufficiently practical and 16 per cent reported that their degree had little value on the job market. However, 8 per cent merely said they would need more education to get into the career they were pursuing, and the same proportion responded that job training was not the role of a university. The remainder gave a variety of other answers.

These preliminary findings about further education plans, the content of high-school and university education, and the work-world relevance of university training, appear somewhat contradictory. On one hand, we note that most of the high-school respondents and over one-third of the university graduates were planning to return to school. The majority of those returning to school were doing so for work or career-related reasons. These results reflect a very high level of commitment to education among Canadian youth, a commitment premised on the belief that higher education will improve one's work or career opportunities.

However, only one in three university graduates were certain that their education had actually provided adequate preparation for the job market (high-school sample members were not asked this question). Thus, while remaining committed to the general belief that there is a clear connection between educational attainment and labour-market success, many of these university-educated youth were also beginning to question whether their own education was adequate.

One response to such cognitive dissonance might be an increase in cynicism, a more critical questioning of the meritocratic beliefs about education and work. Further analysis of these panel data will allow a test of this hypothesis. However, these Year-1 results highlight an alternative response that does not involve a questioning of the educational belief system, that is, dealing with one's doubts by deciding to get more education. In short, recognition that university degrees may no longer guarantee a good job is widespread among university graduates. But there is little evidence so far that the changing labour market for youth has had a significant effect on the educational belief system itself. Instead, young Canadians continue to pursue higher education, committed to the belief that this is how one gets ahead.

And what of the apparently contradictory fact that only a minority of graduates suggested that labour-market and career concerns should be the most important things taught in high-schools and universities? Many of these young people appear to believe that educational institutions should equip one with general knowledge, well-developed intellectual abilities, and social skills, rather than merely with specific job-related skills. Such opinions are not unexpected, given that a liberal-arts emphasis has been fairly prominent in Canadian educational curricula for some time. Advocacy of a 'well-rounded' education is also part of the Canadian educational belief system.

But is this preference for a liberal-arts type of education by a large proportion of graduates not at odds with the widespread belief that education is the avenue to labour-market success? We must distinguish between education credentials and education content in order to make sense of these results. A large majority of Canadian youth appear convinced of the need for higher education credentials if one wishes to get ahead in the work world. Getting a diploma or a degree is generally recognized as a necessary prerequisite. Some of these young people, but certainly not all, are also of the opinion that specific work-related skills should be taught in school. Others recommend a more general education. None of this negates the fact that Canadian youth place great stock in higher education, and that they believe that their future work opportunities will be influenced by their educational attainment.

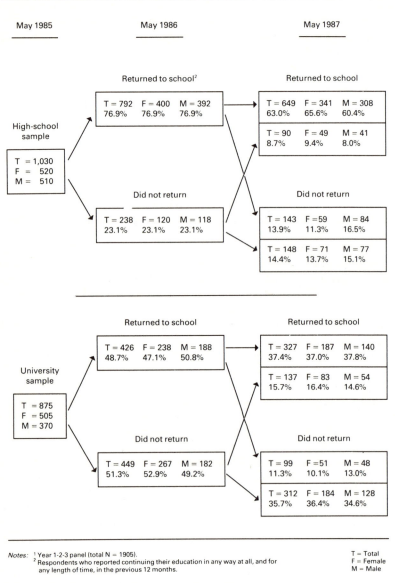

Notes: [1] Year 1-2-3 panel (total N = 1905).
[2] Respondents who reported continuing their education in any way at all, and for any length of time, in the previous 12 months.

T = Total
F = Female
M = Male

Figure 7.1 Education paths by sex by sample, 1985–7[1]

Leaving school

We begin our analysis of the transitional process by examining the educational paths followed by the 1,905 young people who participated in all three waves of the panel study. A very large majority of the 1,030 high-school graduates had continued their education in some form in the year following completion of the first questionnaire. While 81 per cent of the high-school sample reported plans to return to school in Year 2 (table 7.2), 77 per cent had actually returned (figure 7.1). By May 1987 somewhat fewer were attending school, but non-students still only made up 28 per cent of this sample. Gender differences were non-existent in Year 2 but, by Year 3, young men were slightly more likely to have left school.

A large proportion of the high-school graduates continuing in school in Year 2 (46 per cent) had returned to high school (results not shown), considerably more than had reported such plans the previous spring. Some of these individuals might have been 'terminal' Ontario grade-12 students who switched into an academic grade-13 programme. But this group would also include those who failed some subjects and returned to complete their high-school education, either full-time or part-time. Others, perhaps seeking entry to post-secondary educational institutions, might have returned to improve their grades. By Year 3 (May 1987), most of the high-school sample had moved out of the secondary-school system; but 10 per cent of those reporting some educational activity were still attending high-school.

Asked about the typical transition out of high-school, most of us might describe a relatively abrupt exit – after writing final exams, students graduate and then either enter a new educational institution or move into the labour force. Our results suggest a more gradual, extended transition process. Some of the explanation lies in the 'cafeteria' approach to educational curriculum described by Jane Gaskell earlier in this volume. High-school seniors exercise considerable choice in filling their timetable. These choices may not always add up to the package needed for entry into college or university; additional courses may have to be taken later. In an environment where higher education is becoming the norm, the opportunity to repeat courses in which one has done poorly, or to switch into an academic programme, can also lead to a prolonging of exit from the high-school system.

But not all of these high-school seniors prolonged their exit from the secondary-school system. About one-third (28 per cent) of those continuing in school in Year 2 had gone to university, compared to 20 per cent to community colleges or technical schools (results not shown). By Year 3, 48 per cent of the students in the high-school sample were reporting university attendance, compared to 32 per cent in colleges or technical schools. The high level of college and university attendance, and the relative preference for the latter, mirror aggregate statistics showing expanding college and university enrolments over the past decade, and a rising proportion of Canadians holding a university degree (Statistics Canada, *The Daily*, 1 March 1988: 15).

If we turn to the university sample, 37 per cent of these graduates had expressed intentions, when first surveyed (May 1985), to return to school in the fall. However, a larger proportion (49 per cent) had actually returned in Year 2 and, by Year 3, over half (53 per cent) reported some educational activity in the previous twelve months (figure 7.1). Some of this discrepancy between plans and outcomes may be due to the manner in which questions are answered. When responding to a question about education plans in the next year, most respondents might answer with (relatively) full-time education in mind. When asked about education in the previous year, sample members would use a broader frame of reference and report educational activity which might not have been considered in the earlier response (e.g. part-time education). However, it is also quite likely that some respondents changed their plans and decided to stay on in school.

In Year 2, 80 per cent of the university sample staying in school were reporting university-based studies, compared to 8 per cent in colleges or technical schools, and 12 per cent in other educational institutions (results not shown). Among those continuing on in university, three out of five (62 per cent) had begun graduate programmes, while the remainder had completed some more undergraduate work. Some of the latter had moved into a new area of study, while others had completed additional courses in their original area.

A year later, 70 per cent of the continuing students in the university sample were enrolled in a university programme, while 12 per cent were attending a college or technical school. Among the group still attending university, 57 per cent were in graduate studies and 43 per cent reported undergraduate work. Thus, staying in the university system (and pursuing graduate studies) was the most common continuing education choice. But we also find that at least some university graduates follow a non-traditional educational pathway into the college/technical school system.

While graduate studies, generally full-time, appeared to be the most common choice for continuing university-sample members, these data show that other options were also explored by some students. Many reported part-time education in combination with labour-force activity. By Year 3, part-time students were more common than full-time students. And, as noted above, some graduates changed programmes, and others shifted into the community college/technical school route. But what is most noteworthy about these findings is the very high level of continued educational activity among these graduating university students. Again, the transition out of school appears to be a prolonged affair.

One final observation on figure 7.1 is necessary. While 14 per cent of the high-school sample dropped out of the educational system after Year 2, almost 9 per cent came back in after having been absent for a year. In the university sample, 11 per cent left school after Year 2, but almost 16 per cent re-entered the education system. Thus, there is considerably more movement in and out of school among these young respondents than cross-sectional analyses of school attendance would reveal.

In summary, the slow movement of high-school seniors out of the secondary school system, the very high level of continuing education within both samples, and the return to school of significant numbers of young people after they have left for a year clearly suggest a prolonging of the transition process. This blurring of the boundary between student and labour-force roles is accented, of course, by the widespread tendency for both high-school and university students to work part-time while attending school.

Entering the labour force

Our results suggest that there no longer is, if there ever was, a critical juncture at which young people leave school and become a member of the labour force. Instead, the transition from school to work is a long process, the boundaries between the role of student and (paid) worker are unclear and, given recent trends in part-time higher education, it is always possible to return to school after some years out of the education system. Nevertheless, there is merit in comparing the labour-market experiences, and also the work values and other attitudes, of those who have largely left school and those who have not. There is also value in considering separately those youth still in the process of transition.

Our method involves the development of a four-category typology of transition, based on the degree to which an individual has continued to participate in the educational system (table 7.4). Group 1 contains those respondents who reported seven or more months of full-time education, the minimum required for enrolment in two terms at a secondary or post-secondary institution, in both years of the follow-up study. Group 4, on the other hand, contains sample members who reported no full-time education, and no more than two months of part-time education, in either Year 2 or Year 3 (most of this part-time education was in Year 2, and most was job-related).

Members of Group 3 had been in the educational system to some extent in Year 2, but had left by Year 3 (no full-time education and no more than two months of part-time education). Group 2, then, is the residual category, with a mixture of school and labour-force participation in both years. Thus the two middle categories in this typology reflect the blurred transition process we have begun to document. Groups 1 and 4, the end-points on this continuum, distinguish between those who stayed in school and those who left.

Table 7.4 displays average months of full-time and part-time education and work, and average months of unemployment, for each of these four groups of respondents. Results from the high-school and university samples are presented separately. Although it is recognized that these averages are merely summaries of complete distributions (e.g. an average of 1.4 months of unemployment is based on a large number of individuals who had never been unemployed and a smaller number who had been without work for a longer period of time), it is apparent that members of these four groups were reporting very different education and labour-market experiences.

Table 7.4   A typology of transitions from school to work for 1985: high-school and university graduates: education, work, and unemployment experiences

	Average number of months			
	1 Full-time education both Years[1]	2 Education and work both Years[2]	3 Education in Year 2 but not Year 3[3]	4 Employment both Years[4]
High-school sample				
Year 2 (1985–6)				
FT education	8.8	3.6	5.9	0.0
PT education	0.1	1.7	2.6	0.3
FT employment	1.1	3.5	3.0	7.0
PT employment	5.5	4.8	5.4	2.8
Unemployment	1.4	1.7	2.0	1.5
Year 3 (1986–7)				
FT education	8.8	4.7	0.0	0.0
PT education	0.1	1.6	0.1	0.1
FT employment	2.1	4.1	7.0	8.8
PT employment	5.2	4.2	3.7	1.8
Unemployment	0.8	1.3	1.5	1.4
(n)	(375)	(331)	(160)	(164)
University sample				
Year 2 (1985–6)				
FT education	8.7	1.9	2.9	0.0
PT education	0.1	1.8	3.8	0.1
FT employment	2.5	6.9	6.7	9.0
PT employment	4.0	2.6	3.0	1.6
Unemployment	0.5	1.0	1.1	1.2
Year 3 (1986–7)				
FT education	9.4	2.6	0.0	0.0
PT education	0.2	3.7	0.1	0.1
FT employment	1.7	7.4	9.5	10.2
PT employment	4.8	2.4	1.8	1.2
Unemployment	0.3	0.6	0.7	0.6
(n)	(140)	(236)	(136)	(363)

[1] Group 1 = 7+ months of full-time education in both years.
[2] Group 2 = mixed school/labour market both years.
[3] Group 3 = mixed school/labour market in Year 2, no full-time, but up to 2 months part-time education in Year 3.
[4] Group 4 = no full-time, but up to 2 months of part-time education in both years.
FT = full-time
PT = part-time

Group 1, in both the high-school and university samples, contains the traditional 'student', averaging around nine months of full-time education in both years of the follow-up study. For both samples, part-time education is of little consequence, in either year. As for full-time work, one or two months of full-time employment per year (probably in the summer) is the limit for the typical student. But part-time employment is much more common, with four or five months per year being the norm, for both samples.

Group 4, by definition, reported no full-time schooling and only negligible amounts of part-time education. Having left school, most of these respondents were seeking full-time employment. University graduates were somewhat more successful in this respect, averaging 9 and 10.2 months of full-time work in Year 2 and 3 of the study. High-school graduates in Group 4 reported averages of 7.0 and 8.8 months of full-time work in these two years respectively. Thus there is evidence that additional educational credentials have some value, at least in terms of months of work, and that both the high-school and the university members of this group were settling into their labour-force roles over the 24-month period of the study.

By Year 3, individuals in Group 3 had left school. They were reporting a considerable amount of full-time work (7.0 and 9.5 months in the high-school and university samples, respectively), but not quite as much as members of Group 4 who had a one-year advantage in terms of full-time labour-force experience. In fact, if we compare Group 3's education and work activities in Year 3 with the Year 2 activities of Group 4, we see few major differences. What separates Groups 3 and 4, in both the high-school and university samples, is simply the prolonging of exit from the educational system by one year.

Group 2, while also mixing work and school over the 24-month period of this study, seems to have done so in a different manner. Looking first at the high-school sub-sample, we note roughly equal amounts of full-time and part-time work (about four months) in each year. This group also reported more full-time than part-time schooling in each year (about four months, on average, compared to less than two months). The higher average for full-time education in Year 3 reflects the inclusion in this group of those sample members who had dropped out of school in Year 2 and then returned in Year 3 (see figure 7.1). In the university sub-sample, we also observe considerable mixing of school and work. But here full-time work is more common than part-time work, while part-time education is a bit more widespread than full-time schooling. The university members of Group 2 have moved somewhat further into the labour-force role than have their high-school counterparts.

Nevertheless it is apparent that both high-school and university members of Group 2 are in an ambiguous position somewhere between the school role occupied by the 'students' in Group 1 and the labour-force role filled by the 'workers' in Group 4 (and Group 3, by Year 3). While the students in Group 1 are postponing their exit from the educational system, these members of Group 2 appear to be in a prolonged process of exit. There have probably always been 'perpetual students' who did not want to leave school and enter the labour force. But the size of Group 2 (32 per cent of the high-school sample and 27 per cent of the university sample) suggests that we are observing a much broader phenomenon, one which is influenced more by the labour market than by the work values of youth.

Unemployment

Table 7.4 also shows that the education and age advantages held by university graduates translated into considerably less unemployment than was reported by members of the high-school sample. In both samples, 'students' (Group 1) reported somewhat less unemployment than did those who had left school or who were in the process of doing so. It is also apparent that unemployment declined from Year 2 to Year 3. Some of this is due to the general decline in unemployment between 1986 and 1987. But sample members were also a year older (with more education and work experience), and this should have improved their labour-market opportunities to an extent. Looking only at Group 4, we note that the average amount of unemployment experienced by university graduates dropped from 1.2 to 0.6 months between Year 2 and Year 3. For high-school graduates in Group 4, the decline in unemployment was minimal (from 1.5 to 1.4 months, on average). Again, this is evidence of a labour-market advantage held by older, more educated youth.

As noted earlier, these averages cover all members of each of these groups. Hence, an average of 1.4 months of unemployment could mean everyone in the group reported this amount. It could also mean that one-quarter of the group reported 5.6 months, on average, while the remainder had never been unemployed. In fact, 34 per cent of the high-school sample reported at least some unemployment in Year 2, compared to 32 per cent in Year 3. In the university sample, the comparable figures were 31 and 20 per cent. Further analysis (Krahn 1988: 63) revealed sizeable numbers who had experienced unemployment in one year of the study but not the other. Hence, a total of 48 per cent of the high-school sample and 40 per cent of the university sample reported at least one period of unemployment over the 24 months of this study.

It is clear from these statistics that a period of joblessness is part of the transition from school to work for a very large minority of both high-school and university graduates. Furthermore these periods of unemployment are often of considerable length. Considering only those who had been unemployed, high-school-sample members reported an average of 4.7 months of unemployment in Year 2 and 3.7 months in Year 3, compared to 3.4 (Year 2) and 2.9 months (Year 3) for the university sample. Thus university graduates faced a lower probability of unemployment and, if unemployed, tended to be jobless for a shorter period of time.

Table 7.5 provides a more detailed picture of unemployment among female and male respondents and in each of the three cities, displaying the percentages unemployed at the time of the survey and at some earlier time during the year in question. Given the time of year when data were collected

Table 7.5   Unemployment experience by sex and city by sample, 1985–1987*

	Year 2		Year 3	
	Unemployed in past 12 months but not now	Currently unemployed	Unemployed in past 12 months but not now	Currently unemployed
	%	%	%	%
High-school sample				
Female	21.5	13.1	20.4	11.9
Male	19.1	14.7	20.0	11.0
Edmonton	21.1	10.4	21.6	10.6
Toronto	18.6	13.5	17.2	9.5
Sudbury	20.9	24.6	20.9	17.1
Total	20.3	13.9	20.2	11.5
University sample				
Female	26.3	4.8	17.1	4.6
Male	23.0	8.6	13.5	5.1
Edmonton	23.8	6.7	16.9	5.5
Toronto	25.8	4.0	12.3	3.4
Sudbury	26.6	11.7	19.5	6.3
Total	24.9	6.4	15.6	4.8

* Year 1–2–3 panel (N = 1,905)

(May of 1986 and 1987), calculation of official unemployment rates for these samples is difficult. In May many post-secondary students are between school and summer jobs, some might be continuing in school, and others might be seeking a permanent job. Although respondents were specifically asked whether they were 'out of work and looking for work', a few of those who answered 'no' might not have wanted a job at the time. Thus, while we know how many respondents were unemployed, we cannot clearly identify those who should be excluded when calculating an official unemployment rate. Hence the percentages reported in table 7.5 are based on the total sample (or sub-sample) in question; official unemployment rates might be somwhat higher.

Gender differences in current unemployment are small in both samples in both years. The only exception to this pattern is found among university graduates in May 1986, when males were considerably more likely to be unemployed (8.6 versus 4.8 per cent). An explanation of this difference is not immediately apparent. However, there are substantial city differences in unemployment which reflect the strength of the local economies. For example, in Year 2 almost 25 per cent of the Sudbury high-school sample was unemployed, compared to a much lower rate of joblessness in the other two cities. The only exception to the pattern of greater unemployment in Sudbury is for Year 3, when only 6.3 per cent of the Sudbury university sample was unemployed compared to 5.5 per cent in Edmonton and 3.4 per cent in Toronto. This might mean that a larger percentage of the Sudbury university sample had moved away, given the limited job opportunities in this single-industry resource community.

Occupational attainment

Part-time jobs during the school term and summer jobs are a central part of North American youth culture. By the time young people graduate from high-school or university, many have accumulated considerable work experience. In this respect, the transition from education into the labour market is less abrupt in Canada and the United States than in Britain, where part-time work among students appears to be less common (Ashton 1988: 9–10). Generally student workers have been employed in a fairly distinct youth labour market, largely composed of part-time, service-sector jobs. On leaving school most of these young people would seek jobs with more career potential. But concerns about shrinking work opportunities for youth suggest the hypothesis that, today, many young people who have left school are still working in the student labour market.

Thus the first question we address in this analysis of the occupational attainment of our sample members is whether those who have left school and those who are still 'students' are occupying distinctly different labour markets. We then go on to look more closely at the occupational location of those who left school completely. Exactly what kinds of jobs are recent graduates obtaining? To what extent does a university education provide access to high status-jobs? This leads directly into a third question about gender differences in occupational attainment.

Table 7.6 compares the occupations reported by Groups 1 and 4 in our transition typology, the 'students' and the 'graduates', at the time of the Year 2 survey (May 1986). By focusing on the May 1986 occupations of Group 1, we are describing the part-time or summer jobs of students who we know returned to their studies for at least another year. While these individuals are clearly students, we recognize that we are probably describing the upper end (in terms of age) of the student labour market, since most of these youth were back in a post-secondary education institution in the fall of 1987. But, since our concern is with whether graduates leave this labour market, the omission of teen-age workers and the comparison to older graduates who have completely left school, is appropriate.

There are clear differences between the high-school and university samples in terms of participation in clerical, sales and service occupations (table 7.6). About two-thirds of the former were employed here, compared to one-third or less of the university graduates. Within each educational level there are further significant differences between the student and employee sub-groups, with relatively more students reporting clerical, sales, or service jobs.

Table 7.6   Year 2 (1986) occupations of student and employee sub-groups by education level[2]

Occupation	High school		University	
	Students[1]	Employees	Students[1]	Employees
	%	%	%	%
Managerial/administrative	0.3	0.7	2.5	10.9
Science/engineering/maths	2.2	–	8.5	23.1
Social sciences	2.5	–	7.6	5.0
Teaching	1.9	–	31.4	26.5
Medicine/health	1.6	1.3	3.4	1.9
Artistic/literary/recreational	5.1	3.3	3.4	2.2
Clerical	22.6	30.7	20.3	12.8
Sales	22.0	17.0	5.9	9.2
Service	28.0	21.6	9.3	4.5
Manual/blue collar	13.7	25.5	7.6	3.9
Total	100.0	100.0	100.0	100.0
(n)	(314)	(153)	(118)	(359)

[1] Chi-square test for differences between groups ($p < .01$).
[2] The student subgroup includes respondents who reported 7 or more months of full-time education in both 1985–6 and 1986–7, and who held a job in May 1987. The employee subgroup consists of only those panel members employed full- or part-time in May 1987 and who reported no full-time education and a maximum of 2 months' part-time education in both 1985–6 and 1986–7.

Looking more closely at the high-school sample, we observe that those who had left school, compared to continuing students, were more likely to be clerks or manual workers. Considerably fewer members of this group reported sales and service occupations. For youth with only high-school credentials, advancement into clerical and manual labour/blue-collar jobs may be the extent of potential upward mobility in the first few years after graduation. The higher concentration of continuing students in sales and service jobs (50 per cent in total) gives some indication of how much employers in the booming retail, restaurant, fast-food and personal service industries rely on part-time student help.

We also observe the early effects of post-secondary education for high-school students. What clearly sets the student and employee sub-groups apart is the small proportion (6.6 per cent) of the former who, only one year after graduating from high-school, went into science, social science and teaching jobs. These are probably the summer jobs of those high-school graduates who entered university in the fall of 1985. In contrast, nobody in the employee sub-group reported such occupations in 1986. In fact, only 5 per cent of those high-school graduates who had left school completely in 1985 were in a professional or managerial position a year later.

As for university graduates, teaching is the largest occupational group for both students and employees. Among continuing students, teaching assistantships in university would be included here but, for those who left school completely, the size of this occupational group simply reflects the large number of education graduates in the original sample. However, clerical work is a more important source of employment for the students (20.3 per cent, compared to 12.8 per cent of employees). To a lesser degree, service and manual jobs are also more common among students. In contrast, much larger proportions of the employee sub-group report jobs in management and in the professions. Jobs in these areas often provide access to internal labour markets where employers would be seeking individuals willing to work full-time, something most continuing students could not do.

We began by asking whether young people leaving school manage to move quickly out of the clerical, sales and service jobs of the student labour market they inhabited on a part-time basis while in school. For high-school graduates, the answer appears to be 'no'. Ignoring full-time/part-time status for now, we note that 69 per cent of the employees (Group 4 in our transition typology) were still reporting clerical, sales or service jobs a year after graduating. Only 5 per cent had found managerial or professional jobs. The only upward movement we observed was a small shift into clerical and manual/blue-collar positions. Only 36 per cent of the 'students' in the university sample reported clerical, sales or service jobs, compared to 27 per cent of those who had really left school. Thus the majority of university-educated youth, whether continuing in school or not, have left the student labour market as we have defined it. But it is noteworthy that more than one in four had not, despite having obtained a university degree. This is one indicator of underemployment among university-trained youth, a topic to which we return below.

Year 2 results from our panel study provided the best assessment of the student labour market. Year 3 data are more relevant to a discussion of the labour-market opportunities for those who left school completely in 1985 (Group 4 in our typology). The jobs reported in May 1987 by 142 high-school and 341 university graduates are shown in table 7.7. After up to 24 months of post-graduation labour-force participation, where in the occupational structure are these young workers located? How does their distribution compare to that of the 1987 Canadian labour force as a whole?

Comparing table 7.7 totals (females and males combined) with the 'employee' results in table 7.6, we can see that the high-school-versus-university differences observed after 12 months have been maintained a year later. Using the Canadian labour force as a bench-mark, we observe university graduates to be concentrated in teaching, science/engineering/ maths professions, and managerial/administrative jobs. This is consistent with the composition of the university sample, the majority of which was drawn from the education, engineering, science, and business faculties. Lacking the educational credentials required for managerial and professional jobs, the high-school graduates who terminated their education

Table 7.7 Year 3 (1987) occupations of respondents reporting no further education after graduating in 1985[1] by education level and gender, and occupations of employed labour force, Canada, 1987

Occupation	High-school graduates[3]			University graduates			1987 Canadian labour force[4]
	Female[2]	Male	Total[3]	Female[2]	Male	Total	
	%	%	%	%	%	%	%
Managerial/ administrative	–	3.9	2.1	10.3	20.3	14.4	11.6
Science/ engineering/ maths	–	–	–	10.3	47.1	25.2	3.4
Social sciences	1.5	–	0.7	9.4	1.4	6.2	1.9
Teaching	–	–	–	39.4	10.9	27.9	4.2
Medicine/health	1.5	–	0.7	3.0	0.7	2.1	4.8
Artistic/literary/ recreational	–	2.6	1.4	2.0	0.7	1.5	1.9
Clerical	50.0	11.8	29.6	12.3	1.4	7.9	16.5
Sales	21.2	9.2	14.8	7.9	10.9	9.1	9.4
Service	22.7	21.1	21.8	4.4	2.9	3.8	13.7
Manual/blue collar	3.0	51.3	28.9	1.0	3.6	2.1	32.6
Total	100.0	100.0	100.0	100.0	100.0	100.0	100.0
(n)	(66)	(76)	(142)	(203)	(138)	(341)	

[1] See table 7.4.
[2] Chi-square test for differences between males and females in each sample ($p < .01$).
[3] Chi-square test for differences between high-school and university samples ($p < .01$).
[4] Source: Statistics Canada, *The Labour Force*, December 1987, catalogue 71–001: 101.

tend to be found in lower-status white-collar and manual jobs. Clearly the high-school and university graduates who have made the transition from school into full-time or part-time employment inhabit very different segments of the labour market.

There are also significant gender differences documented in table 7.7, although small sample sizes require cautious generalizations. Within the high-school sample, half of the females were in clerical jobs, while half of the males were in blue-collar manual jobs. The constrained opportunities faced by the younger generation of less educated workers seem to be perpetuating traditional gender-based occupational segregation.

If we turn to the university group, the significant gender differences also reflect entrenched patterns of occupational segregation. The overrepresentation of males in science/engineering/maths occupations is primarily a function of the largely male (88 per cent) sample of engineering graduates in this study. Similarly, the large proportion of women in teaching jobs is a direct consequence of the high number of women in our sample of education graduates. But gender-influenced choice of university programme does not explain the low proportion of women in science occupations (10.3 per cent), since women and men were roughly equally represented in the original sample of science graduates. And only 10 per cent of female graduates, in contrast to 20 per cent of males, held managerial positions in 1987 – despite the fact that women made up half of the business graduates in the sample.

Underemployment

A smooth transition from school to work obviously involves more than merely finding a job; the type of job clearly matters. It is important to look beyond employment status to the match, or discrepancy, between skill requirements of available jobs and the educational credentials of new labour-market entrants (Smith 1986). We should be as concerned about underemployment and its potential social effects (Burris 1983), as about youth unemployment itself.

Underemployment can be defined and measured in a number of ways (Clogg *et al.* 1986). We have already introduced the concept in noting that 27 per cent of the university graduates who had completely left school were still employed in clerical, sales or service occupations two years later (table 7.6). Thus failure to obtain work in one's area of training is an objective indicator of a difficult transition process. So too is the desire to work full-time when only part-time work is available. Subjective indicators would include self-assessments of a job as not being related to one's education and training, or as not requiring one's skills and abilities.

In our brief assessment of underemployment, we focus on Year-3 data in order to include in our analysis at least some graduates who had spent a full two years away from school. Looking first at only those working when surveyed in spring of 1987, we find that 33.6 per cent of the high-school and 15.2 per cent of the university-sample members were in part-time jobs. As we might expect, part-time work declines as we move across the four categories of the transition typology (table 7.8). Almost equal proportions of the continuing students (Group 1) in the high school (45 per cent) and university samples (42 per cent) were employed part-time. However, for each of the next three groups, the level of part-time employment in the university sample was only about one-half of that in the high-school sample. In brief, while part-time jobs are very common among youth, young people with higher educational credentials (and who are also older) are less likely to be found in them. In addition, part-time work clearly becomes less important as youth move out of the education system.

Table 7.8   Underemployment in Year 3 (May 1987) by transition location[1] by education level

	Full-time education, both years	Education and work, both years	Education in Year 2; not Year 3	Employment both years
High-school sample				
% (of currently employed) in PT job when surveyed	44.6 (267)[2]	39.8 (236)	23.5 (136)	12.6 (143)[3]
% of those currently employed PT who would prefer FT work	53.0 (119)	53.9 (94)	75.0 (32)	76.5 (18)[3]
% of currently employed who agree that:				
My job lets me use my skills and abilities[4]	37.9 (264)	41.9 (236)	42.2 (135)	49.6 (141)
My job is directly related to my education and training[4]	21.6 (264)	22.5 (236)	22.4 (134)	27.7 (141)
University sample				
% (of currently employed) in PT job when surveyed	42.1 (76)	19.8 (197)	13.4 (127)	7.3 (342)[3]
% of those currently employed PT who would prefer FT work	36.7 (32)	65.8 (39)	82.4 (17)	80.0[3] (25)
% of currently employed who agree that:				
My job lets me use my skills and abilities[4]	59.4 (74)	60.9 (197)	66.1 (127)	65.6 (340)
My job is directly related to my education and training[4]	56.2 (73)	56.3 (197)	63.0 (127)	62.2 (341)

[1] See table 7.4.
[2] Sub-sample sizes (on which percentages are calculated) in parentheses.
[3] Differences across transition categories are statistically significant (chi-square test; $p < .05$).
[4] Respondents answered on a scale of (1) strongly disagree – strongly agree (5); scores of '4' and '5' are combined to obtain % agreeing.

On the other hand, as young people move away from the education system, those working part-time are much less likely to be doing so by choice. Along with part-time work itself becoming less common, table 7.8 also shows a much greater preference for full-time work, among those in part-time jobs, across the four transition categories. Between 75 and 82 per cent of those who had left school completely either one (Group 3) or two years earlier (Group 4) reported that they would prefer full-time work. But even among those who were much less removed from the education system (Groups 1 and 2), involuntary part-time employment was relatively frequent. Thus, the overall level of involuntary part-time work was high in this study – 58 and 64 per cent of all the part-time workers in the high-school and university samples, respectively, stated that they would prefer a full-time job. National statistics for adult populations generally show less than 30 per cent of part-time workers reporting a preference for full-time work (Krahn and Lowe 1988: 54).

A large minority (42 per cent) of employed (part-time and full-time) high-school-sample members agreed that their job let them use their skills and abilities, while only one-half as many (23.1 per cent) agreed that their job was related to their education and training. But over 60 per cent of the employed university graduates agreed with both of these statements. Thus there are large, statistically significant differences between the high-school and university samples in terms of self-assessed underemployment, particularly for the statement about the relationship between education and one's job. Within the university sample arts graduates were least likely to agree with these statements, education graduates were most likely to agree, and business, engineering and science graduates fell somewhere between (results not shown). While these faculty differences were statistically significant, gender differences (in both the high-school and university samples) were not.

Individuals who had left school completely were a little more likely to say that their skills and education were relevant to their job, but the differences across the four transition categories were not statistically significant in either sample (table 7.8). In short, we observe a considerable amount of self-assessed underemployment, particularly within the high-school sample, with only a minor tendency for this to decrease as young people make the transition from school into the labour market. Sizeable proportions of those who have been out of school for a year or two are still employed in jobs which they feel to be beneath their skills and/or training.

Participation in government-sponsored labour-market programmes

Canadian labour market policy, at both federal and provincial levels, is not particularly integrated or sweeping in its scope. It is implemented through a range of small-scale, relatively short-term programmes, aimed at specific, often disadvantaged, groups. Active labour-market policies such as those found in Scandinavia and some European countries are largely absent. With respect to youth, Canada has nothing like Sweden's Youth Team legislation or Britain's Youth Training Scheme (Lowe 1986). None the less, there are some government-sponsored training and job-creation programmes in existence, and it would be useful, for comparative purposes, to see how extensively they are used by recent high-school and university graduates.

We present only descriptive results from our data, and leave the question of whether participation in such programmes eases the transition from school to work for subsequent analyses.

In both of the follow-up surveys, respondents were asked whether they had been 'employed in a government-sponsored job creation programme at any time during the past year?' Those who answered 'Yes' were asked to name the programme. Only a small minority of the total high-school sample reported such involvement in either Year 2 (7.7 per cent) or Year 3 (11.1 per cent). Relatively more of the university sample had participated in Year 2 (17.1 per cent) but, by Year 3, only 10.3 per cent reported employment in a government-sponsored programme.

Part of the greater university participation in Year 2 can be traced to the several dozen education graduates in the Edmonton sub-sample who took part in the Alberta Teacher Internship Program during that year. This programme was introduced as a response to a sudden decline in demand for teachers in Alberta, and lasted only for a short while. Thus it resembled many other Canadian job-creation strategies, introduced to solve a pressing problem rather than as part of some larger, long-term training and labour-market adjustment strategy. Such an approach means that high-unemployment areas are more likely to receive government funding for job-creation programmes. It also helps explain why, in both years of the follow-up study, Toronto respondents were significantly less likely to report participating in such programmes, compared to Edmonton and Sudbury sample members. Obviously Toronto's booming economy would also provide more jobs for recent graduates, and so reduce participation in whatever job-creation programmes existed.

The teacher intern programme, designed to provide on-the-job experience for those education graduates who had been unable to find a permanent position, was exceptional in that it was a full-year programme. About three-quarters (76 per cent) of participants in government-sponsored job-creation programmes in Year 3 reported four months or less of involvement (the length of time question was not asked in Year 2). Summer programmes aimed at providing jobs for students are very common in Canada. In this study, for example, the Alberta government's Student Temporary Employment Program (STEP) accounted for about one-quarter of all the participation reported by respondents in both years.

A variety of federal programmes such as SEED (Student Employment Experience Program), which had employed several dozen sample members, were also listed. Only a handful of respondents reported participation in the Katimavik community service programme which the federal government cancelled during the course of the study (Krahn and Lowe 1987). A considerable number mentioned Canada Employment and Immigration (CEIC), without specifying a particular programme; this suggests that some might have been including visits to CEIC employment centres in their answer. Hence, our low estimates of participation in government-sponsored job creation programmes may still be too high.

Finally, only two respondents in Year 2 and one in Year 3 mentioned apprenticeships, although it is possible that a few of the high-school graduates might have entered an apprenticeship and not reported it in response to this question. While apprenticeship systems are well developed in Germany, and to a lesser extent in Britain, they play a very small part in the school–work transition in Canada, despite chronic shortages of workers in some skilled trades.

The general impression our survey results give then is that there are a limited number of government-sponsored job-creation schemes in Canada, that those that exist are often put in place to solve an immediate problem rather than as part of some larger training strategy, that many are intended to provide summer employment for students, and that relatively few high-school and university graduates participate in such schemes. In addition, these results highlight the fact that apprenticeships are uncommon in Canada.

Changing values and attitudes?

We began with a discussion of what sample members thought high-schools and universities should be teaching, but then moved away from such subjective issues to focus on the education and labour-market experiences of respondents. With the insights provided by these analyses we can now return to consider some other work and school-related attitudes. More specifically, we analyse work values, attitudes toward new technologies, job-entitlement beliefs, and attributions of blame for poverty and youth unemployment.

The panel design of this study provides the opportunity to examine attitudinal change over a 24-month period of transition, something few other studies of youth values can do. Our earlier findings also highlighted the importance of distinguishing between those who left school and those who stayed on. Hence, in considering attitude change, we compare the 'students' and the 'employees' identified in our typology of transition (table 7.4, Groups 1 and 4). The two groups which combined work and school over the 24 months of this study are omitted from tables 7.9 to 7.11. With few exceptions, their responses reflected their middle status in the transition continuum. In addition, distinct differences between the work and education experiences of high-school- and university-sample members and evidence of some gender differences strongly suggest that gender and education level should be controlled in these analyses.

There has been relatively little research on the transition from school to work in Canada. Consequently, the analyses reported below are largely exploratory, although a few general hypotheses do help us decide which of the many findings to discuss. The sub-sample differences clearly point to some interesting areas of further research. However, the overall levels of

Table 7.9 Change in work values (1985–1987) by transition location[1] by education level by gender

		Percentage agreeing[2]			
		Full-time Education both years		Employment both years	
		1985	1987	1985	1987
If I could earn $15 an hour, I would take any job					
High-school	F	39.3	30.3	55.8	36.4
	M	49.4	33.9	55.2	40.2
	T	44.0	31.0	55.5	38.4
University	F	12.2	7.3	25.9	13.3
	M	17.5	10.3	30.3	11.0
	T	14.4	8.5	27.7	12.4
I am not ready for a long-term commitment to a job					
High-school	F	26.4	41.8	18.4	10.4
	M	33.3	47.1	18.6	16.1
	T	29.6	44.3	18.5	13.4
University	F	7.3	8.5	13.8	15.1
	M	16.1	22.4	15.2	14.5
	T	10.9	14.3	14.4	14.8
I would do just about any kind of work if it was a steady job					
High-school	F	12.0	11.9	28.9	16.9
	M	17.3	12.1	19.8	21.8
	T	14.5	12.0	24.1	19.5
University	F	8.5	1.2	12.0	10.1
	M	10.5	6.9	6.2	4.1
	T	9.4	3.6	9.7	7.7
I would rather collect welfare than work at a job I don't like					
High-school	F	7.5	4.5	7.9	6.5
	M	8.7	8.6	10.5	8.0
	T	8.0	6.4	9.3	7.3
University	F	0.0	2.4	3.2	2.3
	M	1.8	5.2	5.5	2.8
	T	0.7	3.6	4.1	2.5

[1] See table 7.4.
[2] Respondents answered on a scale of (1) strongly disagree – strongly agree (5); scores of 4 and 5 are combined.
F = Female, M = Male, T = Total

agreement with each of the attitude measures are also important, since they allow crude comparisons to the findings from the British transition study discussed elsewhere in this volume.

Work values

Table 7.9 displays the percentage of sample sub-groups, distinguished by education level, gender and transition location, agreeing in 1985 and again in 1987 with each of four work-value statements. These measures, replications or modifications of items used in a 1974 national study of work values (Burstein *et al*. 1975: 91–3), are intended to index, in order, instrumentalism, general job commitment, desire for job security, and selectivity regarding jobs.

We would expect instrumentalism, an orientation to work as a means to an end, as primarily a source of income, to be higher among those who left school than among those who continued their education. Individuals motivated primarily by money would, we presume, be more inclined to leave school and look for a full-time job. Those seeking intrinsically rewarding work would be more likely to continue in school to obtain the credentials needed for entry into such a job or career. Table 7.9 shows differences in the predicted direction, for both the high-school and university samples. Just prior to graduation (Year 1), 44 per cent of the high-school students who eventually went on in school agreed that they would take any job that paid $15 an hour. But 55.5 per cent of their peers who left school agreed. In the Year-1 university sample, almost twice as many of those leaving school (27.7 per cent), as compared to those who stayed (14.4 per cent), agreed with this statement.

The much lower level of agreement with this sentiment in the university sample might be explained similarly, since university graduates, by definition, chose (four years earlier) to continue in school. However, for many university graduates, $15 an hour might be less than what they believed they could earn. Hence disagreement with this measure could merely signify a higher self-assessed earning potential. More interesting, perhaps, is the observation that for all sub-groups in both the high-school and university samples, agreement with this statement declined between 1985 and 1987. Intrinsic job rewards may become more important as young people grow older and more experienced, or $15 an hour may become less attractive, or both may be occurring. Whatever the explanation, there is evidence here of a maturational effect.

A large majority of both the high-school and university sample members were ready for a long-term commitment to a job (table 7.9). In only one sample sub-group – Year-1 high-school graduates who remained in school – did more than a small minority (29.6 per cent) agree that they were not ready for such a commitment. Two years later, even more members of this group (44.3 per cent) were expressing unwillingness to think about work in a long-term way. But, with the exception of these high-school graduates who chose to continue their education, it appears that most young people are ready and willing to make the transition from school to work. Hence, it would be inappropriate to argue that a prolonged transition from school to work for large numbers of youth is due, primarily, to their unwillingness to commit themselves to an adult work role.

In Year 1 of the study relatively few respondents agreed that they would be willing to do almost any job so long as it provided security. Two years later, the percentages had declined even further. The 'students' and 'employees' in the university sample differed very little in this regard but, in the high-school sample, those who had left school were more likely to agree (24.1 versus 14.5 per cent in Year 1; 19.5 versus 12.0 per cent in Year 2). Despite this, the overall impression is that, while job security might be a serious concern among youth, it has not become so serious as to override all other considerations about a job. On the other hand, only a handful of respondents in either sample admitted that they would 'collect welfare' before taking a job they did not like. Thus, there is also little evidence of young people being highly 'picky' about the jobs they would take.

Finally, there are some gender differences in work values observed in table 7.9, but they do not reflect a systematic pattern. In some cases they are found only among the continuing students (e.g. instrumentalism among high-school sample members in Year 1). In others the gender differences reverse when comparing continuing students and those who left the education system (e.g. the importance of a steady job for Year 1 high-school students). Thus the most appropriate general conclusion would probably be that gender is not a major determinant of work values. However, our earlier observation of significantly different labour-market outcomes for female graduates suggests that further analyses of change in such values, as a consequence of differential labour-market experiences, might be a fruitful area of research.

Attitudes to new technologies

There is no doubt that the technological revolution now transforming the workplace will have profound implications for the next generation of workers. It is therefore important to examine the attitudes of recent graduates toward automation, computers and new technologies in general. The three items used to measure receptivity to acquiring computer knowledge and skills are adapted from Fife-Schaw *et al.* (1986). Table 7.10 contains the responses of those high-school- and university-sample members who remained in the education system and those who left immediately after graduation (Groups 1 and 4 in the typology in Table 7.4), broken down by gender. Year-1 results for these items cannot be provided since these questions about new technologies were only included in the Year-2 and Year-3 questionnaires. Since very little change in response to these items was observed between Year 2 and Year 3 (results not shown), only Year 3 data are presented.

Table 7.10   Attitudes to new technology by transition location[1] by education level by gender, 1987

		Percentage agreeing[2]			
		Full-time education both years		Employment both years	
		High-school	University	High-school	University
I want to learn more	Female	70.6	84.1	56.6	74.8
about how to use	Male	66.1	75.4	56.3	79.7
computers	Total	68.6	80.6	56.5	76.7
It is not worth the	Female	5.0	3.7	10.5	6.0
effort to learn	Male	6.9	7.0	2.3	2.1
about new	Total	5.8	5.0	6.2	4.4
technology					
I think training in a	Female	77.1	67.1	70.1	65.1
new technology	Male	73.6	77.2	71.3	82.8
would help me in	Total	75.4	71.2	70.7	72.2
the future					

[1] See table 7.4.
[2] Respondents answered on a scale of (1) strongly disagree – strongly agree (5); scores of 4 and 5 are combined.

The main conclusion drawn from this table is that Canadian youth, both high-school and university graduates, and both those who chose to stay in school and those who left, are highly receptive to new technologies. A large majority stated that they wished to learn more about using computers and they believed that training in new technologies would be of value to them in the future. Very few agreed that it was not worth the effort to learn about new technology.

Within both samples, continuing students were more likely to want to learn more about computers than were those who had left the education system, but the difference between these two groups was larger among high-school graduates. A larger proportion of university-sample members compared to high-school graduates agreed with this statement as well. However, greater university receptivity to new technologies in general (first and second statements in table 7.10) was not as apparent. Again, there are some gender differences in this table, but they do not form a single, inter-pretable pattern. In short, the major finding here is that willingness to work with new technologies and recognition of the value of training in this area are both widespread among recent high-school and university graduates in Canada. Analyses reported elsewhere (Lowe and Krahn forthcoming) demonstrate that a large majority of both the high-school and university samples had received some computer training while in school.

Job-entitlement beliefs

Given the degree to which Canadian youth value higher education and believe in the link between education and career success, we would expect widespread commitment to the idea that good jobs are due to those who work hard and train for them. Furthermore, we would predict feelings of job entitlement to be more pronounced among those who had invested, or were investing, more time in school. Thus, agreement with such statements should be more common among university than among high-school sample members, and among continuing students within each education level. Also, we would expect those who stayed in school to express higher levels of job entitlement in Year 3 than they did at the outset of the study.

These hypotheses are tested in table 7.11 where responses to two general measures of job entitlement are cross-tabulated by transition location, education level and gender. The two statements are modified versions of items originally developed by Derber (1978). The first has a universalistic perspective: everyone has the right to a job commensurate with their education. The second expresses a more individualistic and meritocratic view: only those who worked hard in school deserve a good job.

At the outset of the study (Year 1), a large majority of the high-school sample expressed agreement with these statements, compared to slightly less than one-half of the university graduates (table 7.11). Thus, as expected, entitlement beliefs are common among graduating Canadian students. But our hypothesis about university graduates being more committed to such beliefs is not supported. We predicted a greater sense of entitlement among those respondents who continued in school. This was the case in the high-school sample where, in both Year 1 and Year 3, about 10 per cent more 'students' than 'employees' agreed with each of these statements. But, in the university sample, this pattern of differences between 'students' and 'employees' was evident for only the more individualistic entitlement measure, and only in Year 3.

Finally, we hypothesized that continuing students would be even more convinced of their job entitlement after two more years in school. Instead, the percentage of continuing students who agreed with this statement dropped between Year 1 and Year 3, in both samples. Entitlement beliefs also declined between Year 1 and Year 3 among those who had completely left the education system. Thus, whatever the educational choices made, there is evidence that entitlement beliefs decline as young people grow older (this would also account for the observed university–high-school differences).

These longitudinal results show a large majority of young people leaving high-school believing that an investment in higher education will pay off in a good job. Those who continue on in school are even more convinced of this.

Table 7.11   Change in job entitlement beliefs and explanations of poverty/unemployment (1985–1987) by transition location[1] by education level by gender

| | | Percentage agreeing[2] | | | |
| | | Full-time education both years | | Employment both years | |
		1985	1987	1985	1987
Everyone has the right to the kind of job that their education and training has prepared them for					
High-school	F	84.1	76.3	72.4	63.6
	M	75.9	65.3	73.6	63.2
	T	80.3	71.2	73.0	63.4
University	F	56.8	49.4	52.5	44.5
	M	35.1	36.2	42.7	31.3
	T	47.8	43.9	48.6	39.2
If someone has worked hard in school, they are entitled to a good job					
High-school	F	71.6	55.5	56.6	42.1
	M	69.8	47.1	63.2	40.2
	T	70.8	51.6	60.1	41.1
University	F	47.6	42.7	51.6	35.8
	M	47.4	37.9	41.3	25.5
	T	47.5	40.7	47.5	31.7
Young people are too choosy about jobs they will take[3]					
High-school	F	52.0	54.8	64.4	67.5
	M	52.9	61.5	53.8	64.4
	T	52.4	57.9	58.8	65.6
University	F	50.0	39.0	39.6	45.4
	M	41.4	50.9	43.8	58.3
	T	46.4	43.9	41.3	50.6
Most poor people are poor because of their own lack of effort					
High-school	F	21.4	24.6	27.0	37.7
	M	29.9	37.4	29.1	33.3
	T	25.3	30.5	28.1	35.3
University	F	16.3	12.2	13.4	21.9
	M	15.5	12.3	18.3	28.5
	T	15.9	12.3	15.3	24.5

[1] See table 7.4.
[2] Respondents answered on a scale of (1) strongly disagree – strongly agree (5); scores of 4 and 5 are combined.
[3] In Year 1 (1987), this statement was part of a series preceded by the statement 'Youth unemployment is high in Canada because. . .'. In Year 3 (1987) it was used alone and without the introductory statement.
F = Female, M = Male, T = Total

But with age comes more job-search experience, more knowledge of the labour market and of how jobs are obtained, and a more realistic assessment of one's own chances of finding a good job. Our results show that many of these young people had been unemployed at some time. They also show substantial numbers working part-time while desiring a full-time job, or working in jobs where their education was of little relevance. Thus, for quite a few sample members, labour-market experiences contradicted beliefs that 'if someone has worked hard in school they are entitled to a good job'.

Faced with such contradictions, some young people might still hang on to their beliefs, although some kind of psychological reaction might be expected. Resentment, anger and cynicism are among the possibilities. Derber's (1978) study of job-entitlement beliefs among unemployed youth focused on the potential for political radicalism. Subsequent analyses of these panel data will address these possibilities, but the results presented here highlight a very different outcome. They suggest that a common response to the realization that not everyone gets the job for which they trained is to dispense with the belief that one is entitled to such a job.

Explanations of unemployment and poverty

In a previous analysis of explanations of youth unemployment among Year-1 Edmonton-sample members (Lowe *et al*. 1988), we noted the prevalence of both individualistic and structural explanations. In table 7.11 we compare the responses of the various sub-samples, over time, to one of the more individualistic explanations: 'Young people are too choosy about jobs they will take.' Over half of the high-school sample agreed with this statement, compared to somewhat fewer but still a very large minority of university graduates. More important, however, is the greater endorsement of this belief in Year 3 than in Year 1, particularly for those sample members who had completely left school. Additional labour-market experience appears to be associated with more individualistic explanations of how the labour market operates, and of why some participants are less successful than others.

Table 7.11 also displays responses to a very individualistic explanation of poverty in general, adapted from previous studies of this topic (Feagin 1975; Feather 1974). Compared to the explanation of youth unemployment, there was considerably less agreement with this statement which blames the poor for their own predicament. Over one-quarter of the high-school graduates agreed, while university-sample members were less willing to express such a sentiment. But once again, the change over time (more agreement in Year 3), especially for those who had not continued in school, attracts our attention. While not all that large, this change supports our observation that more labour-market experience may lead to greater endorsement of individualistic explanations of how the labour market really works.

In summing up, our exploratory analyses suggest that Canadian youth place great value on higher education, that many leave high school believing that higher education entitles one to a good job, and that, in time, such beliefs are undermined. We have also observed that many of today's graduates encounter difficulties in their transition from school to work. The decline in entitlement beliefs may well be a consequence. However, none of this appears to lead to a questioning of the value of higher education itself. Instead, young people may simply become more individualistic in their assessment of how the labour market operates, reasoning that education is a prerequisite for access to better jobs while individual effort distinguishes those who finally get them from those who fail.

The transition to adulthood

We conclude with a brief look at one last aspect of the transition process, the taking on of adult relationships and family roles. Moving from school to work requires more than merely finding a job consistent with one's educational qualifications and occupational aspirations. It is also linked to a young person's developing an independent adult status. Gainful employment is a prerequisite to leaving the family home, setting up one's own household, moving into new relationships and, perhaps, raising a family. While we do not fully explore these relational dimensions of the transition process in this paper, some of the more pertinent findings from our study are summarized below.

Virtually all (96.4 per cent) of the high-school-sample members had been living with their parents when first surveyed in May 1985. Two years later (May, 1987) these living arrangements had changed a bit, but 81.6 per cent still lived with their parents. In contrast, a larger proportion of the university-sample members had established independent living arrangements. In May 1985 48.1 per cent reported living with their parents. This had dropped to 33.1 per cent two years later. While fewer university graduates remained at home with their parents, one in three still seems high, given that these sample members averaged over 25 years of age in Year 3 of the study. But these findings are consistent with the national trend in the 1980s for growing numbers of young people to prolong living with their parents (Boyd and Pryor 1988).

A variety of factors can influence the decision to move out and set up one's own residence. Obviously a respondent's financial situation had a direct bearing on his or her living situation. Those with full-time jobs were more likely to live on their own; conversely, full-time student status was associated with continued dependence on one's parents. Housing costs must also be taken into account. A much higher proportion of Toronto respondents in either sample lived with their parents in all three years. Thus in May 1987, only 21.1 per cent of university-sample members in Sudbury and 25.9 per cent of those in Edmonton lived with their parents, while in Toronto the comparable figure was 47.2 per cent. This comes as no surprise, given that Toronto had the most expensive accommodation in Canada at the time.

In May 1985 all sample members were living in one of the three cities surveyed. Over the next 24 months, university graduates were much more likely to have moved to other cities to find employment or to obtain further education. Over 40 per cent had left. Sudbury-sample members were most likely to have moved (78 per cent were no longer in Sudbury), while Toronto graduates were least mobile (76 per cent were still in the Toronto area), reflecting the relative number of job opportunities for university graduates in the three labour markets covered by the study. As for high-school sample members, 91.9 per cent were still in the same city. Younger, and more likely to still be in school, this group had stayed much closer to home. However, even within this group, Sudbury-sample members were most likely to have left their home community (24 per cent had moved elsewhere).

In the relatively young high-school sample, we find little evidence of marriage or cohabitation (with someone of the opposite sex) throughout the 24 months of the study. Fully 93.2 per cent of this group of high-school graduates were still single in 1987. Those who had left school completely were more likely to have moved into a permanent relationship but, even within this group, only 12.4 per cent were married or living with someone else. Among the older, university-educated respondents, movement into a permanent relationship was somewhat more common with 32 per cent reporting that they were married or living together in 1987. Again, those who had completely terminated their education were somewhat more likely to be in this group (38 per cent).

In sum, despite some evidence of prolonged dependence on parents for accommodation (at least in Toronto), many of the university graduates in this study were finding jobs, moving out of their parents' home, and entering new relationships. Precisely how these major changes in the life course of young adults may be delayed by specific labour-market experiences, such as underemployment or unemployment, or by the decision to obtain more education, is a question still to be addressed with these data.

Summary and conclusions

We began by questioning whether the process of transition from school to work for Canadian youth might have been affected by changes in the global and national economies, and by patterns of industrial restructuring. More specifically, has labour-market entry become more difficult for youth? Have institutions which traditionally bridged the gap between school and work broken down, as observers of some other Western industrial economies suggest? Our exploratory analysis of data from a 24-month panel study of high-school and university graduates in three Canadian cities provides some general answers.

We found a remarkably high proportion of both high-school and university graduates in the three cities continuing in the education system, many in quest of a first or second university degree. Gender seemed to have little bearing on these educational plans, but socio-economic background did influence the decision to go on in school. Job and career-related reasons were given by the majority of both men and women for staying in school. However, these data do not show young people staying in school because they believe they will not find a job. Instead, it appears as if a common response to a tight labour market is a decision to get more education in order to improve one's labour-market opportunities.

Among the universty sample members, only one in three stated that their education had prepared them adequately for the job market. But willingness to criticize the system was not accompanied by any apparent undermining of belief in the labour-market value of higher education. When asked about what high-schools and universities should be teaching, a significant minority mentioned job-related concerns but roughly equal numbers also favoured a more general, liberal-arts type of education. Thus, while there was not a consensus over the direction in which the education system should be moving, the vast majority of these young people continued to believe in the value of higher education and to see it as the key to career success. In fact, many were investing in even more education.

The experiences of previous generations have given rise to an outmoded image of the transition from school to work: having completed school, successive cohorts of graduates, diploma in hand, enter the labour market seeking work. Our data suggest a much more gradual transition process. Very large numbers of young people work part-time while attending school. Many continue on for further education, either full-time or part-time. Some change programmes or go to different types of schools. Some drop out for a year and then return to school. In short, we believe that the transition from school to work has become a much more prolonged affair.

Our analytic strategy was to construct a four-group transition typology, with the two extreme groups representing full-time students and full-time labour-force participants. The middle groups contained those sample members who reported a mixture of work and school over the 24 months of the follow-up study. A careful look at the amount of work, school and unemployment reported by these four groups revealed the degree to which work and school roles were blurred for a very large proportion of young people.

These data show that most high-school graduates who left school completely were still working in the same kind of clerical, sales and service jobs held by students attending school. University graduates, on the other hand, were much more likely to have left this rather distinct 'student labour market', although a sizeable minority were still in such jobs two years after leaving school. Thus higher education does lead to improved occupational chances, something which most of these young people appeared to believe. But our data also highlight continuing gender differences in occupational outcomes, in both the high-school and university samples. Young women are no longer underrepresented in higher education (although fewer go on to graduate studies), but there is still a distinct tendency whereby gender-influenced educational choices and post-graduation hiring patterns translate into gender-based occupational segregation.

Youth unemployment was a major concern when this study began but had declined somewhat by Year 3. While our survey did not uncover huge numbers of unemployed youth, we did find that almost one-half of the sample members had experienced unemployment at some point over the 24 months of the follow-up study. Those who had been unemployed, particularly high-school-sample members, reported fairly lengthy periods without a job. High-school students were more likely to report involuntary joblessness and, as we would expect, Sudbury high-school-sample members encountered the most difficulty in finding a job.

Our data suggest that underemployment may come to be the more serious problem for Canadian youth. For example, about one in four of the university graduates who had left school completely were still reporting clerical, sales or service occupations in Year 3 of the study. At the same time, one-third of the employed high-school graduates and 15 per cent of the employed university graduates were in part-time jobs. Over 60 per cent of these labour-force participants stated that they would prefer a full-time job. A large minority of the university graduates and well over half of the high-school sample members claimed that their job was not related to their education and did not make use of their skills and abilities. In other words, using both objective and subjective indicators, we observe a considerable degree of underemployment among these young people, although university graduates were less likely to be in this position.

Young people appear to be prolonging their exit from school, moving in and out of programmes and educational institutions and simultaneously filling student and work roles. Many are encountering difficulty finding satisfactory full-time work after leaving school. At the same time, we detect some evidence of prolonged dependence on parents, a trend influenced by extended periods of formal education, labour-market-entry problems and, in some locations, the high cost of housing.

In short, the process of transition from school to work appears to be changing. Unlike the situation in many European countries, there are few large-scale job-creation or training schemes directed at youth in Canada. Our results reflect the short-term nature of such programmes, many of which provide mainly summer employment for continuing students. There are also very few apprenticeship programmes in this country. Thus the problems of transition from school to work are not significantly reduced by government-sponsored job-creation or training programmes.

The behaviour patterns of youth in the 1970s led some observers to suggest that, for many, the first few years after leaving school were a 'moratorium' period of youthful adventure, experimentation, and shopping around in the job market (Osterman 1980:26; Denton *et al.* 1980). This no longer appears to be the case. If anything, the prolonged transition from school to work for recent cohorts of graduates reflects an 'involuntary moratorium'. We find young people expressing a serious and immediate commitment to both higher education and employment. While more are staying on in school, much of this behaviour is a response to the belief, based on experience, that good jobs are harder to get. As for those who have left school and are still not settled into the career of their choice, it is certainly not for lack of trying. Underemployment is seldom chosen.

The problem is certainly not one of work values and attitudes. Our data show a high level of commitment to work, a willingness to learn about new technologies, and a very strong belief in the value of higher education. Job-entitlement beliefs are high among recent high-school graduates. But they clearly diminish over time, probably because of problematic experiences in the labour market. Hence, we are not observing a situation where young labour-market entrants are overly choosy about the jobs they will take.

Assessing the growing labour-market problems faced by British youth, Willis (1986: 156) argues that there is now 'an enforced decoupling of the education system and the labour market'. He and others basically argue that the institutions which traditionally linked school and work have collapsed. We cannot say the same for Canada. While the graduates we studied obviously face constraints and barriers, many following a long and circuitous route out of the classroom into a job, there is little evidence that the school–work transition has completely broken down. Rather, the process has been prolonged and made more difficult. And to the extent that current trends towards more part-time job creation in lower-level service sectors continue, the chances of eventually entering a rewarding career path may have been reduced. But the majority of Canadian youth continue to believe in higher education, and to act accordingly. This belief, reinforced by a very strong individualistic value system that identifies higher education as the 'way to get ahead', may be an important stabilizing factor.

Notes

1 We wish to acknowledge the financial support of the Social Sciences and Humanities Research Council of Canada, the Alberta and Ontario governments, the Solicitor General Canada, the cities of Edmonton and Toronto, the University of Alberta and Laurentian University, and the Royal Bank of Canada. We thank Karen Hughes, Scott McLean and Lindsay Redpath for their research assistance.

References

Anderson, D. S. and Blakers, C. (eds.) (1983). *Youth, Transition and Social Research*. Canberra, Australian National University Press.
Anisef, P. J., Baichman, E. Northrup, D., Rhyne, D. and Tibert, J. (1986). *Models and Methodologies Appropriate to the Study of Outcomes of Schooling in Ontario's Multicultural Society*. Ontario, Ministry of Education.
Anisef, P. J., Paasche, G. and Turrittin, A. H. (1980). *Is the Die Cast? Educational Achievement of Ontario Youth: A Six-Year Follow-up of the Critical Juncture High School Students*. Toronto, Ontario Ministry of Colleges and Universities.
Ashton, D. (1988) 'Sources of variation in labour market segmentation: a comparison

of youth labour markets in Canada and Britain', *Work, Employment and Society*, 2: 1–24.

Ashton, D. N. and Maguire, M. J. (1986). 'Young adults in the labour market', Research paper No. 55, Department of Employment. London, HMSO.

Boyd, M. and Pryor, E. (1988). 'The cluttered nest: the living arrangements of young Canadian adults.' Paper presented at a joint session of the Canadian Population Society and the Canadian Sociology and Anthropology Association, Windsor, Ontario.

Braungart, R. G. and Braungart, M. M. (1986). 'Youth problems and policies in the 1980s: some multinational comparisons', *International Sociology* 1: 359–80.

Brown, P. and Ashton, D. N. (eds.) (1987). *Education, Unemployment and Labour Markets*. London, Falmer Press.

Burris, V. (1983). 'The social and political consequences of overeducation', *American Sociological Review* 48 (4): 454–67.

Burstein, M., Tienharra, N., Hewson, P. and Warrander, B. (1975). *Canadian Work Values: Findings of a Work Ethic Survey and a Job Satisfaction Survey*. Ottawa, Information Canada.

Clark, W., Laing, M. and Rechnitzer, E. (1986). *The Class of 82: Summary Report on the Findings of the 1984 National Survey of the Graduates of 1982*. Ottawa, Supply & Services Canada (catalogue #S2-168/1986E).

Clogg, C. C., Sullivan, T. A. and Mutchler, F. E. (1986). 'Measuring underemployment and inequality in the work force', *Social Indicators Research*, 18: 375–93.

Dayton, C. W. (1981). 'The young person's job search, insights from a study', *Journal of Counselling Psychology*, 28: 321–33.

Denton, F. T., Robb, A. L. and Spencer, B. G. (1980). *Unemployment and Labour Force Behaviour of Young People: Evidence from Canada and Ontario*. Toronto, University of Toronto Press.

Derber, C. (1978). 'Unemployment and the entitled worker: job entitlement and radical political attitudes among the youthful unemployed', *Social Problems*, 26: 26–37.

Education in Canada: A Statistical Review for 1985–86 (1987). Ottawa: Supply and Services Canada.

Feagin, J. R. (1975). *Subordinating the Poor*. Englewood Cliffs, NJ, Prentice Hall.

Feather, N. T. (1974). 'Explanations of poverty in Australian and American samples: the person, society or fate?', *Australian Journal of Psychology*, 34: 309–23.

Fife-Schaw, C., Breakwell, G. M., Devereaux, J. and Lee, T. R. (1986). 'Attitudes to new technology: social and psychological correlates', paper presented at the British Psychological Society Annual Conference, University of Sheffield.

Foot, D. K. and Li, J. C. (1986). 'Youth employment in Canada: a misplaced priority?' *Canadian Public Policy*, 12: 499–506.

Gaskell, J. (1987). 'Education and the labour market: the logic of vocationalism', in T. Wotherspoon (ed.), *The Political Economy of Canadian Schooling*. Toronto, Methuen.

Greenberger, E. and Steinberg, L. (1986). *When Teenagers Work*. New York, Basic Books.

Grootings, P. (1986). 'Sociology of youth and sociology of work and the study of transition from school to work'. Paper presented at the XI World Congress of Sociology, New Delhi, India.

Hartmann, J. (1987). 'Transition from school to work: the Swedish case 1976 to 1985.' Research report, Department of Sociology, University of Uppsala, vol. 4.

Heberlein, T. A. and Baumgartner, R. (1978). 'Factors affecting response rates to mailed questionnaires: a quantitative analysis of the published literature'. *American Sociological Review*, 43: 447–62.

Heinz, W. R. (1987). 'The transition from school to work in crisis: coping with threatening unemployment', *Journal of Adolescent Research*, 2: 127–41.

Hogan, D. P. and Astone, N. M. (1986). 'The transition to adulthood', *Annual Review of Sociology*, 12: 109–30.

Krahn, H. (1988). *A Study of the Transition from School to Work in Three Canadian Cities: Research Design, Response Rates and Descriptive Results*. Population Research Laboratory, University of Alberta.

Krahn, H. and Lowe, G. S. (1987). 'Youth action', *Policy Options Politique*, June: 13–14. (1988) *Work, Industry and Canadian Society*. Scarborough, Nelson Canada.

Looker, D. (1985). 'Fuelling a gender-segregated labour market: gender and the transition from school to work'. *Transitions to Work*. Winnipeg: Institute for Social and Economic Research, University of Manitoba.

Lowe, G. S. (1986). 'Job line for youth', *Policy Options Politique*, June: 3–6.

Lowe, G. S. and Krahn, H. (forthcoming) 'Computer skills and use among high school and university graduates', *Canadian Public Policy*.

Lowe, G. S., Krahn, H. and Tanner, J. (1988). 'Young people's explanations of unemployment', *Youth & Society*, 19: 227–49.

Mason, G. (1985). 'Introduction', *Transitions to Work*. Winnipeg: Institute for Social and Economic Research, University of Manitoba.

Osterman, P. (1980). *Getting Started: The Youth Labor Market*. Cambridge, MA, MIT Press.

Picot, W. G., Wannell, T. and Lynd, D. (1987). *The Changing Labour Market for Postsecondary Graduates 1976–1984*. Ottawa, Supply & Services Canada (catalogue # 89-518).

Porter, J., Porter, M. and Blishen, B. (1982) *Stations and Callings: Making it Through the School System*. Toronto, Methuen.

Radwanski, G. (1987). *Ontario Study of the Relevance of Education, and the Issue of Dropouts*. Toronto, Ontario Ministry of Education.

Roberts, K., Dench, S. and Richardson, D. (1987). *The Changing Structure of Youth Labour Markets*. Research paper no. 59, Department of Employment. London: HMSO.

Senate of Canada (1986). *Youth: A Plan of Action*. Report of the Special Senate Committee on Youth.

Smith, H. (1986). 'Overeducation and underemployment: an agnostic review', *Sociology of Education*, 59: 85–99.

Statistics Canada, *The Daily* (catalogue # 11-001E).

Walker, S. and Barton, L. (eds.) (1986). *Youth Unemployment and Schooling*. Milton Keynes, Open University Press.

Willis, P. (1986). 'Unemployment: the final inequality'. *British Journal of Sociology of Education*, 7: 155–69.

8

Transitions to work: results from a longitudinal study of young people in four British labour markets[1]

John Bynner

Context

Fifteen years ago, the transition from school to adult employment in the UK was relatively straightforward. Well over half the population left school at 16, and most went on to full-time jobs. Of those staying on at school, about two-thirds pursued the academic route (GCE A level) with a view to higher education, and the others went into further-education colleges to take vocational courses. Unemployment was virtually unknown; nor were there any government training schemes. Training occurred either on the job through apprenticeship schemes – overwhelmingly the province of boys – or off the job through day-release at colleges. Advanced qualifications, however, were rare. Only 10 per cent of the National Child Development Study 1958 cohort (Fogelman 1985) who were 23 in 1981, had obtained a degree, and only 7 per cent a vocational qualification; 26 per cent had not obtained any qualification at all.

Over the following years, the transformation of this situation has been dramatic. The collapse of the youth labour market both in the UK and in other European countries is one feature of the change which has been well documented (e.g. Junankar 1987; Gray and King 1986; Ashton *et al.* 1987). It has been estimated that in the mid 1980s, 12 million young people under the age of 25 in EEC countries were unemployed. In Britain alone, the percentage in full-time jobs steadily declined from 71 per cent in 1975 to 37 per cent in 1988: from 1982–6 the percentage of unemployed was constant at 12 per cent per annum (DES 1989).

The response of the government has been a series of initiatives, designed to raise skill levels and make young people more employable (DES,1981). Outside school, for the substantial proportion who leave the education system at 16, traditional apprenticeships, youth jobs and unemployment are being replaced by the Youth Training Scheme (YTS). This started as a one-year scheme aimed at reducing youth unemployment and could be entered either through an employer or through a government-accredited agency such as a local authority. Now it has evolved into a two-year scheme based exclusively in employment. With an investment of £1000 million per annum it is designed to equip the whole school-leaver population – 600,000 in all – with the new skills that industry needs.

Much of the inspiration for YTS comes from the three-year West German apprenticeship scheme – a comprehensive system of employer-based training which similarly targets the whole school-leaver population, but which has recently come under increasing strain (Heinz 1987). The difference in the government's eyes is that YTS is concerned more with imparting 'generic' skills, such as use of new technology and 'enterprise', of value to employers generally, rather than the more narrow occupationally based skills associated with the traditional apprenticeship – 'time serving' as one White Paper (DES 1986) describes the British version.

To justify the investment of effort and to validate the claims of YTS, a comprehensive reappraisal of vocational qualifications – currently over 200 – has also been undertaken and a National Council for Vocational Qualifications (NCVQ) set up to co-ordinate and standardize them (DES 1986). The follow-through back into education is the Technical and Vocational Education Initiative (TVEI) aimed at 14-to-18-year-olds and there is also now a core curriculum, established through the 1981 Education Reform Act and designed to cover 70 per cent of school time in all state schools. Higher education too is to play its part with much greater responsiveness to the needs of employers. Greater reliance will be placed on the 'contract' principle, whereby the university or polytechnic delivers the programme that the government's funding bodies believe the country needs (DES 1986).

Most of the above refers to developments in the English educational system which is centrally funded but locally run through local education authorities (LEAs) in schools and further-education colleges. Many of these have taken major initiatives themselves to reform the school curriculum in vocationally useful directions, e.g. the Hargreaves report (ILEA 1984), but have resisted the vocationalism of government plans which tends to see occupational-skills training as the prime function of educational experience (e.g. see Edwards 1983).

In Scotland the education system is organized on a different and more centralized basis through a department of state, the Scottish Education Department, and operates under different legislation. As Raffe and Courtenay (1988) point out, although similar trends towards vocationalizing the school curriculum and training school-leavers have taken place there (TVEI and YTS extend to Scotland), school-based pre-vocational education has taken a different form through a '16+ Action Plan'. This is a programme comprising a large number of short (eight-week) modules in vocationally relevant skills for which the Scottish National Vocational Certificate (SCOTVEC) is awarded. The consequence has been much higher staying-on rates than in English schools to date and the tendency to delay entry into YTS for a year. But in any event, as entry into higher education takes place a year earlier than in England, the pre-vocational and academic routes run in parallel throughout the whole school career. Some would claim, moreover, that the whole ethos surrounding vocational education in Scotland is different (Ryrie 1981).

The government intervention in education and the labour market in relation to skills training is based on the premiss that work opportunities follow skills wherever they are available. Much of the research has pointed in a different direction, particularly Ashton and Maguire's (1986) study of four labour-market areas in the UK. This shows dramatically how opportunities, regardless of qualifications, are deeply affected by local economic conditions. Moreover, other structural determinants to do with race, gender, education and class also play a crucial role in job opportunities (Roberts *et al.* 1987, Roberts 1987). Changes in labour-market conditions – some cyclical – can also dramatically affect young people's prospects at the time when they are starting a career. The growth of homeworking, part-time employment among adult women generally, higher priority placed on qualifications when jobs are scarce, the growth of the new service sectors, are just four examples of the segmentation of the labour market and its transformation over time (Ashton *et al.* 1987; Ashton 1988).

16–19 initiative

To what extent are the new patterns of transition to employment affecting young people's lives? Are they getting employment; how do they view their prospects and what do they think about the world of work? To what extent are situations and attitudes affected by local economic conditions and how do gender, age and educational achievement play a part in shaping them?

The 16–19 Initiative, launched in 1986 by the UK Economic and Social Research Council, gives us an opportunity to find out. This is a study of economic and political socialization which involves a follow-up over two years of two cohorts of young people aged 15–16 and 17–18 respectively in four UK labour markets: Kirkcaldy (in Scotland), and Swindon, Sheffield and Liverpool (in England) (for full details, see Bynner 1987). Data are being collected by postal questionnaire, interview and ethnographic study. The research is centrally co-ordinated and carried out locally by four university teams: the University of Surrey (for Swindon), the University of Sheffield (for Sheffield), the University of Liverpool (for Liverpool) and the

Table 8.1   Response rates

	Original base (a)	Obtained base (b)	Completed question- naire (c)	Response rates c/b%
Swindon				
I	825	695	559	80
II	825	747	661	88
Total	1,650	1,442	1,220	85
Sheffield				
I	855	731	529	72
II	895	823	691	84
Total	1,750	1,554	1,220	79
Liverpool				
I	825	649	491	76
II	825	716	603	84
Total	1,650	1,365	1,084	79
Kirkcaldy				
I	825	707	598	85
II	825	787	698	89
Total	1,650	1,494	1,296	87
Total survey				
I	3,330	2,782	2,177	78
II	3,370	3,073	2,653	86
Grand total	6,700	5,855	4,830	82

I = Older cohort aged 17–18
II = Younger cohort aged 15–16

Universities of Dundee and Edinburgh (for Kirkcaldy). A research agency is employed to carry out the large postal surveys.

Samples

The samples comprise 1,600 young people selected at random from the full set of state-school records in each of the four areas. In the case of the younger cohort (15–16) these were up to date because all of them were still at school. For the older cohort, the majority of whom had left the education system, the records were up to two years out of date.

For all young people selected, an introductory letter was sent notifying them of the survey and asking them to tell us if they did not wish to take part. Only 3 per cent took this option, and the remaining 97 per cent were sent questionnaires. One postal reminder, followed by a visit by field-workers was used to maximize response. Table 8.1 shows the final response rates. 82 per cent of the achievable sample (i.e. those who could be located) sent back completed questionnaires. The response rate was higher for the younger cohort than the older cohort and was higher for males rather than females. Analysable data were obtained from 4,830 young people in total.

A useful check on the representativeness of the sample was obtained through comparisons with the National Youth Cohort Study, which the Manpower Services Commission has recently published (Courtenay 1988). The proportions of different occupations in the 16–19 Initiative and in the Youth Cohort Study for the same areas matched quite closely.

In addition to the postal questionnaire data, interview data were obtained from over a hundred informants in each area. The interviews were carried out by the local university research teams and usually took about an hour to complete.

The findings which are reported here are based mainly on the first round of postal data collection in 1987, when the two cohorts were 15–16 and 17–18 years old respectively, and a limited amount of interview data. Tables report comparisons across the four areas and within a number of other sub-divisions connected with gender, cohort and educational attainment.

Area characteristics

The four areas in which the research was conducted were selected to represent sharply contrasting labour-market characteristics. They also have quite different cultural and political traditions, reflecting the North–South split in England and the Anglo-Scottish border. These differences become critically important in interpreting some of the findings, especially those to do with education and employment prospects.

Swindon
This is a prosperous town in the 'golden crescent' of British new-technology industry in the south-west of England. Traditionally Swindon's economy was closely tied to the railways through a major railway engineering works but, when this closed, despite a temporary increase in unemployment, the town soon recovered, picking up large numbers of service industries and new-technology industries to fill the gap. A striking feature of Swindon is its large housing estates which at one time were rented from the local council and also tended to deliver votes for the Labour Party. With the recent affluence of the South of England, such political loyalties no longer exist.

Sheffield
This was the heart of Britain's steel industry, a nineteenth-century develop-ment where light steels and associated goods such as cutlery and machine tools were produced in quantity and renowned throughout the world. Faced with competition from the Far East, and new manufacturing methods, this industry rapidly declined and the city underwent a period of unemployment from which it is only slowly recovering. It has long traditions of strong political identity manifested in the election of councils who have tended to resist central government control. By chance it is also the location for the Manpower Services Commission's main headquarters

(now Training Agency) which is responsible for organizing the Youth Training Scheme (YTS).

Liverpool
Famed for its pop music, large youth population and Irish connections, Liverpool has been in economic decline for most of this century. It was a flourishing port in the nineteenth century and large numbers of associated maritime industries grew up around it, including shipbuilding. None of these activities are now central to the economy of Liverpool which has been subjected to continuing long-term unemployment and industrial decline. It is one of the targets for new government initiatives to revive the inner cities, particularly in relation to the large West Indian population which also resides there. It has a reputation for militant left-wing politics and usually elects a Labour council. Until World War II, it voted Conservative.

Kirkcaldy
This is an area of Fife in Scotland, in between the major cities of Dundee and Edinburgh, which has a mixed economy originally based on the coal industry, now much reduced, and traditional manufacturing in such fields as linoleum. It has now taken new directions with light industry and new technology. This means that from one part of Kirkcaldy to the other there are marked variations in both the styles of life and economic well-being. On many economic indicators, Kirkcaldy corresponds closely to the 'national average' for Scotland, making it a particularly appropriate choice for the Initiative. Politically the area is mixed, except that in company with most of Scotland its current political stance is anti-government.

The striking contrast between the areas in prosperity and economic life are not reflected surprisingly in some other key characteristics. For example, analysis of census data shows that roughly comparable proportions of adults in all of them are in the different social classes with no evidence, for example, of Swindon being more middle class than the others. Similarly the proportions in the different age groups, males and females, married and single, is much the same except that Liverpool has a slightly higher single population. The one characteristic where differences do occur is in the extent of home ownership. A higher proportion of Swindon residents own their own homes than their counterparts in Sheffield, Liverpool and Kirkcaldy who more frequently live in council-rented accommodation.

Education – work transitions

The major transition point in UK education is in the fifth year of secondary school in England and the fourth year in Scotland. This is the time when young people have the option of continuing with full-time education or leaving to get a job. As noted earlier, only fifteen years ago, most took the latter option and got a job. The collapse of the youth labour market has meant that in place of full-time employment most young people who leave school now confront a variety of options including YTS. With the removal at the end of 1988 of social-security benefits (the dole) from those unemployed school-leavers who refuse to take up the scheme, the government intends to involve virtually the whole school-leaver cohort in YTS which is intended to cater for both boys and girls equally. At the time our older cohort were in a position to enter YTS, it was a one-year scheme that had two major forms, employer-based, or local community-based. Now the scheme lasts two years and is intended to be based exclusively in employment.

Occupational statuses

The older cohort were asked about their occupational situation in three-month intervals over the two years since they were in a position to leave school. Table 8.2 shows the pattern of occupational change for males and females and in each of the four areas by comparing occupations at five intervals in the period April–June 1985 to April–June 1987.

The most notable feature of the male/female differences was the tendency for more females to stay on in full-time education and for more males to go into full-time jobs. Levels of unemployment and YTS entry barely differed between the sexes, with about a quarter of both sexes involved in them. This appears to support government intentions for YTS, that it serves both sexes equally. The apprenticeship schemes that it replaces were aimed almost exclusively at males.

The striking difference in the table is the pattern of differences between areas. First, only in prosperous Swindon were substantial numbers in the sample getting full-time jobs: even at the end of the two years, in spring 1987 when the sample was 17–18 years old, less than a third were in full-time employment in Sheffield, Liverpool and Kirkcaldy compared with over a half in Swindon. In the first year after leaving school the lack of youth jobs was even more apparent. In the spring of 1986, two-fifths of the young people in Swindon had a full-time job, and in the other areas the proportion was less than a fifth.

Over this period the prominence of YTS in areas with low job prospects is evident with over a third of the sample involved in Sheffield and Liverpool by the autumn of 1985. Take-up was substantially lower in Swindon and Kirkcaldy.

The other option for the school leaver, unemployment, also varied between the areas, and the rate fluctuated across time, rising to 9 per cent in Swindon, 14 per cent in Kirkcaldy and 20 per cent in Sheffield and Liverpool.

What about staying on in education? Surprisingly the rate did not vary markedly between the three English areas, dropping from between 40 per cent and 50 per cent in full-time education in the autumn of 1985 to roughly 30 per cent by the spring of 1987. In Scotland the picture was different: 62 per cent of young people were in full-time education in the autumn of 1985, but only 33 per cent in the spring of 1987. This accounts for the delayed take-up

Table 8.2 Occupational statuses post-15*

	Apr. May June 1985				Oct. Nov. Dec. 1985				Apr. May June 1986				Oct. Nov. Dec. 1986				Apr. May June 1987				Total (100%)
	Un	YTS	Job	Ed	Un	YTS	Job	Ed	Un	YTS	Job	Ed	Un	YTS	Job	Ed	Un	YTS	Job	Ed	
Female %	12	8	4	76	6	28	12	53	13	22	19	46	11	17	34	37	18	15	31	36	1,030
Male %	14	7	8	71	7	27	18	47	13	25	23	39	14	17	38	32	16	15	39	30	1,028
Swindon %	5	3	14	76	3	18	32	47	5	11	40	43	6	6	52	36	9	3	55	32	527
Sheffield %	18	10	5	66	10	38	11	41	14	30	18	37	19	18	31	31	21	13	36	29	503
Liverpool %	12	14	4	70	9	34	9	48	12	28	19	40	16	24	31	37	20	18	35	28	462
Kirkcaldy %	8	5	4	82	4	21	10	64	9	26	17	47	10	22	31	37	14	18	34	33	566

* Because of rounding, percentages do not always add up to exactly 100%.
Un = Unemployed
YTS = Youth Training Scheme
Job = Job
Ed = Full-time education

of YTS in Scotland and reflects the success of Scotland's pre-vocational 16+ Action Plan in keeping young people in school.

Finally, part-time work, a common option in Canada (Ashton 1988) barely existed in the sample as a main occupation: less than 5 per cent were currently engaged in it. Half of the sample had never had a part-time job.

Mobility between occupations

To what extent are the occupational decisions taken at age 16 reversed subsequently? Table 8.3 tabulates the older cohort's occupations in the autumn of 1985 against their subsequent occupations in spring 1987 and suggests that, although there was quite a lot of movement between occupations among leavers, mobility across the great divide between leaving and continuing with full-time education was virtually nil.

Again, area differences are striking. Thus among the unemployed in Swindon over two-thirds had moved into a full-time job; in Kirkcaldy just one-half had moved – but equally into jobs and YTS; in Liverpool and Sheffield 59 per cent of those who were unemployed in 1985 were still unemployed in 1987.

The greatest stability over the two years was shown for full-time work – this time in all areas. Even in Sheffield, where the stability was weakest, 76 per cent had retained a full-time job. It looks as though once a 'toehold' is gained in the labour market, it is not too difficult to hang on to it.

Of those staying on in full-time education, there was evidence of some later one-way traffic into the labour market, either direct or via YTS. But again there is marked regional variation; of those staying on only half were still at school in 1987 in Kirkcaldy compared with 72 and 71 per cent in Swindon and Sheffield respectively.

An obvious explanation of the movement out of education and the disincentive to return is financial. Even the YTS allowance of £28.50 (in 1987), though half the average youth wage (Courtenay 1988), or dole money of not much less is better than getting nothing which returning to school would have entailed. The situation will change now that the government has removed the right to dole money from unemployed school leavers who refuse to go on YTS. It remains to be seen whether YTS will be the preferable option or whether there will be a move back to education as in other countries.

Occupational stability

A final gloss on the post-16 occupational patterns is provided by a measure of how short-term or long-standing the experience of each occupation was. Table 8.3 gives the percentages of those who spent more than twelve months in each of five occupations: unemployed, YTS, full-time education, full-time job and part-time job. In Liverpool, Sheffield and Kirkcaldy young

Table 8.3   Changes in occupational status from autumn 1985 to spring 1987*

Occupational status autumn 1985	Occupational status spring 1987				
	Un	YTS	Job	Ed	Total (100%)
Swindon					
Un %	33	0	67	0	18
YTS %	12	14	68	7	95
Job %	8	0	91	1	141
Ed School %	2	1	24	72	107
FE %	5	3	30	63	146
Sheffield					
Un %	59	12	28	0	49
YTS %	23	23	51	1	183
Job %	22	2	76	0	140
Ed School %	4	9	9	77	60
FE %	12	2	30	57	49
Liverpool					
Un %	59	15	21	4	41
YTS %	25	34	41	1	149
Job %	11	3	84	3	172
Ed School %	9	9	25	58	41
FE %	5	12	22	61	38
Kirkcaldy					
Un%	47	26	26	0	29
YTS %	21	23	49	7	115
Job %	5	0	93	3	327
Ed School %	8	15	26	50	29
FE %	24	17	37	23	40

* Because of rounding, percentages do not always add up to exactly 100%.
Un = Unemployed
YTS = Youth Training Scheme
Job = Full-time job
Ed = Full-time education
FE = Full-time Further Education College

people were not only less likely to get a job than young people in Swindon, but less likely to hold on to it for more than a year. On the other hand, in Sheffield and Liverpool (not Kirkcaldy) they were more likely to be unemployed for more than a year. In Swindon, and to a lesser extent Kirkcaldy, unemployment seems to be more in the nature of a temporary staging post than a permanent career disadvantage. There were less marked differences for full-time education, except that Kirkcaldy's superior staying-on rate over the English areas is evident.

Table 8.4 Whether spent more than 1 year in occupation by area (total who had experienced an occupation)

Occupational status now	Swindon	Sheffield	Liverpool	Kirkcaldy
	%	%	%	%
Unemployed	15 (143)	25 (242)	27 (183)	10 (194)
YTS	28 (125)	32 (259)	37 (245)	29 (270)
Full-time education	49 (418)	49 (356)	52 (334)	58 (474)
Full-time work	59 (333)	36 (195)	38 (176)	34 (231)
Part-time work	3 (124)	6 (53)	10 (48)	7 (62)

Note: Figures in brackets are bases for percentages.

Career trajectories

The last analysis takes us directly to one of the main analytic tools developed in the study, 'career trajectory'. One of the aims of the 16–19 Initiative is to construct a typology of adolescent careers and to chart their progress over the period 16–19. From the analysis of patterns of change as reported by individuals in the older cohort over the two-year period since the last year of compulsory schooling, five major career trajectories were identified.

Academic

Continuing in education full-time past 16 on the General Certificate of Education (GCE) A-level route, i.e. taking exams which lead to university entrance.

Non-academic

Staying on past 16 but not doing courses leading to a higher education outcome: typically retaking earlier examinations or pre-vocational and vocational courses often at further education colleges – the 'new sixth formers'.

Job

Traditional transition of entry into a job almost immediately after leaving school at the minimum age.

YTS to Job

The new two-step transition involving entry into a training scheme (one year at the time the data were collected) on route to a full-time job.

Unemployment/training

Experience of unemployment or training over the whole period but no lasting experience of full-time work.

Table 8.5 gives an analysis of these career trajectories by area, sex and educational attainment.

Table 8.5   Career trajectory by area and educational attainment*

	Ed Ac	Ed Non-Ac	Ed → FT job	YTS → FT job	Unempl/ Training	Total 100%
Females %	27	22	13	13	31	988
Males %	17	19	19	14	31	1,010
Swindon %	20	20	33	12	16	518
Sheffield %	21	15	9	18	37	488
Liverpool %	20	20	11	11	38	444
Kirkcaldy %	17	27	10	12	33	548
Ed Ach 1 %	56	25	7	4	9	569
Ed Ach 2 %	15	31	16	16	22	513
Ed Ach 3 %	2	16	19	19	44	513
Ed Ach 4 %	0	6	17	12	65	531

* Because of rounding, percentages do not always add up to 100%.
Note: Ed Ac = Full-time academic education
   Ed non-Ac = Full-time non-academic education
   ED → Full-time job = From full-time education into full time job
   YTS → Full-time job = From YTS to full-time job
   Unempl/Training = Unemployment or training; no experience of full-time job
   Ed Ach = Educational Achievement in quartiles (1–4)

The figures amplify the conclusions about occupational patterns drawn earlier. We can see yet again the persistence in Swindon of the traditional school-to-job trajectory and its virtual disappearance (10 per cent) in every other area. But we can now also see that in confirmation of national studies (e.g. Courtenay 1988; Clough *et al.* 1988) it is marginally more common for boys than for girls, girls having the greatest tendency in all areas to stay on in full-time education.

The crucial role of educational attainment in underpinning career trajectory is also evident. Using a measure of educational attainment derived from exam results in the Certificate of Secondary Education (CSE) and the General Certificate of Education (GCE) O-level in England and O-grade and 'highers' in Scotland,[2] the sample was split into four groups defined by quartile ranges. It can be seen that few in the bottom attainment group (4) continued with education and in all others as high a proportion as two-thirds of this group had failed to establish any career (unemployment/ training). At the other extreme, among the highest attainers (group 1), over three-quarters were continuing with education.

Reasons for career choice

Why do some young people stay on in education and others leave? Clearly educational attainment has quite a lot to do with it as does family background. Another important incentive for leaving, as we noted earlier, is

Table 8.6 Satisfaction with present situation and education received by career trajectory, area and cohort

% satisfied	Swindon	Sheffield	Liverpool	Kirkcaldy
	%	%	%	%
Academic	85 (110)	77 (107)	87 (88)	74 (107)
Non-academic	80 (109)	86 (72)	70 (90)	72 (152)
Job	73 (165)	74 (44)	61 (51)	71 (53)
YTS to job	77 (61)	73 (86)	68 (50)	72 (66)
Unemployment/training	70 (105)	53 (203)	51 (190)	57 (197)
Older males	78 (266)	66 (253)	59 (244)	65 (312)
Older females	74 (284)	64 (259)	69 (245)	70 (263)
Younger males	72 (316)	66 (313)	64 (274)	68 (329)
Younger females	76 (333)	73 (362)	75 (327)	76 (359)

Note: For older cohort answers related to present situation; for younger cohort to education received.

money. Once young people have experienced a wage or a YTS allowance, or even dole money, they are unlikely to exchange it for education with no financial benefit to them. Such affluence, as it exists, was accentuated in Swindon with relatively high proportions in full-time jobs: two-fifths of the older cohort there had incomes of over £60 per week, compared with a tenth in Sheffield and Liverpool and a fifth in Kirkcaldy.

Reactions to past experience may also play a part in career choice, though to what extent this is *post hoc* rationalization for decisions made is impossible to judge. Table 8.6 shows the percentages of older cohort respondents in each career trajectory who said they were very or fairly satisfied with what they were currently doing.

Although the overall levels of satisfaction were surprisingly high, there were some notable exceptions. In Sheffield, Liverpool and Kirkcaldy, dissatisfaction in the unemployment/training group was widespread – a product presumably of frustrated career choice in these areas. Dissatisfaction was far less evident in Swindon, suggesting that unemployment is not perceived as such a problem there. Compare for example the 49 per cent of the unemployed in Liverpool who were dissatisfied with their present situation compared with the 13 per cent who expressed this feeling in the academic trajectory there. The comparable figures for Swindon were 30 and 15 per cent.

The table also shows male/female comparisons for both the older and the younger cohort. The younger cohort who were all at school were asked how satisfied they were with the education they had received.

There was no clear difference between males and females in satisfaction with the present situation. On the other hand, marginally more younger cohort females expressed satisfaction with the education they had received than males – a possible foundation for the females' superior staying-on rates. Perhaps girls simply like being at school more than boys!

Table 8.7   Views about area by area by cohort

	% agreeing		
	---	---	---
	Difficult to get a job locally[1]	Likely to move out of the area to get a job[2]	Total 100%
	%	%	
Younger cohort			
Swindon	14	48	660
Sheffield	48	52	683
Liverpool	67	64	601
Kirkcaldy	45	59	694
Older cohort			
Swindon	8	45	554
Sheffield	56	51	527
Liverpool	64	70	485
Kirkcaldy	50	57	597

[1] Respondents agreeing that it was 'very difficult' to get jobs locally.
[2] Respondents agreeing that it was 'very likely', or 'quite likely' that they would want to move out of the area to get a job in the future.

Young people's reasons for occupational choices are probably most affected by their own appraisal of their likely prospects in the labour market. We asked both the younger and the older cohort how difficult it was to get jobs locally and how likely it was that they would want to move out of the area to get a job. As table 8.7 shows, perceptions reflected labour-market realities with two-thirds in Liverpool seeing great difficulty in getting jobs, compared with a half in Sheffield and under a tenth in Swindon. The likelihood of moving home confirmed this pattern of labour-market pessimism, with two-thirds of Liverpudlians saying they were likely to move out of the area to get a job, compared with just over half of the young people in Sheffield and Kirkcaldy and just under a half in Swindon.

So what do young people expect to be doing if it is not full-time work? Are they expecting to get educated or trained instead? We asked both the younger and the older cohort what they were expecting to be doing in one year's time. Table 8.8 compares the younger and the older cohorts' answers in different sub-groups.

For the younger group there were few differences between boys and girls: full-time education followed by YTS was seen as most likely, followed by a full-time job. It is notable, though, that only 12 per cent of girls and 20 per cent of boys expected this – the occupation that fifteen years ago 60 per cent would have entered. This pattern holds broadly between the areas except that expectations of staying on in education were higher in Liverpool and Kirkcaldy than Swindon and Sheffield. In Sheffield expectations were towards YTS and in Swindon to further education and full-time jobs.

Table 8.8 Expectations by sex, cohort, area and occupational status now by cohort

	Unemp	YTS	School	FE college	HE	FT Job	PT Job	Other	Total (100%)
	%	%	%	%	%	%	%	%	
Older cohort									
Females	4	1	1	14	8	60	4	9	1,056
Males	5	1	1	9	10	65	2	7	1,047
Swindon	1	0	1	6	9	72	3	8	551
Sheffield	5	1	1	8	9	62	4	11	504
Liverpool	8	1	2	11	9	56	2	10	466
Kirkcaldy	4	2	0	19	10	60	2	4	502
Unemployed	15	3	0	7	0	52	10	18	317
YTS	9	4	0	4	0	73	3	10	265
School	1	0	5	26	42	19	1	8	415
FT FE	1	1	1	39	8	42	2	10	218
FT Job	0	0	0	1	0	94	1	6	751
PT Job	6	2	0	6	2	58	20	10	52
Younger cohort									
Females	1	28	34	19	0	12	3	2	1,391
Males	1	29	31	14	0	20	2	4	1,232
Swindon	1	21	24	26	0	22	4	3	658
Sheffield	1	38	23	18	0	15	2	3	680
Liverpool	1	28	42	12	0	12	2	3	597
Kirkcaldy	1	26	44	11	0	13	3	3	688

Note: Unemp = Unemployed
FE = Further Education
FT Job = Full-time job
PT Job = Part-time job

Surprisingly, expectation of a full-time job was not markedly higher in Swindon than it was in other places, though boys were more optimistic than girls in this respect.

For the older cohort a different picture emerged. As we might expect, far more expected to be in a job in Swindon than other places: 72 per cent of boys in Swindon, compared with 56 per cent in Liverpool. But compare this with the reality: only half of the older cohort in Swindon and one-third in Liverpool had actually got a full-time job. It seems that optimism about one's prospects in the labour market remains strong, despite experience – a powerful disincentive against returning to education.

The only education featuring in their expectations was further education, mentioned by about 10 per cent, and university, mentioned by the same proportion. It is here that English and Canadian occupational patterns and preferences diverge most sharply. In Canada well over four times the British numbers would be expecting to continue their education post-18 (Ashton 1988).

For the older cohort, expectations are also compared between the occupational categories. The superiority of YTS over unemployment in relation to perceived job prospects is apparent. University outcomes were strongly related to attendance at school post-16 rather than at further-educational college. But even so, less than half of the young people at school planned to go to university. The rest, together with those in further education colleges, expected either to be in further education again or in a job. Finally, those in a full-time job expected to stay in one (over 90 per cent) – a further example of the toehold phenomenon referred to earlier.

The exploration of reasons for career decisions taken at 16 was undertaken only with the small interview sample. Most people claimed that the decision was their own. Of those who acknowledged any influence on it, family was most frequently mentioned; teachers and careers officers rarely (less than 10 per cent). The main reason for staying on at school was 'the best option available'. Reasons for leaving were more diffuse with 'best option' and 'only option' being mentioned most, plus the desire to get work. 'Only option' was more common for girls than for boys, perhaps pointing to the greater external influence girls experience over the choices they make than boys (Griffin 1985; Wallace 1987). More girls also acknowledged pressure from friends as a reason for leaving school; parental pressure was marginally more evident for staying on at school than leaving but was mentioned by very few.

Type of job/training scheme

Each young person who said they were currently in a job was asked to describe the nature of the work and the kind of organization who employed them. A list of some 60 occupations was elicited which were classified into six categories ranging from professional/technical/managerial at one end to

Table 8.9   Type of job held by area by sex*

Job	Type of Job							
	Males				Females			
	Sw	Sh	Li	Ki	Sw	Sh	Li	Ki
	%	%	%	%	%	%	%	%
Professional, technical and managerial	9	6	8	3	6	0	4	1
Clerical/administrative	16	16	17	12	63	64	68	49
Skilled manual	52	56	55	71	25	14	15	47
Semi-skilled manual	4	4	3	3	4	5	1	8
Unskilled	19	19	17	12	2	18	13	6
Total (100%)	164	84	64	116	126	89	80	88

* Because of rounding, percentages do not always add up to exactly 100%.
Sw = Swindon
Sh = Sheffield
Li = Liverpool
Ki = Kirkcaldy

unskilled at the other. (The classification was derived from Ashton and Maguire 1986 coupled with the market-research classification which had been used for parents' occupation.) Table 8.9 compares the distribution of jobs for males and females in each of the four areas. The table nicely reflects the segmentation of the labour market for males and females, with the most common category of occupation for girls being clerical/administrative compared with skilled manual for boys. Interestingly there were barely no differences in the distribution of occupations between the English areas. On the other hand in Kirkcaldy substantially fewer were involved in clerical/ administrative tasks and relatively more in skilled manual work.

For those young people on government training schemes (YTS) we also asked for details of the kind of work they were being trained to do (using a classification derived from Banks and Ullah 1987). We classified all the 40 training schemes mentioned into eight categories. Table 8.10 shows their distribution in each area for males and females. This table shows much the same picture as the previous one, in pointing to skilled manual work as being the province for boys and clerical/administrative work being much more commonly taken up by girls. With the exception of more females tending to be trained in sales than males, there were few other differences. The results are interesting though in pointing to the continual gender-based segmentation of the labour-market, particularly as far as skilled jobs are concerned. This is now being underpinned by YTS – a scheme that makes a great deal of equal opportunities. It looks as if the separate routes for boys and girls into employment are going to be, if anything, reinforced by YTS.

Table 8.10   Type of training undertaken by area by sex*

	Training Scheme							
	Males				Females			
	Sw	Sh	Li	Ki	Sw	Sh	Li	Ki
	%	%	%	%	%	%	%	%
Administrative & clerical	25	11	22	16	46	36	33	49
Health and community	7	7	8	5	0	5	13	14
Sales	0	0	4	2	0	10	11	4
Catering	0	0	6	0	0	8	7	0
Agriculture/horticulture	8	7	12	7	0	3	0	0
Transport	0	7	2	2	0	0	0	6
Skilled manual	50	32	31	38	9	5	18	12
Semi or unskilled manual	0	29	8	23	9	18	9	18
Unemployed	0	7	6	0	9	10	7	2
Total (100%)	18	28	51	56	11	39	45	51

* Because of rounding, percentages do not always add up to exactly 100%.
Sw = Swindon
Sh = Sheffield
Li = Liverpool
Ki = Kirkcaldy

Work values

The most distinctive feature of British post-16 transitions is the values that accompany them. The near universal appeal in Canada of extended education (Ashton 1988) gives way in Britain to a deep-rooted commitment to getting paid employment at the earliest possible opportunity. Many writers have noted that for male working-class adults in Britain, identity is intimately tied to the idea of being in work (e.g. Willis 1977; Wallace 1987). Unemployment is therefore a serious blow to male self-esteem, typically compensated for by a kind of perpetual adolescence, whereby identities are sustained through acts of bravado and story telling. For girls, a job becomes the essential means of maintaining personal autonomy; in its absence there is withdrawal back into the private world of the home where a domestic role is expected (Griffin 1985; Wallace 1987). These values which are linked to a work ethic that has a long history in the UK (Furnham 1986), spill over into feelings of powerlessness to affect the course of events and fatalistic resignation to the lack of proper work (Coffield et al. 1986). There is also much hostility to YTS which is seen as exploitative, and ambivalence about work with new technology, the teaching of which forms a central plank of YTS (Raffe and Smith 1987).

Assessment of such attitudes and values among the Initiative samples was undertaken by a series of opinion items to each of which the respondent indicated agreement or disagreement on a five point scale[3]. Four composite

Table 8.11 Opinions about work*

	Males	Females	Younger	Older	Sw	Sh	Li	Ki
	%	%	%	%	%	%	%	%
Support for new technology								
1. I think a technical training will help me in the future	57	43	49	49	46	46	53	51
2. It is not worth the effort to learn about new technology	6	7	7	7	6	6	8	7
3. I want to learn more about how to use computers	64	62	62	64	64	60	61	66
4. I would like to have a job involving new technology	48	29	36	40	38	34	39	43
Work Commitment								
1. A person must have a job to be a full member of society	39	32	32	40	34	33	39	37
2. Having almost any job is better than unemployment	60	60	62	58	64	58	52	66
3. Once you've got a job it is important to hang onto it even if you don't like it	44	44	43	46	36	42	44	54
4. If I didn't like a job I'd pack it in even if there was no other job to go to	14	13	15	14	14	15	16	11
5. A person can get satisfaction out of life without a job	42	43	42	43	43	43	43	39
Support for training								
1. It is much better to get some kind of training than to go straight into a paid job	56	56	62	47	52	51	56	59
2. Youth training schemes are just slave labour	48	47	44	52	38	45	58	50
3. Youth training schemes are better than the dole	73	75	79	69	80	74	65	76
4. Going on YTS is the best way for 16 and 17 year olds to eventually get a job	38	42	41	37	35	44	36	43
External locus of control								
1. Getting a job today is just a matter of chance	24	29	25	28	16	26	33	30
2. It is bad luck that causes people to be poor	18	12	15	14	14	13	15	17
3. Being successful at work is just a matter of luck	6	7	7	6	5	7	9	6
4. Getting on at work really depends on other people	43	34	37	39	37	34	40	43
Sample size (100%)	2323	2468	2642	2163	1209	1212	1086	1289

* Respondents answered on a scale of (1) strongly agree (2) agree (3) undecided. (1) & (2) are combined.

scales were constructed from these items: 'support for new technology', 'work commitment', 'support for training' and 'external locus of control'. The constituent items are shown in table 8.11 which also shows the percentages of boys and girls in each cohort and each area who gave positive endorsement of the item, i.e. they strongly agreed or agreed on the whole with it.

The overall picture is one of attitude consistency for both sexes across all areas, but there are interesting exceptions. Fewer females endorsed the value of technical training than did boys, and fewer girls wanted a job involving new technology. Overall though, the picture was one of a positive view of new technology, with few young people rejecting its value. Learning about computers was particularly favoured by both sexes. With respect to work commitment, there was ambivalence, with Kirkcaldy expressing the strongest commitment. Getting a job and hanging on to it was more frequently stressed in Kirkcaldy than in other places. In relation to support for training, the main difference was a markedly more positive attitude to YTS coming through from the younger cohort than the older cohort, suggesting increasing acceptance of it. Most young people seemed broadly in favour of training schemes, with Liverpool lagging behind somewhat; 16 per cent of respondents there agreed that 'youth training schemes are just slave labour', compared with less than half everywhere else. On the other hand, both Liverpool and Swindon young people shared the same position in relation to the idea that 'going on YTS is the best way to get a job'. For probably very different reasons they tended to reject this view.

Finally, the items labelled 'external locus of control' showed few differences, except that in Liverpool young people appeared to have more fatalistic attitudes than those in other places. 'Getting a job today is just a matter of chance' was endorsed more frequently there than in other areas.

To take the analysis of these results further, composite scores for the items under each heading are compared for area, sex, cohort, educational attainment and career trajectory. Each scale was dichotomized at its median to produce a positive and negative attitude. Table 8.12 shows the percentages in the sample who gave the positive response in the different groups.

As far as sex differences were concerned, clearly males tend on average to be more favourably disposed towards new technology than females. On the other hand, males were no more likely to be committed to work, to support training, or to have fatalistic views about employment. In relation to age, the only notable difference was for training, with the younger group adopting a more positive attitude to it than the older group.

With respect to educational attainment, now split between high and low attainment, there was a clear tendency for the high-attainment group to favour new technology more than the low-attainment group but in sharp contrast to be less committed to work. More of the low-attainment group were also negative about training. Fatalistic attitudes were also more common in the low-attainment group, suggesting that education may give young people a greater sense of control over their lives.

Table 8.12   Attitudes by sex, area and educational attainment

	Supports new tech- nology†	Work commit- ment†	Supports training	Economic locus of control† (fatalistic)	Sample size (100%)
	%	%	%	%	
Males	54	51	43	46	2,323
Females	39	51	45	39	2,468
Younger	45	49	50	43	2,642
Older	45	53	37	42	2,163
Swindon	44	48	48	36	1,209
Sheffield	43	49	46	41	1,212
Liverpool	47	48	36	44	1,086
Kirkcaldy	49	59	46	49	1,259
* low attainment	32	62	35	50	1,119
high attainment	60	45	39	42	1,044
* Academic	63	40	33	29	410
Non-academic	57	48	40	35	420
Job	39	64	24	44	311
YTS to job	42	59	52	45	261
Unemployed/training	37	57	38	50	734

* = Older cohort only.
† = top half of the scale i.e. those respondents scoring above the median score.

Finally, career trajectories: support for new technology was strongest among young people in the full-time education trajectory and weakest among the unemployment/training group. Work commitment was weakest in the academic-career trajectory, and strongest among those that entered a full-time job. Support for training was strongest among those who had got a job at the end of it and weakest among those in a full-time job, or in unemployment/training. These groups too showed most fatalism about employment.

Conclusion

From the results presented, a number of broad conclusions about school–work transitions in the UK can be tentatively drawn. First, a finding which comes through from earlier studies (e.g. Ashton and Maguire 1986), but which is reinforced even more strongly here, is the significance of the labour-market in connection with occupational outcomes. In the one really prosperous area of the UK's 16–19 Initiative, Swindon, job prospects are good whether a young person pursues them after leaving school or through a YTS scheme; even if unemployment is experienced, it does not last for long. In other areas of the country such as Sheffield and especially Liverpool, the picture could hardly be more different. In these areas, although much the same proportion of young people leave the educational system at 16, far larger numbers enter unemployment after leaving school or get involved in training schemes. Once a job has been established – a toehold in the labour market – then the young person is likely to hang on to it. It is those who have failed to make the transition to work who face the most serious long-term difficulties.

These features of local labour markets are reflected in the expectations young people have of their prospects in them. Thus, although there is more optimism about employment in all places, especially among the younger cohort, than the employment situation warrants, there is much greater gloom in depressed areas like Liverpool and Sheffield than in a relatively prosperous place like Swindon.

The worth of government training schemes like YTS also has to be judged in labour-market terms. Although young people in the South-east of England may be better disposed to YTS than those in the North, there is far less of a need for it for them now. Recent evidence suggests that the demand for youth labour is now rising again to the point where YTS is seen as an expensive luxury that employers can do without. The government's hope of introducing a 'training culture' into the UK on continental lines (DES 1986) are being yet again dashed by employers' beliefs that all the training needed can be supplied on the job over a relatively short period of time. This is at a time when, as our cohort comparisons show, young people are becoming more favourably disposed towards training. Junankar's (1987) conclusion that youth unemployment is a temporary phenomenon which waxes and wanes depending on the buoyancy of the economy gains support from our findings. The last-in first-out principle dictates that, at times of economic stress, young people are the last to get unskilled and semi-skilled jobs and the first to lose them. Hence, at the time that the survey was conducted, youth unemployment had a real meaning in the North of England and Scotland, with all the consequences this implies (Banks and Ullah 1987), but in the South it has only a notional existence.

Another variation is between forms of education and training in different locations and the policies for 16+ education that lie alongside them. On many indicators Sheffield and Liverpool appear to be suffering from the same level of economic difficulty but, in relation to YTS in Sheffield, take-up is higher, outcomes are better and attitudes are more positive. The strong commitment of the local Sheffield Council to develop comprehensive and effective YTS programmes must be a factor here.

Kirkcaldy falls somewhere in between Swindon and the other two English areas on many indicators and differs interestingly with respect to education. We find that much larger numbers of young people stay on at school beyond the minimum age in Kirkcaldy than do in England. This is no doubt because of the appeal of Scotland's pre-vocational 16+ Action Plan, which has no exact counterpart in England. There is also a stronger work commitment among Scottish young people. In the English areas, despite the massive transformation of the labour market for young people that has occurred over the last ten years or so, there is little evidence that this has diminished the desire to get a job in places where it is difficult. Much the same proportions of young people stay on at school in Swindon as in Sheffield and Liverpool. The figures are not that much different from those prevailing ten years ago. Work clearly still has great attractions, even though the reality may well be unemployment or training schemes and little prospect of a full-time job.

This is, of course, in striking contrast to most other European countries and to Canada where the desire for extended full-time education is much stronger. It suggests that more concerted efforts are needed in Britain to bring about a change in values than have hitherto been recognized. Until recently there was a financial incentive for leaving school and going on the dole, but this cannot be a sufficient explanation of why so many young people take this step. More significant is the values that they still cling to. Getting a job is still central to adult identity for those boys and girls, and especially amongst those who have the least prospect of getting one – the low attainment group. There is a queer twist of fate that prospects are worse where desire is strongest and one can only see as the outcome, a growing frustration.

The distinctive Scottishness of many of our findings is one element of an understanding of the whole UK occupational scene, but within England the unique character of localities and the labour markets operating in them also comes through. Swindon is an industrial town that has 'taken off' through the benefits of new-technology investment in the South of England. Home owners' affluence and confidence characterize it, even though many young people expect to leave the town at some time in their lives to get a job. In the North of England we have all the symptoms of fundamental decline; unemployment and poor prospects and large numbers of young people involved in training programmes. In Sheffield, where the collapse of steel manufacturing is relatively recent, good use appears to be made of 'temporary' training measures and the signs of recovery are all there. In contrast, in Liverpool, where the decline has been occurring for very much longer, there are few signs of economic optimism and confidence returning. Much more radical programmes of reconstruction and education may be required to combat the pessimism of the young people there and make pre-vocational education and training effective.

In summary, the picture of British occupational transitions is one of opportunity structures that are strongly dependent on where you live. Extended education is one way out of the morass of unemployment but is still chosen by relatively few young people. Training schemes, if organized well, are another. Where unemployment is low, however, the demand for young people to fill jobs rather than to go on to training schemes remains strong. This is a distinctly British phenomenon which suggests a failure, almost unique among advanced nations, to recognize the value of extended education and training. How to bring about the necessary value change among employers and the young people they seek to employ is the challenge to be met.

Notes

1 The research reported here was supported by a grant from the UK Economic and Social Research Council.
2 The English scoring system was developed by the Research and Statistics Division of the Inner London Education Authority and the Scottish system by the Centre for Educational Sociology at the University of Edinburgh.
3 The first three sets of items and the composite scales constructed from them were developed in earlier work by colleagues in the Initiative, Glynis Breakwell *et al.* (1988) (New Technology and Training) at the University of Surrey and Michael Banks and P. Ullah (1988) (Work Commitment) at the Studies in Applied Psychology Unit at the University of Sheffield. The 'locus of control' items are derived from Furnham 1986.

References

Ashton, D. N. (1988). 'Sources of variation in labour market segmentation: a comparison of youth labour markets in Canada and Britain, *Work, Employment and Society*, 2, 1–24.
Ashton, D. N. and Maguire, M. J. (1986). *Young Adults in the Labour Market*. London, Department of Employment Research Paper, No. 55.
Ashton, D. N., Spilsbury, M. and Maguire, M. J. (1990). *Restructuring the Labour Market: Its Implications for Youth*. London, Macmillan.
Banks, M. and Ullah, P. (1987). *Youth Unemployment: Social and Psychological Perspectives*. London, Department of Employment, Research Paper No. 61.
Banks, M. and Ullah, P. (1988). *Youth Unemployment in the 1990s: and its Psychological Effects*. London, Croom Helm.
Beloff, H. (ed.) (1986). *Getting into Life*. London, Methuen.
Bynner, J. M. (1987). 'Coping with Transition', *Youth and Policy*, 22, 25–8.
Clough, E., Gray J. and Jones, B. (1988). 'Curricular patterns in post-compulsory provision: findings from the Youth Cohort Study', *Research Papers in Education* 3, 27–41.
Coffield, F., Borrill, C. and Marshall, S. (1986). *Growing Up at the Margins: Young Adults in the North of England*. Milton Keynes, Open University Press.
Courtenay, G. (1988). *England and Wales Youth Cohort Study: Report on Cohort 1, Sweep 1*. Sheffield, Manpower Services Commission.
DES (1981). *New Training Initiative*. Department of Education and Science. Cmnd 9135, London: HMSO.
 (1985). *Higher Education: Meeting the Challenge*. Department of Education and Science, Cmnd 9823, London: HMSO.
 (1986). *Working together: Education and Training*. Department of Education and Science, Cmnd 9823, London: HMSO.
 (1989). *Statistical Bulletin* 1/89, London, Department of Education and Science.
Edwards, A. D. (1983). 'The reconstruction of post-compulsory education and training in England and Wales', *European Journal of Education*, 18, 7–20.
Fogelman, K. (1985). *After school: the Educational and Training Experiences of the 1958*

Cohort. NCDS Working Paper No. 3. City of London University, Social Statistics Research Unit.

Furnham, A. (1986). 'Economic locus of control', *Human Relations* 39, 29–43.

Gray, D. and King, S. (1986). *The Youth Training Scheme: The First Three Years.* Research and Development Series No. 35. Sheffield, Manpower Services Commission.

Griffin, C. (1985). *Typical Girls?* London, Routledge & Kegan Paul.

Heinz, W. R. (1987). 'The transition from school to work in crisis: coping with threatened unemployment', *Journal of Adolescent Research,* 2, 127–41.

ILEA (1984). *Improving Secondary Schools* (The Hargreaves Report) London: Inner London Education Authority.

Junankar, P. N. (1987). 'The British Youth labour market in crisis', *International Review of Applied Economics.* 1, 48–71.

McGurk, H. (ed.) (1988). *What Next? An Introduction to Work on Young People.* London: Economic and Social Research Council.

Raffe, D. and Courtenay, G. (1988) '16–18 on both sides of the border' in Raffe, D. (ed.) *Education and the Youth Labour Market (Schooling and Scheming).* Lewes: Falmer Press.

Raffe, D. and Smith, A. (1987). 'Young people's attitudes to YTS: the first two years, *British Education Research Journal,* 13, 241–60.

Rawson, S. (1986). 'A Janus-headed revolution in education and training' in Ranson, S., Taylor, B. and Brighthouse, T. (eds.) *The Revolution in Education and Training.* Harlow, Longman.

Roberts, K. (1987). 'Young People in society', *Youth and Policy,* 22, 15–24.

Roberts, K., Dench, S. and Richardson, D. (1987). *The Changing Structure of Youth Labour Markets.* Department of Employment Research Paper 59, London, DES.

Ryrie, A. C. (1981). *Routes and Results,* Edinburgh, Scottish Council for Research in Education.

Wallace, C. (1987). *For Richer for Poorer: Growing Up in and out of Work,* London, Saxon House.

Willis, P. (1977). *Learning to Labour: How Working Class Kids get Working Class Jobs.* London, Saxon House.

9

Youth and labour markets: promises of comparative research on transition processes

Walter Heinz

Introduction

Sociological research on the organization and long-term effects of school-to-work transitions signals a theoretical shift from structural models of labour-market behaviour to theories of social reproduction (Bourdieu), structuration and agency (Giddens) and social embeddedness of action (Granovetter). These theories, despite their differences in dealing with macro–micro relationships, emphasize the interrelation of opportunity structures, social action and the life course. Social transitions as recurring status passages in the life course require a level of sociological analysis where social structure and individual action are conceptualized in reference to each other. Society provides normative and institutional frames as well as material resources, whereas individuals take up options and attempt to accommodate to choices and outcomes. Transitions in the life course, like job entry, are socially constructed and vary in the degree they are formally organized. The two societies under review – Britain and Canada – traditionally have relied on little systematic vocational training between school and work. School leavers who do not continue to secondary or post-secondary education have to cope with an abrupt role change – from student to unskilled worker. Only recently the British government, by introducing a Youth Training Scheme, (YTS) has attempted to create opportunities for vocational preparation for a growing number of youth who do not find a job after leaving school at the age of 16. In both societies you become a worker not after an extended period of vocational training but by on-the-job training and the accumulation of work experience.

In this short essay similarities and differences between the processes of becoming a worker in Britain and Canada will be elaborated by introducing a third society that has a well-organized transition pattern, West Germany. From this vantage point it will be possible to mark down the specific relationships that are formed between respective transition processes, labour-market segmentation and the social stratification of the labour force. In order to conduct such a three-fold comparison it is not necessary that the features of school-to-work trajectories are identical, it will be sufficient if the structural properties are equivalent (Kohn 1987).

All the contributions to this volume assume that the processes by which young people attain their positions in the labour market depend on the structured interaction of education, training, recruiting strategies of firms, and the amount of governmental intervention to promote equal opportunity. Furthermore, they emphasize the importance of orientations of youth towards education and work for understanding preferences for and resistance to the various features and outcomes of the transition sequence.

Transition patterns and the stratification of the work force

Comparative analyses of transitions as presented in this volume shed light on the specific forms capitalist labour relations take by stratifying the labour force at job entry and by determining further employment careers. The pathways integrating youth into the employment system shape their social identity and to a large degree the social relationships they will develop inside and outside the firm (cf. Maurice *et al.* 1986).

In West Germany hiring and promotion are related to the occupational qualification. In Canada and to a lesser extent in Britain, the firms cannot draw on specific skills workers have acquired before entering employment. Therefore they have to set up an internal training mechanism to provide their employees with the qualifications the company needs. The social status of the employee thus depends less on the level of certified vocational competence but more of the length or time he or she has been a member of the organization. In total contrast to this internal strategy, the West German apprenticeship system provides manual and most non-manual workers with certified competence and instills work norms that are taken for granted at employment entry. The polyvalent skilled workers are already equipped with practical and theoretical skills that make organizational socialization less important in West German firms than in British and Canadian companies. In marked difference to these societies, the work system organized in West Germany supports the occupational identity established by apprenticeship training. Consequently, for the social position of the employee the level of vocational training he or she has received is a decisive factor, they tend to have a wider span of control over their job and more responsibility quite early in their work life, they depend less on non-occupational, bureaucratic supervision in the firm in order to do their job.

Vocational training and education must be regarded as the corner-stone of the social fabric in which work careers are established and by which the firm stabilizes and legitimizes the stratification of the work force. Not so in Britain and Canada: work experience accumulated within the firm is the main criteria for wages, job security and careers. The status level is determined by seniority and the internal organization of jobs is the reference point for socialization and division of the work force. Whereas the social relations of work concentrate on the occupational dimension which connects training practices, employment channels and social positions in West Germany, in Britain and Canada social relations centre mainly on work experience.

From comparing the three societies a fairly clear picture emerges: the division of labour and the employment prospects are influenced by the specific pathways by which youth is socialized for work. The social relations created by the interplay of labour markets, training and education vary from society to society depending on the fusion of cultural traditions and institutional networks that define the relative importance of schooling, vocational training or work experience for getting ahead. Transition patterns do not just coexist with schools, firms and the labour market, they mediate institutional structures and social action by reproducing social stratification and by socializing youth for work.

Labour-market segmentation and the relevance of training

For the purpose of developing our threefold comparison further it is useful to introduce the notion of labour-market segmentation (cf. Edwards 1980, for a comparative perspective see Sengenberger 1987). The basic idea is that the labour market is divided into several parts which have a specific structure, are more or less separated from each other and have different income as well as employment prospects. The main division is between internal and external labour markets, the former being regulated by the company, the latter by market forces. This distinction, however, only holds for countries like the USA or Canada where a decentralized system of industrial relations exists and the regulation of employment relation by law is relatively weak. The concept of a 'dual labour market' which has been differentiated into a dependent and independent sector within the *primary* market with high wages, job security, and promotion rules, and a *secondary*, sometimes also called 'casual' market with low wages, high employment risks and no promotion opportunities, is more suitable for comparative purposes. Segmentation results from a combination of unequal employment conditions and unequal access to jobs, and thus it creates permanent social inequalities.

The West German labour market can be described by the combination of qualification requirements and company size. This leads to a relatively simple, but realistic fourfold classification: casual-labour market in small firms; casual-labour market in large firms; skilled-labour market; firm-specific or internal labour market.

Because of the paramount importance of vocational skills, the third segment plays a key role in the allocation of workers and shows a high interdependence with the fourth segment – the internal labour market. The qualifications acquired in the system of Vocational Education and Training (VET) also opens access to the skilled and firm-specific segments as well. A recent cohort study in West Germany (Blossfeld and Meyer 1988) demonstrates the impact of this school–work trajectory on the work histories of employees: less than a fifth of the job changes have depended on the operation of internal labour-market mechanisms. This leads to the conclusion that, in contrast to Canada and Britain, labour-market segmentation in West Germany is not a consequence of firm size and seniority rules but the result of qualification barriers between the primary and the secondary sector.

Therefore the competence acquired and certified by VET is not only important at job entry in the skilled and firm- specific segments of the labour market, but also for the entire employment history. Thus, the vast majority of school leavers who take the VET pathway act according to the rules and social relations which promise them access to jobs in the primary sector.

In Canada internal markets dominate the segmentation process, applicants for jobs are selected according to their educational level (high-school diploma, college degree) and promotions occur according to seniority rules. In Britain, while secondary educational qualifications are important for entry to skilled blue-collar and white-collar jobs, vocational training certificates are not of great importance. Those without qualifications who leave at 16 start as unskilled workers and are trained, step by step, to become employees with firm-specific qualifications. This transition pattern carries not only the risk of becoming dependent on a single firm, but also of being moved into the casual segment during economic crisis. It is doubtful whether the introduction of YTS will break through this labour-market mechanism as long as more emphasis is not put upon general education or on vocational training regulated and certified by bodies independent of single companies. When young people are selected for unskilled entry jobs, they are not interested in formal vocational certificates because they know that they are recruited for a sequence of jobs for which a series of on- the-job training experiences will do. Employers in turn hire and promote on the basis of the level of education and work experience and thereby build a core labour force which has to adapt to changes in technology by acquiring the necessary skills on an *ad hoc* basis.

In contrast to this allocation system, skilled-labour markets operate on occupational qualifications and the readiness for further training which are both acquired in the VET system that is regulated by a universalistic standard. These qualifications furthermore permit job changes within and between firms without disadvantages for the employee. From the point of view of companies it is more efficient in the long run to invest in apprenticeship training because it creates a labour force which disposes of an in-built potential to adapt to changed markets or lines of production.

Increased participation in secondary and post-secondary education in West Germany since the education reforms in the early 1970s has not weakened the dominance of the skilled-labour-market segment. Nowadays about two-thirds of all school leavers enter apprenticeship training, mostly those who do not continue into post-secondary education. But many young people with higher educational levels opt for VET, too, among them young women who consider an apprenticeship for office, bank or insurance jobs.

One reason for the popularity of this transition pattern lies in its paramount role as a conveyor belt between education and work, making it a meaningful investment even for those youths who plan to continue with higher education. Another reason is the high rate of unemployment especially among untrained workers which has reinforced the belief that VET is a necessary prerequisite for labour-market entry. A third reason is the opportunity to acquire further occupational credentials as a master craftsman or industrial technician on the basis of VET which opens the way to becoming a supervisor or setting up one's own firm.

Recruitment and employment careers in West Germany are strongly influenced by initial vocational credentials; they are relatively independent of general education. In Canada the situation is the reverse, education has an independent effect on employment opportunities. In Britain, apart from those who enter a recognized apprenticeship, some training and work experience affect the worker's career only if it results in an improved position in the job market so that he or she may stay with a firm long enough to acquire and make good use of seniority.

So we may conclude that there is a strong relationship between the various structural properties of labour-market segmentation in the three societies and the relative importance of vocational training. West Germany differs from Britain and Canada in respect of the skilled segment, as Maurice Sellier and Silvestre (1986: 15) have shown in their comparison of France and West Germany: 'the system of occupational training has a powerful autonomous influence on work force stratification'. Thus further comparative research on transition patterns and employment histories should look at the specific relationship between labour-market segmentation and training and its impact on timing, content and outcomes of school-to-work transitions.

So far we have mainly dealt with a relatively static description of the current transition structures in the respective societies. In view of demographic shifts, increased labour-force participation of women, and an up-grading of skill requirements, there are crucial policy issues which may be phrased in a question: more general education or more vocationalism?

A period of deskilling seems to have given way to a period of up-grading of skill requirements in the three societies under review. In Canada this has led to more post-secondary education, but not to a nationwide introduction of a sequence of vocational courses between high-school graduation and work: there has been rather the creation of vocational and academic tracks within high schools. Britain has responded in two ways. First, for the small number of apprentices it has introduced a modular system of training which incorporates a broader range of skills. Second, for many of the remaining school-leavers, it has introduced YTS as a nationwide and firm-based trajectory. In doing this Britain attempts to emulate part of the West German apprenticeship concept but thereby makes the prospects of trainees very dependent on the internal labour markets of companies. In West Germany the response to changes in technology and to the trend towards service industries is a modernization of VET curricula, for example, by combining various formerly distinct metal, electric and office occupations into newly designed respective basic occupations which require more intellectual training and an extension of VET to four years. These developments correspond to the orientations of young people that to get ahead it is important to have a high level of education and to return to college in Canada, to acquire work experience in Britain and to combine secondary education with VET credentials in West Germany.

Despite the various adjustments of the transition processes to economic and technological changes, employment opportunities, however, have improved only slowly for the job-entry cohorts in the three societies. Depending on the trade learned and the local labour market West German youth run into problems finding full-time employment after VET, many of them have to settle with part-time and temporary jobs and some have to endure spells of unemployment (Heinz 1987). In Britain the ties between school-leaving and taking up work have been severed because of the shrinking youth labour market. By introducing YTS instead of offering more general education and raising the school-leaving age, the job prospects of youth have become contingent on local labour markets. Thus, in many cases, YTS is only delaying unemployment or the allocation to the casual segment of the labour market for two years. On the other hand, a majority of British youth do not prefer to continue in school and many resent YTS as long as they are not convinced that these pathways actually improve their position on the labour market. It would be misleading to attribute this perspective only to the orientation especially among working-class youth towards early paid employment. As shown by contributions to this volume, there is virtually little public support and social encouragement to continue in school.

In this respect the situation in Canada is quite different. High-school graduates opt for more educational credentials rather than starting to work right away; even dropouts are motivated to return to school. The orientations of Canadian youth not only mirror structural connections between educational achievements and work careers, they are mediated by socialization experiences young people make who tend to combine education and part-time' employment before and after graduating from high-school.

Our analysis has shown that various transition patterns can be understood by reference to the specific societal combination of education and work values with the institutions of the labour-market. The structural relationships between firms, educational and training systems, and the state constitute specific transition networks and life-course patterns which are reproduced by orientations and options young people follow in the status passage of job entry. Transition patterns differ in the three societies because of structural properties and cultural norms that crystallize around education as professional qualification in Canada, work experience through on-the-job training in Britain, and vocational and educational training in West Germany. These features are embedded in the economic structure of the three societies, a decline of manufacturing and a growing service sector in Britain, a dominant service industry in Canada, and a core of modern manufacturing and a well-developed service sector in West Germany.

Thus the question, more education or more vocationalism, cannot be answered in an either-or fashion. The occupational prospects of youth will depend on an optimal combination of intellectual training, vocational and social skills which are best provided for by staying in school long enough to acquire the base for taking up vocational and professional training that gives occupational identity and relative independence from internal labour markets.

Conclusions: towards comparative transition research

The transition from school to work not only supplies the labour market with employable recruits, it also is a status passage that shapes the life course of each generation to a high degree. The organization of the transition process constructs socialization milieux which mirror the segmentation of the labour market. The societies analyzed in this volume represent a variety of organizational patterns, ranging from abrupt to extended rites of passage with different emphasis on and sequences of education, practical and theoretical instruction, work experience and job entry. For future comparative study the relationships between timing, duration and contents of various transition sequences and their bearing on social positions in the employment systems will be a main focus. This calls for mapping the various social contexts of transition patterns and the degree to which status change from student to worker is defined by institutionalized rules and a credential system, and finally for examining the amount of stability and discontinuity the respective transition gives to the life course.

The comparative analyses presented in this volume have succeeded in demonstrating connections between labour market and education in the respective economic and cultural contexts of Britain and Canada. They have shown that different solutions of the problem of job entry are contingent on the way education and training are related to the employment strategies of firms. Furthermore some contributions give an account of how organization of the transition process is intertwined with orientations of youth towards education and work.

The results presented in this volume are building material for developing a comparative analysis of transition processes in societies which display different combinations of education, vocational preparation and job entry. Since the contributions do not apply a common research design, they do not yet meet the requirements necessary for testing hypotheses. Although they demonstrate how transitions are patterned and operate in different societal contexts, it is premature 'to develop generalizations that transcend particular historical experiences in search of more explanatory principles' (Kohn 1987: 728). For the time being we will have to settle with comparative case studies with a twofold perspective on social contexts and life-course effects of transitions. To advance cross-societal research on this topic, an examination of similarities and differences among a limited number of cases, recently suggested by Ragin (1987), is a promising step.

References

Blossfeld, H.- P. and Mayer, K. U. (1988). Arbeitsmarktsegmentation in der Bundesrepublik Deutschland', Kölner Zeitschrift für Soziologie und Sozialpsychologie 40: 245–61.

Edwards, R. C. (1980). *Contested Terrain: The Transformation of the Workplace in America*. New York, Basic Books.

Heinz, W. R. (1987). 'The transition from school to work in crisis: coping with threatening unemployment', *Journal of Adolescent Research*, 2: 127–41.

Kohn, M. L. (1987). 'Cross-national research as an analytic strategy', *American Sociological Review*, 52: 713–31.

Maurice, M., Sellier, F. and Silvestre, J.- J. (1986). *The Social Foundations of Industrial Power: A Comparison of France and Germany*. Cambridge, MA, MIT Press.

Ragin, C. C. (1987). *The Comparative Method: Moving Beyond Qualitative and Quantitative Strategies*. Berkeley, CA, University of California Press.

Sengenberger, W. (1987). *Struktur und Funktionsweisen von Arbeitsmarkten: Die Bundesrepublik Deutschland im internationalen Vergleich*. Frankfurt/New York, Campus.

10

Conclusion: toward an explanation of transition patterns

David Ashton and Graham Lowe

In the Introduction we argued that comparative sociology can help to identify how specific institutional and cultural contexts condition an individual's passage through the life course. In the last chapter Walter Heinz has shown how the particular fusion of cultural traditions and institutional networks which characterizes each society define the relative importance of schooling, vocational training and work experience for making the transition. We now return to this theme, sketching out an explanation of how the emergence and persistence of different institutional structures and cultural traditions in Canada and Britain have resulted in schooling, vocational training and work experience taking on a different significance in each society in determining the outcome of the transition into employment.

Essentially there are three components in our analytic framework: the industrialization trajectories of the two countries; 'organising principles' (Lipset 1986), or sets of institutional relationships which, once established, exert a formative influence on a society; and interrelationships between education and the labour-market, given their obvious interdependence as outlined in the preceding chapters. These three components provide a unified cross-national perspective, in the sense that they underlie differences in the demand for youth labour in the two societies at any given time and in the structure and sequence of transition patterns.

To elaborate how these components are interrelated, the divergent industrialization trajectories followed by Britain and Canada reflect different organizing principles. For example, as the first industrial nation Britain could draw on its medieval apprenticeship system to provide skilled labour.

Canada, as a white settler state and a late industrializer, has a history of recruiting skilled labour from abroad in the form of immigrants. Of course, class relations and political institutions must also be taken into account, for it is in these arenas that education–labour-market links become most apparent. How does a ruling élite handle the problem of providing an educated and trained workforce? What is the role of a democratic state in establishing an educational system that at once meets the needs of employers as well as the rising aspirations of its citizens? More basically, how do schools and labour-markets both reflect and affect the enduring features of class structure?

Clearly our explanatory efforts are limited by not having the benefit of a systematic, cross-national research design that would yield fully comparable data. Thus the line of argument below is tentative, although the analytic framework from which it is derived can usefully point the way for future cross-national research.

As sociologists we are well aware of how our own values and social circumstances influence our definition of the 'problem' of transition. We therefore begin with a brief critical examination of the ways in which British and Canadian scholars have conceptualized the research problem.

In Canada the problem, as viewed by Krahn and Lowe, concerns the transition of all high-school and university graduates. To complete the picture, one could also include those enrolled in non-university post-secondary institutions. Their four-fold typology focuses on two issues: the lack of a critical juncture in the school–work transition in Canadian society; and a relatively prolonged transitional process which blurs the lines between student and (paid) worker roles. Looking at Britain, Bynner is typical of other researchers in that country in that he defines the 'transition' in terms of the traditional distinction between those who enter the labour-market (i.e., get a job on leaving school at 16) and those who pursue an academic career either in the sixth form or in university. For the latter, the distinction between student and worker is crystal clear. Significantly university students are excluded from Bynner's analysis, as they have been from all previous studies of the transition in Britain. It is widely assumed that British university students are a privileged group with significantly better life chances than anyone who left school at age 16. However, Bynner does point to the creation of three new youth statuses: the non-academic vocational sixth-former, the YTS trainee, and those who had not experienced work. In short, these two contrasting definitions of the school–work transition reflect basic cross-national differences in educational and labour-market institutions and accompanying values.

The Canadian focus on both high-school and university students undoubtedly reflects the fact that the latter educational route is far more common, and therefore less élitist, in Canada. Within the British-research tradition it is much less problematic to mount a major study which (in spite of the efforts of the principal investigators) excludes those in private education, universities and polytechnics. These observations highlight the extent to which the values and power structures of the two societies influence the scholarly enterprise, especially how sociologists conceptualize their problems. Comparative studies, by engendering an awareness of such issues, enable us to transcend the constraints imposed by our immediate social context on problem definition. The implications for future research are clear: Canadian studies of the transition can benefit by including high-school dropouts; British studies need to encompass university and poly-technic students.

Throughout this volume we have argued, following the work of Marc Maurice and his colleagues (1986) that transition patterns should be conceptualized at the societal level in terms of the interrelations of the educational and training institutions and the labour-market structures and recruitment practices of employers. In Britain the transition pattern created by these linkages was characterized by a clean break between school and work at 16 with clearly defined routes leading into the various segments of the labour-market. The Canadian transitional routes by contrast have been less clear cut and the transition from school to work less abrupt.

In order to explain these linkages between the educational system and the labour market, we shall focus historically on the factors which shaped current institutional structures. Specifically, this means investigating the formative influences on the linkages between the educational system and labour market in the nineteenth century, paying careful attention to the industrialization trajectories followed by the two societies. This approach will illuminate the 'organising principles' which then structured subsequent developments (Lipset 1986).

Explaining transition patterns – Britain

As the first industrial nation Britain's manufacturing base was characterized by labour-intensive industries which created a strong demand for young workers. As the early history of British manufacturing attests, literacy was a prerequisite for only the more skilled jobs which employed proportionally few youth. Vocational training was the responsibility of the employers, utilizing the apprenticeship system inherited from the medieval guilds. The (private) educational system was shaped by the demands of the middle classes for an education which would secure their children a respectable place in the social order. The working class was catered for either by church schools or the private 'dame' schools. The latter provided basic literacy and numeracy – all that was required for most working-class jobs. When the state extended compulsory education to the masses in the late nineteenth century its primary objective was to exert moral control over them (Gardner 1984).

Throughout most of the twentieth century the ruling élites maintained this organizing principle. It became embedded in a tradition of educating various social groups for their respective places in the social order. The advent of universal secondary education to the working class during World War II maintained these different routes into the labour-market in the form of secondary-modern, technical and grammar schools. The introduction of comprehensive education in the 1960s and 1970s was an attempt to break with this form of educational stratification by injecting the values of equality of opportunity into the system. However, forces of tradition combined with pressures from the labour-market resulted in internal stratification within the comprehensive schools. The system of examining at age 16, combined with a strict academic curriculum, differentiated those who were academi-cally 'successful' from the majority who would exit at 16. As Brown documents, the competition for apprenticeships among boys and office jobs among girls differentiated these two groups from those destined for unskilled factory or service-sector work. The result was the maintenance of three distinct channels or routes into the labour-market (Ashton and Field 1976), followed by groups of students Brown (1987) refers to as 'rems', 'ordinary kids' and 'swots'.

Higher education traditionally was a privilege reserved for the children of the upper and middle classes, designed to prepare them for the major professions or leadership in the church, armed forces, civil service or colonial administration. This élitist character was maintained in the mid-twentieth century, even in the face of growing working-class political power and the Robbins Report recommending higher education for all those who were qualified. Moreover, the institutions through which higher education was made available were divided between the academic universities and the more vocationally oriented polytechnics.

Historically this organizing principle for the English educational system has been imposed from the top down, although some local authorities were able to experiment. Such a system could be implemented only by a highly centralized state which abrogated decisions about what was the appropriate form of scientific and technical education for an industrial society.

Against this background the Thatcher administration's reform of the educational system can be seen as an attempt to return to a highly centralized system in which equality of opportunity is displaced by the goal of educating the next generation for their respective locations in the social order.

From the demand side, the key 'organizing principle' was to give employers and unions the responsibility for 'training' the working class. This was achieved in two ways: first, through the apprenticeship system which trained entrants to construction trades, engineering, printing, and so on; second, by on-the-job training, deemed sufficient for unskilled and semi-skilled workers. However, an entirely different approach to occu-pational preparation prevailed for the majority of middle-class and upper-class youth. They were 'educated' – not trained – by private (public) schools, universities or professional bodies over which the ruling class had more direct control. In the case of the private schools selectivity was achieved through the fee structure, in the case of the universities through the dominance of Oxbridge, and in the professions through state licensing of their activities.

The major result of these 'organizing principles' was the creation and subsequent maintenance of a system of well-defined routes linking the educational system to labour-market positions. The system was, of course, subject to periodic strains. The slow modernization of British manufacturing industry during the twentieth century gradually increased the demand for more highly skilled and literate labour. Because this could not be met by the existing supply of graduates, universities and later polytechnics were expanded. This broadened the basis of recruitment into the professions and leadership positions, but did not disrupt the overall system. The institutional links between the educational system and the labour market remained clearly articulated. From the age of 13, if not earlier, most young people knew which route they were going to follow.

The main shock to this system came with the recession in the early 1980s. As the papers by Maguire and Bynner show, the recession and the political handling of its impact effectively decoupled the linkages at the middle and lower levels of the system. This breakdown of institutional structures, in particular the serious shortages of entry-level jobs and apprenticeships, resulted in the problems of youth unemployment and urban riots. The regulatory mechanisms governing the flow of young people from school to work, at least in the middle and lower levels, no longer functioned. Canada did not experience similar problems. What then accounts for the British crisis in the school–work transition?

One of the main reasons for the decoupling of the linkages in Britain was the demise of manufacturing industries, previously one of the main sources of demand for youth labour. The impact of the world recession, exacerbated by the government's policy of maintaining a high value for the pound, led to massive job losses in manufacturing firms increasingly unable to compete on world markets. Together the high pound and the recession combined to reduce manufacturing capacity by 20 per cent. As British firms adjusted to the realities of global markets and new technology, the pattern of labour demand among the surviving firms changed. Firms no longer looked for the sorts of unskilled, semi- skilled or even skilled workers they would have recruited in the 1960s or 1970s. Many of these jobs – once the foundation of the link between school and work for numerous young people – had disappeared. As Brown shows, this industrial restructuring raised questions about the legitimacy of the educational system. The problem took on serious political dimensions when young people, holding an instrumental orientation to school, found that their commitment to education no longer paid off in the form of a good job – or in some cases any job at all. For others the response was to stay in school, motivated by the assumption that achieving better credentials may improve their employment chances. Overall, the result was to crowd those young people who succeeded in entering the labour market into the service sector. However, prospects were brighter for those who sought entry into the more highly rewarded professional, managerial and technical labour-market segments. The continued expansion of these occupations throughout the recession maintained intact established institutional linkages (Ashton, Maguire and Spilsbury 1990).

The British government responded to the crisis by attempting to rebuild the links to the labour market through the Youth Opportunities Programme and later the Youth Training Scheme. For some, such programmes provided a 'bridge to work', as officially claimed; for many others they were just a temporary respite from unemployment. The relative success of this state policy is documented by the 16–19 Initiative, where Bynner distinguishes the new routes which have since been forged; the non-academic route; the two-step transition from YTS to a job; and the unemployment/training route. As his results dramatically show, only a small minority of school leavers now follow the traditional one-step transition at age 16. At best, success has been only partial, for there are still parts of Britain where chronically high unemployment has given rise to an 'underclass' of socially and economically marginal youth.

In public-policy terms, the creation of a centralized system of training for 16- and 17-year-old school-leavers was a major feat. Yet it did not represent a radical break with previous 'organizing principles'. On the contrary, it can be seen as the reassertion of the traditional principle of the state imposing a particular set of institutional arrangements on the relatively disadvantaged segments of society. In this case, the government produced a series of schemes aimed at preparing young people for jobs in the lower tiers of the labour market. There were, however, some new features. For one thing, training was organized through employers, thereby ensuring that work socialization was more consistent with employers' labour requirements. A major innovation was the initial attempts by the Manpower Services Commission to negotiate a tripartite agreement with employers and unions for the provision of training (Marquand 1989). However, in spite of some initial success, the government was later to abandon this strategy in favour of giving employers the dominant role in the delivery of its training schemes. The result was, as Heinz points out, a training scheme which provided a fairly tenuous link in many instances between unskilled 16-year-old school-leavers and firms' internal labour markets.

Explaining transition patterns – Canada

Turning now to Canada, we seek an explanation of the transition patterns in terms of the distinctive trajectory of industrialization followed by Canadian society and the organizing principles adopted in its formative stage. Although Canada developed the basis for an indigenous manufacturing sector in the period around Confederation, in 1867, the major thrust of sustained industrialization did not come until the turn of the century (Laxer 1989). The Canadian labour market did not experience a steadily rising demand for uneducated, low-waged youths, as in Britain. Nor did employers look mainly to local educational institutions to provide more skilled workers, although from the mid-nineteenth century on there was an assumed connection between economic development and educational reform.

As a white-settler society, Canada's major source of labour was immigration. Indeed, throughout much of the nineteenth century the supply of wage labour exceeded the demand; many immigrants drifted to the United States after discovering there were few employment opportunities in British North America. In the latter part of the nineteenth century and into the early twentieth century the labour market for the skilled trades was continental, and these workers moved back and forth across the Canada–US border. For these reasons Canadian employers did not perceive a strong need for a system of training such as that provided by apprenticeships in Britain. Consequently, there was less pressure exerted on the education system, either to reproduce within the schools appropriate forms of occupational socialization or to encourage young people to leave school early.

In the nineteenth century development of schools in Canada was more a product of the local issues and politics and less a result of decisions by a centralized state. The schools were subject to more democratic control and hence concerned more with transmitting a common culture and equipping its pupils as citizens rather than preparing them for a predetermined position in the division of labour. Constitutionally, control was vested in the provinces, thereby preventing the central imposition of a uniform education on the working class of the kind which characterized Britain.

Rapid economic growth, especially in knowledge-based industries, in the immediate post-World-War-II period created a demand for more highly educated labour. No longer could educated immigrants from Britain, the US or Western Europe meet the demand. Thus began a major phase of expansion in higher education. Buttressing this growth of universities, and later community colleges, was the liberal value of equality of opportunity through expanded access to higher education.

Furthermore, in the absence of a well-developed set of institutions for worker training, employers and the state tended to look to the educational system as the means for increasing the supply of qualified labour. Indeed, the absence of a well-developed training culture in Canada has meant that Canadian society is not characterized by the same strict division between education and training as found in Britain. Hence the schools and universities were able to incorporate vocational courses into the curriculum without such courses' having the same stigma attached or facing student resistance as in Britain.

One result was the integration of vocational and academic programmes within the mainstream curriculum through what Gaskell refers to as the 'cafeteria' model. In this model students assume more responsibility for constructing their own curriculum and shaping their own routes into the labour market. But as Gaskell shows, this does not negate the influence of the labour market on the school, given that specific vocational programmes are directly tailored to an occupational niche. Indeed, streaming exists in the Canadian system but in a less overt form than in Britain. The streaming comes from selecting course electives as some students 'steer' themselves towards university and others towards the labour market at age 18. In this sense, student 'choice', not a central education policy, is the basis of educational differentiation.

From the demand side, the basic organizing principle was to make the acquisition of training the worker's responsibility. Until recently, Canada looked to other societies to provide trained workers during major periods of economic growth. As a result, employers tended to focus on providing job-specific skills. Unlike the situation in Britain, there were few institutional structures such as those associated with the apprenticeship system to ensure a supply of skilled workers. In some trades apprenticeships did develop, but in general this approach never took on the prominence it achieved in Britain. This has two important consequences for our understanding of Canadian transitional patterns and how they differ from what we have observed in Britain.

The first is that, unlike their British counterparts, Canadian employers have not put pressure on students to leave school and enter their apprenticeship or training programmes as soon as they reach 16 years of age. On the contrary, Canadian employers prefer to wait until people have obtained post-secondary credentials before investing resources in training them. This also reflects the organization of firm-internal labour markets in Canada. The most extensive training programmes typically are offered by large corporations (and government, to a lesser degree) mainly for middle-level managerial, technical or professional recruits. This adds to the segmentation of the labour market, possibly conferring long-term career advantages on those recent graduates who gain entry into a major employer's internal labour market.

The second is that, as schools and universities took on the task of vocational and academic education, employers could rely on them to provide initial training. As a result they tended to look for school-based credentials when recruiting to identify those with appropriate attributes. By contrast in Britain, because of the rigid division between education and training, many employers remain suspicious of the value of academic credentials for jobs such as apprenticeships (Ashton and Maguire 1980). The age-based requirements for entry to British apprenticeships meant that many young people were recruited for training before their credentials were obtained. A result of this situation, as Gaskell shows, is that Canadian students appear to place a higher value on school-based credentials.

Both of these features of Canadian employers' practices, late recruitment and reliance on credentials, place pressure on students to stay on in education in order to obtain their credentials and hence maximize their choices on the labour market. By contrast in Britain the combination of early recruitment and less reliance on credentials for manual employment encourages young people to leave school at age 16. This behaviour is further reinforced by financial incentives, either in the form of a wage or a training allowance. Canadian students are far less susceptible to these economic pressures to terminate their education, given the widespread availability of part-time jobs.

These national differences in education, training institutions, employers' recruitment practices, and their interrelationship help to explain the divergent transitional patterns found in Britain and Canada. In Canada the key features are a decentralized educational system which provides a range of qualifications and employers who, in the absence of extensive state-sponsored training, rely on educational credentials for late recruitment. These factors partly account for Canadian youth's remaining in the educational system, following the transitional patterns documented by Krahn and Lowe. In Britain, a national educational system geared towards slotting young people into a position in the labour market consistent with their class background, together with pressures from employers to leave school at the earliest opportunity for the 'best' working-class jobs, produces the patterns documented by Bynner. It is perhaps a testament to the strength of these institutional structures that, even when the job market for 16- and 17-year-olds all but disappeared in Britain, the pattern of early school-leaving persisted.

Differences in the institutional linkages supporting particular transitional patterns may also partly account for the relative success of the Canadian system in coping with the impact of the recession. Furthermore, in Canada the vast majority of young people sought employment in the service sector. The major disruptions experienced by manufacturing industries during the recession therefore had a lesser impact on the youth labour market in Canada than in Britain, although some parallels can be drawn with the effect of declining world energy prices on employment opportunities in Alberta. Yet unlike Britain, the impact of the recession in Canada was not exacerbated by an exchange-rate policy which overvalued the currency.

In short, the recession precipitated a cyclical fall in the demand for youth labour in Canada. This was not sufficient to sever the main links between educational institutions and the labour market. As Krahn and Lowe and Tanner show, those following the route from high school into the labour-market were worst affected. High-school dropouts and even high-school graduates faced long spells of unemployment, but not the mass unemployment experienced in Britain. University graduates continued to enter employment, although some may have experienced difficulties in securing appropriate work, a harbinger of growing underemployment in the future. Unlike British youth, who continued to leave school at 16 despite adverse labour-market conditions, there were greater inducements for Canadian youth to continue their education. The result was not a major political crisis of youth unemployment, as in Britain, but rather a short-term problem which required a series of stop-gap measures by both federal and provincial governments. Significantly some of these measures were directed just as much at students as at unemployed high-school leavers.

Even in the wake of the recession, the main transition pathways remain intact in Canada. The problem of high-school dropouts persists, but the main routes are still either through high school and into the lower- and middle-level jobs or through university and college into more promising careers. But will the Canadian labour market be able to absorb the growing proportion of well-educated entrants? The rise of a service economy, advancing automation and possible job deskilling raises the spectre of unfulfilled occupational aspirations for many graduates. The rapid growth of managerial and professional jobs in Canada may not be sufficient to absorb the supply of highly educated young people.

Certainly the same economic forces are in evidence in Britain. Yet the manifestations are quite different, given the lower proportion of post-secondary graduates. The growth in demand for professional, technical and managerial labour has continued but there has been no major increase in the proportions of young people following the academic route which leads to these jobs. One consequence has been a growing shortage of people capable of filling these jobs. However, while the graduates have faced a buoyant labour market, this has not been the case for those who followed the other routes. As Bynner points out, in all areas with the exception of Swindon, the traditional route from school straight to work at age 16 all but disappeared. In its place three new routes emerged, the vocational for those few who chose to remain in education, the two-step YTS route and the training/unemployment route for those who continued to enter the labour market. What we witness here is not so much a movement downmarket, as may well be happening in Canada, but a more radical restructuring of the transition based on new institutional links between education/training and jobs and the marginalizing of groups of young people throughout the labour market. The only outcome common to both societies has been the extension of the transition as young people remain dependent on their parents for longer periods in the struggle to secure a permanent foothold in the labour market.

Finally, what can account for the key differences we have identified regarding young adults' attitudes towards education and training in the two societies? One major similarity is a pronounced instrumental attitude towards education. However, in Canada this leads young people to stay on longer and to display a greater willingness to go back to school or university to continue their education. Canadian youth have a receptive attitude towards education which seems to reflect a more widespread belief in equality of opportunity. In Britain, young people are only too keen to leave school as soon as possible, even in the absence of jobs. Once they have left, there is a strong reluctance to go back and continue their education.

As Tanner has argued, differences in the class structures in the two societies play an important part in any explanation. The structure of industry in Canada and its more recent settlement by waves of immigrants are less likely to produce the traditional working-class community so often found in Britain. Instead he accurately identifies the more widespread commitment to the ideology of equality of opportunity as an important factor. Tanner also points to differences in the organization of educational institutions – between forms of sponsored and contest mobility – as additional explanatory factors.

We have not provided an exhaustive explanation of the differences in the transition patterns between the two societies. Our more limited objective has been to show why a focus on the interrelationships between education and training institutions and the labour market is essential if we are to develop such explanations. It follows from this strategy that policy debates which, as Heinz has pointed out, either focus on education reform in terms of the provision of more or less vocational training or which focus on training provision in terms of more or less education are also misguided. Moreover, policy action which stems from them is bound to be limited in its effectiveness because it is dealing with only one aspect of a complex system. Thus, in Canada, the very extension of educational provision and the success of the educational policies in maintaining a high proportion of young adults in higher education is threatening to create a problem of underemployment. In Britain the introduction of vocationalism has not increased the proportion staying on in school and the country still faces skills shortages in the higher-level occupations. In order to bring about effective change in the structure of transition pathways and in the supply of skilled workers, action is required which comprehends the interdependencies of the educational and labour-market structures. For example, if Britain is to increase the proportion staying on at school substantially, it is clear that this will involve action which inhibits the present recruitment practices of employers which entice young people into the labour market at 16. Similarly, any attempt in Canada either to reduce the problem of underemployment or unpredictability in the transition pathways would require the building of stronger institutional links between the educational system and employers. Moreover, in addition to a concern with ensuring the reproduction of the labour force it must also be emphasized that the linkages so forged between the education system and the workplace also structure the life-course transition of each new generation and their values and aspirations should also form an integral part of the policy agenda.

References

Ashton, D. N. and Field, D. (1976). *Young Workers: The Transition from School to Work.* London, Hutchinson.

Ashton, D. N. and Maguire, M. J. (1980). 'The Function of Academic and Non-Academic Qualifications in Employers' Selection Strategies', *British Journal of Guidance and Counselling*, 8, 2.

Ashton, D. N., Maguire, M. J., Spilsbury, M. (1990). *Restructuring the Labour Market: The Implications for Youth.* London, Macmillan.

Brown, P. (1987). *Schooling Ordinary Kids: Inequality, Unemployment and the New Vocationalism*. London, Tavistock.
Gardner, P. (1984). *The Lost Elementary Schools of Victorian England*. London, Croom Helm.
Laxer, G. (1989). *Open for Business: The Roots of Foreign Ownership in Canada*. Toronto, Oxford University Press.
Lipset, S. M. (1986). 'Historical traditions and national characteristics: a comparative analysis of Canada and the United States', *Canadian Journal of Sociology*, 11: 113–55.
Marquand, J. (1989). *Autonomy and Change: The Sources of Economic Growth*. Brighton, Harvester.
Maurice, M., Sellier, F. and Silvestre, J.-J. (1986). *The Social Foundations of Industrial Power: A Comparison of France and Germany*. Cambridge, MA, MIT Press.

Index